DEVELOPING WRITING
SKILLS IN CHINESE

DEVELOPING WRITING SKILLS IN CHINESE

实用汉语写作

Boping Yuan and Kan Qian

Routledge
Taylor & Francis Group

LONDON AND NEW YORK

First published 2003 by Routledge
11 New Fetter Lane, London EC4P 4EE

Simultaneously published in the USA and Canada
by Routledge
29 West 35th Street, New York, NY 10001

Routledge is an imprint of the Taylor & Francis Group

© 2003 Boping Yuan and Kan Qian

Typeset in 10½/13pt Times by Graphicraft Limited, Hong Kong
Printed and bound in Great Britain by TJ International Ltd, Padstow, Cornwall

British Library Cataloguing in Publication Data
A catalogue record for this book is available from the British Library

Library of Congress Cataloging in Publication Data
A catalog record for this book has been requested.

ISBN 0-415-21583-8 (hbk)
ISBN 0-415-21584-6 (pbk)

目录 Contents

CONTENTS

Preface

Developing Writing Skills in Chinese is a book designed for non-native speakers of Chinese at the post-intermediate level, who may need to write Chinese now or in the near future in a fairly coherent, clear and appropriate style. It can be used below that level as well if great care is taken in restricting access to certain units. The book is written not only as a textbook for classroom use but also as a self-study or reference book for people who are no longer classroom learners but have to write Chinese in their life, work, research, etc.

The book is divided into units according to different functions and situations. The teacher or the user does not have to follow the sequence of the units in the book, and the units can be studied selectively and flexibly according to the user's immediate and future needs. Each unit contains a number of model texts, and each model text is followed by clear notes in English explaining issues related to format, style, relevant expressions and grammar in that text. There are ample practice materials drawing the user's attention to some relevant writing techniques and expressions in the model text. These practice materials include controlled, semi-controlled and free production tasks, which make it possible for the user to digest and consolidate what is learned in each unit in a systematic way. Vocabulary from the texts, the notes and the exercises is given at the end of each unit in the order of appearance, with *pinyin* and English translation provided. There is also a Chinese–English glossary at the end of the book. Answers to the closed exercises are provided. It is strongly recommended that unless the book is used for self-study, classroom learners should keep the section of the answers closed at all times. Self-study users may find it useful to find a competent Chinese-speaking person to mark the open-ended exercises.

It is unrealistic to write a book that attempts to deal comprehensively with the written expressions of all notions and functions available in Chinese. In fact, it is never actually possible to provide the foreign language learner with sufficient model texts to allow him or her to assimilate the necessary facts of language, style and appropriateness that make the path to good writing an easier one for the native speaker of the language. In this book, we focus on those types of writing we think users of the book are likely to encounter in their life, work and studies.

The substance of this book is based on the materials used in Chinese writing classes at the University of Cambridge over the past ten years. We would like to thank the students in the Chinese writing classes for their comments and feedback. We would also like to express our gratitude to Don Starr for his careful review of the draft of the book and his helpful comments. We owe debts of gratitude to Bin Yu for her valuable assistance in helping us complete the book. Our artist, Yuli Hou, provided the book with very nice drawings, for which we feel very grateful indeed. This project is financially supported by a grant from the Universities' China Committee in London, for which we are grateful. Finally, we would like to express our sincere thanks to Sophie Oliver, the Language Learning Editor at Routledge, for her patience with our work and for her encouragement and support throughout the whole project.

第一单元: 卡片
Unit One: Cards

This unit covers the following types of cards: birthday cards, New Year's greeting cards, wedding cards and condolence cards. The language used in card writing is usually rather formal and brief with often incomplete sentences. The general format for these cards is as follows:

recipient's name:

        main message

        closing remark

              sender's name
                 date

1

1.1 生日卡片 Birthday cards

范文 *1, Text 1*

This is a card written to Wang Xiaoli, who is about to celebrate her 20th birthday, by her close female friend similar to her in age.

小丽：

　　祝你过一个丰富多彩的
二十岁生日！

　　生日快乐！

　　　　　　好友：薇萍
　　　　　　2002. 3. 8

Notes to Text 1

a. Between friends of similar age, it is normal to write the recipient's given name without adding terms such as '*dear*' in front of it. Between close friends, if the recipient is older than the writer, terms such as 大哥 (**dà gē**, *elder brother*) or 大姐 (**dà jiě**, *elder sister*) or simply 哥 or 姐 can be added to the recipient's given name to show respect.

b. The verb '过' (**guò**) is often used with 生日 (**shēngri**, *birthday*), 春节 (**chūnjié**, *Spring Festival*), meaning '*to celebrate*'.

c. Note that '二十岁生日' is modified by the phrase '一个丰富多彩的' (*a colourful 20th birthday*).

d. The following are common birthday expressions (when the recipient is either of a similar age or younger):

祝你的生日充满 . . .	**zhù nǐde shēngri chōngmǎn . . .**	*wishing your birthday is full of . . .*
欢乐	**huānlè**	*happiness*
诗意	**shīyì**	*poetic flavour*
浪漫色彩	**làngmàn sècǎi**	*romantic colour*
惊喜	**jīngxǐ**	*pleasant surprise*

2

愿你三十岁的生日给你	yuàn nǐ sānshí suì de shēngri gěi nǐ	*wishing your 30th birthday*
带来...	dàilái...	*brings you...*
幸福和成功	xìngfú hé chénggōng	*happiness and success*
无穷的欢声笑语	wúqióngde huān shēng xiào yǔ	*endless laughter*
满足和暇逸	mǎnzú hé xiáyì	*comfort and contentment*

范文 2, Text 2

This is written by John to his Chinese teacher who is to celebrate his 70th birthday.

> 尊敬的李老师：
>
>   祝贺您七十岁高寿！愿您身体健康，寿比南山！
>
>   学生：约翰 敬上
>   二〇〇二年六月八日

Notes to Text 2

a. When writing to people who are one's senior or superior, the term 尊敬的 is often used before the recipient's name:

尊敬的　　　　李先生/王教授
zūnjìngde　　Lǐ xiānsheng/Wáng jiàoshòu
Respected　　Mr. Li/Professor Wang

b. Note that the pronoun 您 (**nín**) instead of 你 is used to show respect.

c. The phrase 祝贺您...高寿 (**zhùhè nín ... gāoshòu**) literally means '*to congratulate you on your ... high age*', which is a polite way of congratulating an older person on their birthday (usually above 60). Similar expressions include:

祝贺您...大寿/寿辰！
zhùhè nín ... dà shòu/shòuchéng!
Congratulations on your ... birthday!

Therefore, it is more polite to use the expression 祝寿 (**zhù shòu**, *to celebrate a birthday*) rather than 过生日 (**guò shēngri**) when referring to an older person's birthday. For example:

为了给我奶奶祝寿，我给她定了一个大蛋糕。

wèile gěi wǒ nǎinai zhù shòu, wǒ gěi tā dìng le yí ge dà dàngāo.

To celebrate my grandma's birthday, I've ordered a big cake for her.

d. The phrase 敬上 (**jìngshàng**, *sincerely yours*) is used after the signature with one character space in between in a card/letter to one's senior or superior.

e. The following are some other expressions one can use when writing birthday cards to an elderly person (usually aged over 60):

祝您 . . .	zhù nín . . .	*wishing you . . .*
健康长寿	**jiànkāng chángshòu**	*health and long life*
寿比南山	**shòu bǐ nánshān**	*the life is as long as the southern mountain*
福如东海	**fú rú dōnghǎi**	*happiness as great as the eastern sea*
寿如松柏	**shòu rú sōngbǎi**	*live as long as the pine and cypress*
多寿多福	**duō shòu duō fú**	*long life and good fortune*
乐享余年	**lè xiǎng yú nián**	*to enjoy the rest of your life*
像松柏一样长寿	**xiàng sōngbǎi yíyàng chángshòu**	*live as long as the pine and cypress*

Exercises

1 Fill in the blanks with appropriate words:

(a) 你妹妹什么时候_____二十岁生日？

Nǐ mèimei shénme shíhou _____èrshí suì shēngri?

(b) 这个星期六是我爷爷的八十岁_____。我要去给他_____。

Zhège xīngqīliù shì wǒ yéyede bāshí suì _____. Wǒ yào qù gěi tā _____.

(c)

_____张老师：

今年九月七日是您的七十岁____。
祝您____南山，福如____。

您的学生：魏平 _____
二〇〇二年九月六日

2 Write a birthday card to a very good friend of yours who is about to celebrate her/his 21st birthday and who lives in another city.

3 Write a birthday card to your grandmother who is going to be 70 years old and who is in good health.

1.2 贺年卡片 New Year's greeting cards

范文 3, *Text 3*

On the right is a card sent by Lin Weiping to her good friend Wang Shuqin.

> 舒琴：
>
> 在新春即将来临之际，我在此祝你和你们全家
>
> 龙年快乐，万事如意！
>
> 友：维平
> 2002. 1. 18

Notes to Text 3

a. According to the Chinese lunar calendar, there is an animal sign for each year. Altogether there are 12 animal signs, and so they come round every 12 years. If we take the following 12 years as an example, below is a table of the 12 signs corresponding to those 12 years:

Year	Sign	Pinyin	Character
1984	Rat	shǔ	鼠
1985	Ox	niú	牛
1986	Tiger	hǔ	虎
1987	Rabbit	tù	兔
1988	Dragon	lóng	龙
1989	Snake	shé (xiǎo lóng)	蛇（小龙）
1990	Horse	mǎ	马
1991	Sheep	yáng	羊
1992	Monkey	hóu	猴
1993	Rooster	jī	鸡
1994	Dog	gǒu	狗
1995	Pig	zhū	猪

For example, 'the Year of the Dragon' is 龙年 (**lóng nián**).

b. The phrase 在 . . . 之际 (**zài . . . zhī jì**) is a formal expression used mostly in written language. For example:

At the time when I/you/you (plural) *will soon graduate/retire/leave China, I feel very emotional.*

c.   在此 (**zài cǐ**) is also a formal term which is often used in letters and cards, meaning '*here*' and which refers to the card or letter being written.

d.   Relevant expressions

There are many set phrases which people use for New Year's greetings, and it is customary to use the set phrases of this type in even numbers, that is, to write two or four set phrases in a card rather than one or three. Here are some often used ones (they are not arranged in pairs below):

新年好	**xīn nián hǎo**	*Happy New Year*
恭喜发财	**gōngxǐ fācái**	*Congratulations and wishing you prosperity*
恭贺新禧	**gōnghè xīn xǐ**	*New Year congratulations*
新春愉快	**xīn chūn yúkuài**	*Happy New Year*
合家欢乐	**hé jiā huānlè**	*happy family reunion*
一帆风顺	**yì fān fēng shùn**	*smooth progress*
心想事成	**xīn xiǎng shì chéng**	*achieve your heart's desires*
春风得意	**chūn fēng déyì**	*enjoy success*
富贵年年	**fù guì nián nián**	*be prosperous year after year*
年年有余	**nián nián yǒuyú**	*have an abundance every year*
岁岁平安	**suì suì píng'ān**	*have peace year after year*

Exercises for 1.2

1   Fill in the blanks according to the context:

2   Write a Chinese New Year's greeting card to a Chinese friend of yours. The New Year is the Year of the Rabbit.

1.3 新婚贺卡 Wedding cards

Wedding cards are more straightforward in that the language used does not differentiate between young couples or older couples.

范文 *4, Text 4*

On the right is a wedding card sent by Lingfang who is a cousin of Xiaoming.

晓明，丽华：

    喜闻你们即将结为伉俪。在这个大喜的日子里，我们全家祝你们

    喜结良缘，白头到老！

表姐: 玲芳
二○○二年六月八号

Notes to Text 4

a.   The verbal phrase 喜闻 (**xǐ wén**), literally '*happily hear*', can be translated as '*be pleased/delighted to hear*'. It is a phrase which is used in formal writing. For example:

> 喜闻你考上了哈佛大学，在此向你表示祝贺。
> **xǐ wén nǐ kǎo shàng le Hāfó Dàxué, zài cǐ xiàng nǐ biǎoshì zhùhè.**
> *I'm delighted to hear that you've been admitted to Harvard University. Many congratulations.*

b.   The four-character expression 结为伉俪 (**jié wéi kànglì**), meaning '*to become a married couple*' or '*to become husband and wife*', is a formal expression usually reserved for weddings.

c.   The phrase 大喜 (**dà xǐ**) literally means '*big happiness*'. There are a few things which can be called 大喜. Marriage is one of them, and the birth of a boy is another (of course, people may use it for other occasions such as getting a Ph.D. or being promoted to a high position). There is a special character which serves as a marriage symbol, and it looks like this: 囍. It is pronounced 双喜 (**shuāng xǐ**), meaning '*double happiness*' as the character 喜 is written twice.

d. The four-character expression 喜结良缘 (**xǐ jié liáng yuán**) translates as '*to be happily married*'. Literally, 缘 (**yuán**) means '*predestined*' or '*relationship*'. For example:

> 我们分手了，可能我们本来就没有缘。
>
> **wǒmen fēnshǒu le, kěnéng wǒmen běnlái jiù méi yǒu yuán.**
>
> *We split up. Perhaps we were not meant to be together in the first place.*

> 我和烟酒没有缘。
>
> **wǒ hé yān jiǔ méi yǒu yuán.**
>
> *I have nothing to do with smoking and drinking.*

e. Relevant expressions

The word for bridegroom is 新郎 (**xīnláng**), which literally means '*new man*'; and the term for bride is 新娘 (**xīnniáng**), which literally means '*new woman*'. Also, the newly wed couple are often compared to a dragon and a phoenix.

The following expressions are often used on wedding cards and frequently written in pairs (they are not arranged in pairs below):

生活甜蜜	**shēnghuó tiánmì**	*sweet life*
早生贵子	**zao sheng guizi**	*to have a boy soon*
龙凤齐飞	**lóng fèng qí fēi**	*dragon and phoenix fly together*
永偕伉俪	**yǒng xié kànglì**	*be married forever*
百年佳偶	**bǎi nián jiā ǒu**	*be happily married for a hundred years*
白头到老	**bái tóu dào lǎo**	*grow old together*
百年偕老	**bǎi nián xié lǎo**	*be together for a hundred years*
百年夫妻	**bǎi nián fūqī**	*be husband and wife for a hundred years*
夫妻恩爱	**fūqī ēn'ài**	*loving couple*
恭贺新禧	**gōnghè xīn xǐ**	*congratulations on your new happiness*

Exercise for 1.3

Fill in the blanks using appropriate wedding expressions:

顺昌兄：

　　__闻你与戴虹小姐结为____。
　　祝你们
　　　　生活____，____贵子，
　　　　夫妻____，____到老！

　　　　　　　　　　老同学：孟戈
　　　　　　　　　　2001年6月1日

1.4 哀悼卡片 Condolence cards

范文 5, *Text 5*

On the right is a card sent to Professor Song's widow, Mrs Zhang, by Liu Xiaoqing who was a student of Professor Song.

尊敬的张女士：

　惊悉宋教授不幸逝世，无限悲痛，深表哀悼。望您节哀保重。

　　　　　　学生：刘晓清
　　　　　二〇〇〇年五月十号

Notes to Text 5

a. There are various ways to address Professor Song's wife. She can be 宋夫人 (**Sòng fūren**, *Mrs. Song*) or 师母 (**shīmǔ**). The term 师母 is used only to refer to or address one's master's or teacher's wife. It is especially appropriate if the writer is one generation younger than she is and knows her fairly well. If she is a professor or teacher herself, then simply address her as 张教授 or 张老师.

b. The verbal phrase 惊悉 (**jīng xī**) is a rather formal expression meaning '*to be shocked to learn*'. In contrast to 喜闻 (see 1.3 above), this is often used for bad news. For example:

惊悉你母亲身患癌症/你因车祸受伤。
jīng xī nǐ mǔqīn shēn huàn áizhèng/nǐ yīn chēhuò shòu shāng.
I was shocked to learn that your mother was suffering from cancer/you were injured in a car accident.

c. Here, the verbal phrase 逝世 (**shìshì**, *to pass away*) should be used instead of the word 死 (**sǐ**, *to die*), which is one of the taboo words Chinese people try to avoid. As a result, there are many other euphemistic expressions which are usually more formal and indirect. For example:

父亲去世的时候，我才五岁。
fùqin qùshì de shíhou, wǒ cái wǔ suì.
When father passed away, I was only five.

9

我才五岁，父亲就离开了这个世界。

wǒ cái wǔ suì, fùqin jiù líkāi le zhège shìjiè.

I was only five when father left this world.

他和我们永别了。

tā hé wǒmen yǒngbié le.

He left us forever.

癌症残酷地夺去了他年轻的生命。

áizhèng cánkùde duóqù le tā niánqīnde shēngmìng.

Cancer cruelly took away his young life.

d.   The following expressions are often used in condolence cards:

不胜悲痛	**búshèng bēitòng**	*great sorrow*
万分同情	**wànfēn tóngqíng**	*deepest sympathy*
深表同情	**shēn biǎo tóngqíng**	*to express deep sympathy*
深切哀悼	**shēnqiè āidào**	*heartfelt condolences*
深感惋惜	**shēn gǎn wǎnxī**	*to feel the loss keenly*
永垂不朽	**yǒngchuíbùxiǔ**	*to be immortal*

Exercise for 1.4

Fill in the blanks with appropriate words based on the context:

(a)   为了对王老师的逝世表示_____，我们全班送了一个花圈。

      wèile dui Wáng Lǎoshīde shìshì biǎoshì_____, wǒmen quán bān sòng le yí ge huāquān.

(b)   一想到父亲如此突然地_____，我便悲伤万分。

      yì xiǎngdào fùqin rúcǐ tūránde_____, wǒ biàn bēishāng wànfēn.

(c)

> 南河大学：
>
>   ____贵校邓山立教授不幸____，不胜____，并____惋惜。请转达我们对邓教授家属的万分____和深切____。
>
>   邓山立教授永__不__！
>
>   金桥大学中文系
>   二〇〇一年十月八日

Vocabulary

1.1

丰富多彩	**fēngfù duōcǎi**	splendid
好友	**hǎo yǒu**	good friend
充满	**chōngmǎn . . .**	to be full of
尊敬的	**zūnjìngde**	respected
祝贺	**zhùhè**	to congratulate; congratulations
高寿	**gāoshòu**	long life
身体健康	**shēntǐ jiànkāng**	good health
寿比南山	**shòu bǐ nánshān**	may your age be as long as the southern mountain
敬上	**jìngshàng**	sincerely
大寿	**dà shòu**	birthday (for older people)
寿辰	**shòuchén**	birthday (for older people)
祝寿	**zhù shòu**	to celebrate (an older person's) birthday
长寿	**chángshòu**	long life
松柏	**sōngbǎi**	pine and cypress

1.2

在 . . . 之际	**zài . . . zhī jì**	at the time when . . .
新春	**xīn chūn**	New Year
即将	**jíjiāng**	soon; to be about to
来临	**láilín**	to arrive
在此	**zài cǐ**	here; in this
龙年	**lóng nián**	Year of the Dragon
万事如意	**wàn shì rú yì**	everything goes as you wish

1.3

喜闻	**xǐ wén**	to be pleased to hear
结为	**jiéwéi**	to tie the knot; to become married
伉俪	**kànglì**	married couple; husband and wife
大喜	**dàxǐ**	happy event
喜结良缘	**xǐ jié liáng yuán**	happily married
新婚快乐	**xīn hūn kuàilè**	happy marriage
表姐	**biǎo jiě**	cousin (female and older)

1.4

惊悉	**jīng xī**	to be shocked to hear
不幸	**búxìng**	unfortunately; sadly
逝世	**shìshì**	to pass away
无限	**wúxiàn**	boundless
悲痛	**bēitòng**	sadness
深表	**shēnbiǎo**	to deeply express
哀悼	**āidào**	condolences
节哀	**jié āi**	restrain one's grief
保重	**bǎozhòng**	take care of yourself

第二单元: 便条
Unit Two: Notes

As notes are usually written in a hurry to people we know quite well, they are rather informal and sometimes ungrammatical in sentence structure. Usually, there is no need to put any opening or closing remarks; nor is there any need to date the note unless the content of the message makes it crucial to do so. Here we shall cover notes that are written for the following purposes: explaining things, making arrangements, instructing someone to do something, asking for help, apologising for something and giving instructions.

2.1 说明某事 Explaining things

范文 1, Text 1

This is a note written by a mother to her daughter who is coming home with two other friends from her university.

玲玲:

    单位早上来电话,说有(件)急事,(需)要我去处理。午饭(妈妈)已为你们准备好(了),在冰箱里,吃(的)时(候),在炉子上或微波炉里热热(就行了)。

    让你(的)朋友们用你妹(妹)的房间。

    我大概五点左右回来。

妈妈

Notes to Text 1

a. The words in brackets in the above text can be omitted, as it is normal for notes to be brief. Normally, functional words such as 的, 了 and measure words can be omitted in informal writing. Also, conjuctions such as 因为, 如果, 但是 can be shortened to 因, 如 and 但.

b. Often, single syllable verbs are repeated to soften the tone so that whatever is being said does not sound like an order. For example, the meaning of the following two sentences is the same except that the second one carries less force and sounds more friendly:

你热饭，我收拾房间。
你去热热饭，我收拾一下房间。
nǐ qù rère fàn, wǒ shōushi yíxià fángjiān.
You go ahead and warm up the food, and I'll tidy up the room.

The phrase 热热就行了 in the text above means '*warm it up, and it'll be fine*', and cannot be reduced to 热就行了. However, one can say 热一下就行了.

c. Notice that the note is not dated as the information is obvious to the recipient. If there is any ambiguity, it is better to include the date, and sometimes even the specific time (see Model 2 below).

范文 2, *Text 2*

Dongmei works at a university. Her friend Li Yong has come round to pick up some books she has borrowed for him from her university library. Li Yong has just found a note from Dongmei on her desk, on top of the books. Notice that the time is specified at the bottom of the note as Li Yong is an hour late.

李勇：
　　等了你快一个小时，仍(然)不见你来。因我下午有(个)会，只好先走(了)。这些是你要的书，还缺第四册。我已给你预订(了)，估计一周后能拿到。到时(候)我给你打电话。

冬梅
3. 12 下午1:30

Notes to Text 2

a. Whatever is missing is placed after the verb 缺, for example:

这本书缺第15页。
zhè běn shǔ quē dì shíwǔ yè.
Page 15 is missing from this book. (lit. This book lacks the 15th page.)

b. The object of 拿到, which should be 这本书, is omitted.

Exercises for 2.1

1 Cross out the words in the following sentences that can be omitted.
  (a) 明明，我去图书馆还本书。如果有人给我打电话，就说我下午两点以后回来。
  (b) 小李，因为今天晚上有个朋友请我吃饭，我可能晚些回来。

2 Students in your class have decided at a meeting to have an end-of-term party but a fellow student has missed the meeting. Write a note to him/her explaining when and where the party is to be held and what he/she needs to do for the party.

2.2   做安排 Making arrangements

范文 3, Text 3

Wang Ping asks her colleague, Li Xiaoju who works in the same office to look after a visitor for her for half an hour.

小菊：

　　我担心下午2点赶不回来，估计要晚半(个)小时。如(果)报社记者到得(比我)早，请替我招呼一下，并说声对不起。我桌上有(一)些材料，(你)可(以)先让他看看。

王苹

Notes to Text 3

a. In the phrase '替我招呼一下', the object '他' is omitted. It is translated as '*Please look after him for me.*'
b. Notice the omission of '的' in '我(的)桌上有一些材料' (*There is some material on my desk*).

范文 4, Text 4

The following note is from a young woman to her boyfriend:

> 大钢：
>
>   6点在电影院门口见。别忘了！看完电影后去吃火锅，怎么样？
>
> 芳

Note to Text 4

a.   Apparently, the boyfriend knows which cinema it is and must also know what film they are going to see. This note is simply a reminder. So the following phrases are often used in this sort of note: 别忘了 (*Don't forget*), 千万别忘了 (*Whatever you do, don't forget!*), and 一定记住 (*Make sure to remember it*).

Exercise for 2.2

    Several of you have agreed to go to the cinema, followed by a meal in a Chinese restaurant. You cannot reach one friend by phone, so you have gone to her house but she is not in. Write a note about the arrangements, mentioning what film it is, the name of the cinema, the time the film starts, the name of the restaurant and perhaps when and where to meet up.

2.3 交代他人做某事 Instructing people to do things

范文 5, Text 5

Li Jian, duty manager of a hotel, has left a note for his secretary, Wang Yang, asking her to handle a request from a hotel guest.

> 小王：
>
>   请帮318房间的客人确认一下去昆明的机票(机票在信封里)。另外，给他联系几家在昆明的饭店。将价钱、档次、位置等详(细)情(况)尽快告诉客人，并问客人是否需要咱们帮助预定房间。
>
>   这件事就交给你去办了。
>
> 李建
10月6号

Note to Text 5

a. The sentence '这件事就交给你去办了' can be translated as '*I'll leave this matter for you to sort out.*'

范文 6, *Text 6*

A husband leaves a list of things for his wife to do while he is away on a business trip:

秀:
　　　以下几件事，帮我做一下：
(1) 寄我办公桌上的信；
(2) 给我母亲打(个)电话，告诉她我出差了；
(3) 每隔三天浇一次阳台上的花草。
　　　到上海后(会)给你打电话(的)。

小雷

Note to Text 6

a. The construction 会...的 is used to show that one is serious about doing something. 的 is always placed at the very end of the sentence. For example:

我会让小明去看你的。
wǒ huì ràng Xiǎomíng qù kàn nǐ de.
I will ask Xiaoming to go and see you.

Exercises for 2.3

1 Fill in the blanks using the appropriate words from Models 5 and 6 above:
   (a) 有件事想请你＿＿我＿＿一下。我把自行车锁在了咱们办公楼的后面 (右边靠墙)。请你帮我移到附近的车棚里。钥匙在信封里。
   (b) 你是否能帮我＿＿件事?
   (c) 妈妈，请您放心。我＿＿每天给您打个电话＿＿。

2 You are going away for two weeks. Leave a note for your neighbour, who has a key to your house, asking him to:

(a)   return some books to Lao Li, another neighbour;

(b)   water your plants once a week; and

(c)   use anything in your fridge which he finds usable.

2.4   请求帮助 Asking for help

范文 7, *Text 7*

Fang Ming and Liu Hong are studying on the same course at a university and sharing a flat. Here is a note from Fang Ming to Liu Hong:

刘宏：

　　明(天)早(上)我要去机场接我母亲，今晚(我)到我姨妈家住。这样，明早经济学的课(我)就上不成了，劳驾你帮我录下来。我把录音机和磁带放在你(的)书桌上了。

　　多谢！

方明

Notes to Text 7

a.   劳驾 is a colloquial expression often used when asking for help. It can be used both as a verb and as an independent phrase. When used as a verb, the construction is 劳驾 + somebody + do + something (*to bother sb. to do sth.*). It can also be used independently to mean '*excuse me*'. For example, it can be used when you want people in front of you to move aside so that you can get off a crowded bus.

b.   The following expressions may be used to make a request more polite.

我想 . . . , 不知行不行?

wǒ xiǎng . . . , bù zhī xíng bù xíng?

I'd like to . . . I'm wondering if it is ok.

你如果 . . . (的话), 能不能顺便帮我 . . . ?

nǐ rúguǒ . . . (dehuà), néng bu néng shùnbiàn bāng wǒ . . . ?

If you . . . , could you do . . . for me at the same time?

如果不太麻烦的话, 能否帮我 . . . ?

rúguǒ bú tài máfan dehuà, néng fǒu bāng wǒ . . . ?

If it's not too much hassle, could you please help me . . . ?

范文 8, *Text 8*

Zhang Meiqing leaves a note for her flatmate:

文文：
　　有两件事麻烦你：
(1) 今天可能有我的快递，帮我签收一下。
(2) 如小丽来电话，告诉她我在陈国强家。

　　多谢。

美清

Note to Text 8

a. The phrase 麻烦你 literally means '. . . *bother you*', which is a common opening in asking for help. For example:

我想麻烦你一下，你能帮我签收一个快递吗？

wǒ xiǎng máfan nǐ yíxià. nǐ néng bāng wǒ qiān shōu yí ge kuài dì ma?

Can I bother you with something? Can you sign for a special delivery for me?

The verb 麻烦 can also be used in the following phrases when you wish to express your thanks for a favour:

麻烦你了。	给你添麻烦了。
máfan nǐ le.	**gěi nǐ tiān máfan le.**
Sorry for the trouble.	*Sorry to have given you so much hassle.*

Exercise for 2.4

Write a note to a friend and ask him/her if he/she could return a book to the library for you if he/she goes there this afternoon. Explain why you cannot do so yourself and where you have left the book.

2.5 道歉 Apologising

范文 9, *Text 9*

陈老师：
　　这个星期我们合唱团排练占了我许多时间，所以，我的翻译作业至今还没做完，实在对不起。今晚(我)哪儿也不去，把作业认真做好，明(天)早(上)一定交。

刘新平
3月5号

范文 10, *Text 10*

小明：
　　你要的《明清史》我忘带了，十分抱歉。明晚我一定把书送到你家去，希望不会耽误你用书。

建钢

Notes to Texts 9 and 10

a.　The following phrases are often used together with 对不起 or 十分抱歉:

　　　请多多原谅。
　　　qǐng duōduō yuánliàng
　　　Please excuse/forgive me.

　　　请多多包涵。
　　　qǐng duōduō bāohán
　　　Please excuse/forgive/bear with me.

Another common expression for '*I'm sorry*' is 真不好意思 (**zhēn bù hǎo yìsi**), the literal translation of which is '*really embarrassed*'. This expression is very informal.

b. The sentence 希望不会耽误你用书 literally means '*(I) hope it won't delay your using the book*', and can be loosely translated as '*I hope it won't cause you too much inconvenience.*'

Exercises for 2.5

1   You have been ill for the last couple of days, and hence have not finished the writing assignment which is due today. Write a note to your teacher to apologise and indicate in your note when you will be able to hand in the work.
2   You promised a Chinese friend who was visiting the college that you'd find out some information for him/her about train services to Paris. You've completely forgotten until now. Write a note of apology and explanation to him/her.

2.6 给出做事步骤 Giving instructions

Here, we shall only cover informal instructions such as how to operate an appliance and how to get to somewhere. This wording is therefore very different from a manufacturer's manual which is technical in wording and formal in grammatical structure.

范文 *11, Text 11*

Lixian's friend, Xiao Hua, is coming to stay over the weekend, but Lixian won't be around, so she leaves Xiao Hua a note, telling her how to operate the washing machine.

小华：

　　洗衣机在厨房里，洗衣粉在洗衣机旁边的抽屉里。如果有衣服要洗，你尽管用。先接上电源，再把衣服放进去，一定要关好门。然后，将洗衣粉放进左上角的小抽屉里，并把右边的旋钮顺时针转到5。最后将旋钮拉出，机器便会开始工作。大概要洗40分钟。机器停后，等两、三分钟再开门。

　　其它用具都简单易用。你就随便用吧。

丽贤

Note to Text 11

a. When giving instructions, it always involves telling people what to do first, second and third, etc. So words that list things and put things in order are important. In the text above, the following linking words are used to indicate temporal sequence: 先 (*first of all*), 再 (*then*), 然后 (*after that*), 最后 (*finally*).

范文 *12, Text 12*

Zheng Fang has invited Li Ming to have dinner with her in her new house, so she has written him a note with directions:

李明：

　　我们家很好找。从你那儿先乘33路，在美术馆下车。然后换乘7路，在和平里下车。下车后往东走200米左右，在你的右边有一家邮局，过了邮局后的第一条胡同就是我们的胡同(地址：新柳胡同61号)。进了61号大院后，往左拐。第二个门就是我们家。万一找不到，给我们来个电话(号码：76627397)，我去公共汽车站接你。

　　周六见！

郑芳

Notes to Text 12

a. In giving directions, especially general directions, Chinese people like to use 东 (*east*), 南 (*south*), 西 (*west*), 北 (*north*). When it comes to the detailed location, 前 (*in front*), 后 (*behind*), 左 (*left*), 右 (*right*) are used.

b. In Beijing, there are some old style one-storey houses known as 四合院儿, compounds with houses around a square courtyard. In the old days, a compound used to be owned by one well-off household. Nowadays, some compounds are shared by several households, and people who live there refer to their compound as 大院.

Exercises for 2.6

1   The following is an instruction for making egg-fried rice (all the preparation work has been done). Fill in the blanks with appropriate words to indicate the sequence:

_____把油烧热，_____把切碎的葱倒入油内，紧接着倒入打碎的鸡蛋，炒一、两分钟；_____，把剩米饭倒进去，和鸡蛋一起炒几分钟；_____，加一点酱油和少许盐。

2   You are having a birthday party in your place. You have invited some friends. One of them does not know how to get there. Write a note to him/her with directions including the following information: (a) there are two buses that go to your area: one gets there directly but the service is infrequent, while the other runs every five minutes; (b) after getting off the bus, follow the direction for the railway station, then turn left at the first traffic light; and (c) your address and how far it is from the traffic light. Use Model 12 as your guide.

Vocabulary

2.1

单位	dānwèi	work unit
急事	jí shì	urgent matter
处理	chǔlǐ	to see to; to deal with
炉子	lúzi	cooker
微波炉	wēibōlú	microwave oven
仍然	réngrán	still
缺	quē	to be missing; to lack
第四册	dìsì cè	the fourth volume
预订	yùdìng	to reserve
估计	gūjì	to estimate
到时(候)	dào shí(hou)	when the time comes

2.2

担心	dānxīn	to be worried, to be concerned
赶不回来	gǎn bu huílai	can't come back in time
报社	bàoshè	newspaper (as an organisation)
记者	jìzhě	reporter
替	tì	on one's behalf; for
招呼	zhāohu	to look after
材料	cáiliào	material
火锅	huǒguō	hot pot

2.3

确认	**quèrèn**	to confirm
昆明	**Kūnmíng**	[a city name]
联系	**liánxì**	to get in touch; to contact
价钱	**jiàqian**	price
档次	**dàngcì**	grade
位置	**wèizhi**	location
详(细)情(况)	**xiáng(xì) qíng(kuàng)**	details
隔三天	**gé sān tiān**	every three days
浇	**jiāo**	to water
阳台	**yángtái**	balcony
植物	**zhíwù**	plant
锁	**suǒ**	to lock
办公楼	**bàngōnglóu**	office building
墙	**qiáng**	wall
车棚	**chēpéng**	bike-shed
钥匙	**yàoshi**	key

2.4

姨妈	**yímā**	aunt (on mother's side)
经济学	**jīngjìxué**	economics
上不成	**shàng bu chéng**	cannot attend
劳驾	**láojià**	to bother
录下来	**lùxialai**	to record it
录音机	**lùyīnjī**	recorder
磁带	**cídài**	tape
麻烦	**máfan**	to bother; to cause trouble
快递	**kuài dì**	express delivery; express letter or parcel
签收	**qiān shōu**	to sign for
添	**tiān**	to add

2.5

合唱团	**héchàngtuán**	choir
排练	**páiliàn**	rehearsal
占	**zhàn**	to occupy
实在	**shízài**	indeed
交	**jiāo**	to hand in
明清史	**Míng Qīng shǐ**	history of Ming and Qing Dynasties
抱歉	**bàoqiàn**	to apologise; apologies
耽误	**dānwu**	to delay; to take up (time)

2.6

厨房	**chúfáng**	kitchen
洗衣粉	**xǐyī fěn**	washing powder

抽屉	chōuti	drawer
接上	jiēshàng	to connect (power)
电源	diànyuán	power
旋钮	xuánniǔ	knob
顺时针	shùnshízhēn	clockwise
转	zhuàn	to turn
拉出	lāchū	to pull out
用具	yòngjù	appliance
简单易用	jiǎndān yì yòng	simple and easy to use
随便	suíbiàn	to do as one pleases
乘	chéng	to take (e.g. bus, train)
美术馆	Měishù Guǎn	Art Gallery
换乘	huàn chéng	to change (e.g. bus)
往东走	wǎng dōng zǒu	to walk towards the east
胡同	hútong	lane
大院	dàyuàn	compound
烧热	shāorè	to heat up
切碎的	qiēsuìde	chopped-up
葱	cōng	spring onion
紧接着	jǐnjiēzhe	straight after that
打碎的	dǎsuìde	beat-up; beaten
鸡蛋	jīdàn	egg
炒	chǎo	to stir-fry
剩米饭	shèng mǐfàn	left-over rice
酱油	jiàngyóu	soya sauce
少许	shǎoxǔ	a little
盐	yán	salt

第三单元: 私人书信
Unit Three: Personal letters

This unit deals with personal letters. As personal letters are written between friends and family, the style of writing is informal and sometimes includes incomplete sentences. Personal letters cover so many topics that it is impossible to deal with all of them. Here, we introduce only two kinds: (i) letters with a specific purpose and (ii) keep-in-touch letters.

3.1 私人信件格式 Format of a personal letter

范文 *1, Text 1*

琳琳: 　你好！近来好吗? XXXXXXXXXXXXXXXX XXXXXXXXXXXXXXXX. 　祝全家好！ 　　　　　　友: 小方 　　　　　　六月三十号 另: 寄上一张近照。	琳琳: 　你好！近来好吗? XXXXXXXXXXXXXXXX XXXXXXXXXXXXXXX. 　　　　祝 全家好！ 　　　　　　友: 小方 　　　　　　6. 30

Notes to Text 1

a.　When writing to a family member, many kinship terms are used to address the recipient. For example, 亲爱的妈妈 (**qīn'àide māma**, *Dear Mum*);

25

小姨，姨夫 (**xiǎo yí, yífu**; *youngest Auntie, Uncle-in-law*). When writing to friends, given names or full names can be used to address the recipient. For example, 博彬 (**Bóbīn**, [*a given name*]) 王小梅 (**Wáng Xiǎoméi**, [*a full name*]). The term 亲爱的 is usually used among couples, or when addressing someone senior in the family, elderly people and teachers. It is rarely used among friends. Note that after the name of the recipient, a colon is used.

b. Opening remarks are general greetings, including expressions such as:

> 你好！
> **nǐhǎo!** *Hello!*

> 近来好吗?
> **jìnlái hǎo ma?** *How have you been recently?*

> 近来身体好吗?
> **jìnlái shēntǐ hǎo ma?** *Have you been well?*

> 好久不见，很想念您。
> **hǎojiǔ bú jiàn, hěn xiǎngniàn nín.**
> *Haven't seen you for a long time and miss you very much.*

> 好久没收到你的来信，不知近况如何?
> **hǎojiǔ méi shōudào nǐde láixìn, bù zhī jìn kuàng rúhé?**
> *Haven't heard from you for a long time, just wondering how you are getting on.*

Note that the opening remark takes a separate line and it is usually two character spaces (Chinese characters) indented.

c. Closing remarks are expressions of good wishes. The following are often used in closing remarks:

> 祝好！
> **zhùhǎo** *Best wishes*

> 请代我向 . . . . 问好。
> **qǐng dài wǒ xiàng . . . wèn hǎo.** *Please say hello to . . . for me.*

> 祝你全家好！
> **zhù nǐ quán jiā hǎo.** *Wishing your whole family well.*

> 祝你健康！
> **zhù nǐ jiànkāng.** *Wishing you good health.*

> 祝愉快！
> **zhù yúkuài.** *Wishing you happiness!*

> 祝进步！
> **zhù jìnbù.** *Wishing you good progress!*

When writing to older people, the following more polite closing remark is often used:

敬祝安好！
jìng zhù ānhǎo! *Respectfully wishing you are well.*

Closing remarks take up either one or two lines. When it is split into two parts, 祝 or 敬祝 takes up one line (normally positioned in the middle of the page) and the rest of the phrase takes up another line (normally positioned on the left, in line with the first line of the previous paragraphs). An exclamation mark is often used at the end of a closing remark.

d. If writing to friends, either the full name or just the given name can be signed, and sometimes the character 友 (**yǒu**, *friend*) is put in front of the signature. If writing to parents or grandparents, appropriate kinship terms such as 女儿, 儿子, 孙子, 孙女 (**nǚ'er, érzi, sūnzi, sūnnü**; *daughter, son, grandson, granddaughter*) can be put in front of the signatory's name, according to what their relationship is to the recipient. A character space is usually put between the relationship term and the signature.

e. The order of the date is as follows: year, month and day. Obviously, the year is often omitted. You can date the letter in Chinese characters or in numerals. For example: (二〇〇一年)十二月三日/号, (2001年)12月3日/号 or simply 2001. 12. 3. The date is placed either directly underneath the signature or further down in the lower right corner.

Note that if you need to add a sentence or two when the letter is finished, you can find a space anywhere in the letter, preferably in the lower left corner, and add phrases such as: 另 (**lìng**, *p.s.*), 又及 (**yòují**, *p.s.*). For example:

另: 随信寄去咱们的合影。
lìng: suí xìn jìqu zánmende hé yǐng.
P.S. Find enclosed the photos of us.

又及: 还有一事 . . .
yòují: hái yǒu yí shì . . .
P.S. There's another thing . . .

Exercises for 3.1

1 Below is a personal letter (the main text is represented by XXXXXXX . . .) from a granddaughter to her grandmother. The other parts of the letter need to be filled in. Below the letter are four phrases. First, fill in the blanks with appropriate words based on the context, and then place each phrase in the appropriate position in the letter.

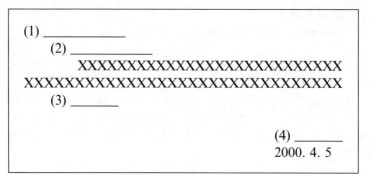

(a)   ____好！
(b)   祝您____健康！
(c)   ____奶奶：
(d)   ____：晓花

2   Translate the following opening and closing remarks into Chinese:

    (a)   I just got your letter yesterday. Knowing that you're doing fine over there, I'm really pleased for you.

    (b)   I haven't heard from you for a long time. I'm just wondering how you are getting on and if you have adjusted to the new environment.

    (c)   Sorry I haven't replied to your letter earlier. I've been really busy with my graduation dissertation recently.

    (d)   Please give my regards to your family.

3.2 信封格式 Format of an envelope

范文 2, Text 2

100081
北京长安大街2号
    《华丰广告编辑部》

        沈建秋　(先生)收

        西安西北外国语大学英文系吴寄
        710061

Notes to Text 2

a. In mainland China, the postcode usually consists of six digits. Place it at the top left-hand corner. The word for postcode is 邮编 (**yóubiān**).

b. In writing the recipient's address, the order is as follows: province, city/county, street or avenue name and number, house/building name and finally flat/house number. The address is often split into two lines. There are no rules as to where the split should be made. If it is a work address, the organisation name can be put on a separate line (see the example above). If it is a big city, then the province name can be omitted. Here are the relevant words for writing out an address:

省	**shěng**	*province*	市	**shì**	*city*
县	**xiàn**	*county*	路	**lù**	*road*
大街	**dàjiē**	*avenue*	楼	**lóu**	*building*
栋	**dòng**	*block*	号	**hào**	*number*
室/宅	**shì/zhái**	*flat/house*			

c. In Chinese, the surname comes first, followed by the given name, and then the title. Titles can be used but are not compulsory. The common titles for a personal letter are: 先生、女士、小姐、同志. The term 同志 is still used in mainland China, although its use is diminishing. If the recipient is a teacher, 老师 is usually used as the title. Please note that kinship terms such as uncle, auntie, should not be used as titles here. Finally, put 收 (**shōu**, *to be received by*) or 启 (**qǐ**, *to be opened by*) after the title if used, otherwise after the name.

d. In writing the sender's address and name, it is fairly normal just to write the surname after the sender's address followed by the word 寄 (**jì**, *sent by*).

e. Sending a letter from an English-speaking country to someone in China, you can still use the above format if the address is written in Chinese characters, so long as you put 'To: People's Republic of China' at an eye-catching position on the envelope. Note that red ink should not be used in writing a letter or envelope as it is regarded as impolite and offensive.

Exercise for 3.2

You are in China doing a summer language course at Beijing University. You live on campus, in Room 3 of Overseas Student Dormitory No. 6 Building, and the postcode is 100081. You are writing a letter to Wang Heping, a Chinese friend of yours. Write out an envelope in Chinese characters. Here is Heping's address in English:

Apartment 2, Building 16,
No. 38 West City Avenue,
Xi'an, 710061

3.3 有具体目的的信函 Letters with a specific purpose

范文 3, Text 3

The following letter is from Cheng Mingde to his former classmate and friend Li Jiahe. Mingde is inviting Jiahe to a spring outing:

嘉禾:

你好！

好久不见了。自从你家搬到城南以后，我便少了一个好同伴。非常想念你。

春天来了，又到了春游的好时候，五月的第一个星期天(2号)，我想约你，还有吴天瑞和张兵一起去城东的孤峰岭春游。孤峰岭周围到处都是郁金香花，风景非常优美。我们每人都多带上些好吃的东西，早晨八点半在我家集合，然后一同出发。希望你能参加这次春游。

请你尽快给我一个回信。

祝

康乐！

明德
4.18

Notes to Text 3

a. When writing an informal invitation to friends and family, the verb 请 or 约 is most frequently used. For example:

我们全家想请你来上海和我们一起过春节。

wǒmen quán jiā xiǎng qǐng nǐ lái Shànghǎi hé wǒmen yìqǐ guò Chūnjié.

Our whole family would like to invite you to Shanghai to spend Chinese New Year with us.

In writing an informal invitation, one can simply explain the event, and add one of the following expressions at the end of the letter:

这是个难得的机会，你来参加吧。

zhé shì ge nándéde jīhuì, nǐ lái cānjiā ba.

This is a rare opportunity, please come to join us.

如果你能来，我将会非常高兴。

rúguǒ nǐ néng lái, wǒ jiāng huì fēicháng gāoxìng.

If you can come, I'll be delighted.

In a formal invitation, the place and time of the event is spelled out first, then one of the following two expressions is added at the end:

敬请光临。

jìng qǐng guānglín.

Your presence is cordially requested.

希望您能准时光临。

xīwàng nín néng zhǔnshí guānglín.

Hope you can honour us with your timely presence. (formal)

b. Here use of 便 is very similar to that of 就. It is often used in written language. As an adverb, it has the meaning of '*then*' or '*therefore*'. For example:

我听到这个消息便立即去医院看他。

wǒ tīngdào zhè ge xiāoxi biàn lìjí qù yīyuàn kàn tā.

Upon hearing the news, I went to the hospital to visit him straightaway.

c. When listing two things, 和 or 跟 is often used. When there are more than two items, 和 or 跟 is placed between the last two items, and at the same time other linking words such as 还有 can be used between the first and the second item as in Model 3 above:

我想约你、还有吴天瑞和张兵一起去...春游。

wǒ xiǎng yuē nǐ, hǎi yǒu Wú Tiānruì hé Zhǎng Bīng yìqǐ qù...
chūnyóu.

I'd like to invite you, Wu Tianrui and Zhang Bing, to ... for a spring outing.

范文 *4, Text 4*

Below is Jiahe's reply to Mingde's letter (as in Model 3), accepting his invitation:

明德：

　　谢谢你的来信。说真的，我这两天正打算同你联系呢。

　　非常高兴接受你的邀约。五月二号去游孤峰岭，好极了！我要带上许多好吃的东西，有几样东西你想也想不到。我一定去，风雨无阻。

　　两周后见！

嘉禾
四月十八日

Notes to Text 4

a. The phrase 来信, (*lit. coming letter*), refers to letters you have received. If this is too confusing, then simply use 信. For example:

> 读了你的(来)信后，我激动不已。
> **dú le nǐde (lái)xìn hòu, wǒ jīdòng bù yǐ.**
> *Having read your letter, I was tremendously excited.*

b. The particle 正 is used here to indicate that something was just about to happen. It is often used before the verbs 想, 要 or 准备, and with 就 in the second half of the sentence. For example:

> 我正想给他打个电话，他的电话就来了。
> **wǒ zhèng xiǎng gěi tā dǎ ge diànhuà, tāde diànhuà jiù lái le.**
> *As I was just thinking of calling him, he rang.*

> 我正想给你写信，你的信却先到了。
> **wǒ zhèng xiǎng gěi nǐ xiě xìn, nǐde xìn què xiān dào le.**
> *I was just about to write to you when your letter arrived.*

c. The following are common expressions used in accepting an invitation:

> 非常高兴接受你的邀请。
> **fēicháng gāoxìng jiēshòu nǐde yāoqǐn.**
> *I'm so pleased to accept your invitation.*

> 能做你的客人，是我的荣幸。
> **néng zuò nǐde kèrén, shì wǒde róngxìng.**
> *Being your guest is my pleasure.*

> 这么好的机会，我怎么能错过呢?
> **zhème hǎo de jīhuì wǒ zěnme néng cuòguò ne?**
> *How can I miss such a good opportunity?*

> 谢谢你的邀请，我一定准时到/出席。*
> **xièxie nǐde yāoqǐn, wǒ yídìng zhǔnshí dào/chūxí.**
> *Thank you for your invitation, and I'll definitely be there on time.*

*到 is informal and 出席 is formal.

d. The phrase 想也想不到 can be loosely translated as '*would never imagine*' or '*cannot possibly think of (no matter how)*'. This construction consists of *verb* + 也 + *the same verb* + *negation word* + *complement*, and can apply to some other verbs. It is often used with 怎么 in front of the first verb. For example:

不知为什么，昨晚我怎么睡也睡不着。

bù zhī wèishénme, zuó wǎn wǒ zěnme shuì yě shuì bù zháo.

Don't know why, I couldn't sleep last night no matter how hard I tried.

我写了好几遍，可怎么写也写不好。

wǒ xiě le hǎo jǐ biàn, kě zěnme xiě yě xiě bù hǎo.

I tried several times, but could not write it satisfactorily no matter how hard I tried.

范文 5, Text 5

Below is Zhang Bing's reply to Mingde's letter (as in Model 3), turning down his invitation:

明德兄：

很高兴收到你的来信。

去孤峰岭春游是个非常好的主意，我一直想去那儿一游。可五月二号那个星期天是我姐姐出嫁的日子，我们全家都要参加她的婚礼，吃她的喜酒。因此，去孤峰岭春游，我就不能奉陪了。非常抱歉。

请代我问老同学们好！

祝

春游愉快！

张兵
4.22

Notes to Text 5

a. This kinship term 兄 (*elder brother*) is only used in the written language. Here, Mingde is not Zhang Bing's real elder brother. The term is used to show their close relationship.

b. The verbal phrase 出嫁 (*lit. marry out*) is used when a woman gets married; when a man gets married, it is 娶媳妇 (**qǔ xífu**), meaning '*take a wife*'. However, 结婚 (**jiéhūn**) can be used in both cases and it is a modern expression. Again, when a woman marries a man, 嫁 is used; and when a man marries a woman, 娶 is used. For example, Xiaohua is a woman and Zhigang is a man:

小花昨天出嫁了，她嫁给了志钢。
Xiǎohuā zuótiān chūjià le, tā jiàgěi le Zhìgāng.
Xiaohua got married yesterday. She married Zhigang.

志钢昨天娶媳妇了，他娶了小花。
Zhìgāng zuótiān qǔ xífu le, tā qǔ le Xiǎohuā.
Zhigang got married yesterday. He married Xiaohua.

小花和志钢结婚了。
Xiǎohuā hé Zhìgāng jiéhūn le.
Xiaohua and Zhigang got married.

c. The phrase 吃喜酒 (*lit. eat happy wine*) means '*to attend a wedding banquet*'. 喜酒 is a term for wedding banquet. The expression 喝喜酒 is equally common.

d. In turning down an invitation, here are some other useful phrases:

Formal:

非常抱歉，那天我已有约，不能奉陪。
fēicháng bàoqiàn, nà tiān wǒ yǐ yǒu yuē, bù néng fèngpéi.
Many apologies. As I already have an appointment that day, I won't be able to be there.

因为我下周末有事，对于你的邀约，只好辞谢。
yīnwèi wǒ xià zhōumò yǒu shì, duìyú nǐde yāoyuē, zhǐhǎo cíxiè.
As I already have a prior engagement next weekend, I have to turn down your invitation with regret.

我不能接受你的邀请，务请原谅。
wǒ bù néng jiēshòu nǐde yāoqǐng, wù qǐng yuánliàng.
Please forgive me, but I am not able to accept your invitation.

Informal:

对不起，下星期天我去不了，因为 . . .
duìbuqǐ, xià xīngqītiān wǒ qù bù liǎo, yīnwèi . . .
Sorry, I can't make it next Sunday because . . .

真不巧，后天我要去上海出差，后天晚上的聚会就不能参加了。
zhēn bùqiǎo, hòutiān wǒ yào qù Shànghǎi chūchāi, hòutiān wǎnshangde jùhuì jiù bù néng cānjiā le.
Unfortunately, I'm going to Shanghai on a business trip the day after tomorrow, so I won't be able to come to the party that evening.

很可惜/很遗憾，周末的春游我无法参加，因为我妈妈病了 . . .
**hěn kěxī/hěn yíhàn, zhōumòde chūn yóu wǒ wú fǎ cānjiā, yīnwèi
wǒ māma bìng le . . .**
*It is a great shame/pity but, because my mum is ill, I shall not be able to
come for the spring outing.*

Exercises for 3.3

1   Complete the following sentences using appropriate phrases/sentences given
in the box below (see relevant notes above for references):

(a)	敬请光临。	(b)	真遗憾......无法前来参加。
(c)	你要是能来，那就太好了。	(d)	务请原谅。
(e)	是我的荣幸。		

(1)   由于下周末我要出席学术会议，无法参加庆祝晚宴，_____。
(2)   本大使馆将于9月30日晚8时在使馆主厅举行国庆招待会，_____。
(3)   下个星期六，咱们大学的同学要在我家聚会，_____。
(4)   能参加你们的婚礼，_____。
(5)   谢谢你邀请我参加你儿子的婚礼，_____我下个星期天要去上海
出差，_____。

2   Imagine a friend of yours is having a birthday party and has sent you the
following invitation. Unfortunately you cannot accept it as you are going
on holiday with your sister just before that. Write a reply to the following
invitation:

晓明：

     你好！八月六号是我二十一岁生日。我父母准备在那天
给我开一个生日晚会。我请了大约二十多人，都是以前的老
同学和朋友。如果你能来的话，我可就太高兴了。晚会大约
七点开始。你可以在我家住一夜，这样，咱们第二天还可以
去看电影。

     盼回音！

                                          友：明亮
                                          七月十六号

3.4 保持联系信函 Keep-in-touch letters

范文 6, Text 6

亲爱的爸爸，妈妈：

你们好！前几天意外地接到奶奶的电话，我真是高兴极了。她说爸爸最近出差去了北京，想必已经回来了吧。妈妈的书编得怎么样了？

我一切都很好。上周休了几天假，和几个朋友一起去爬了泰山。我们在山上呆了一夜，第二天早上看了日出。那景色十分独特，使人陶醉不已！下次你们来济南时，如果有兴致，我可以陪你们再爬一次泰山。

这个星期也不知忙些什么，不知不觉就快到周末了。对了，我们公司的小李这个星期天要给我介绍一个女朋友！我已同意去见面。等见完后，如果有眉目的话，会告诉你们的。

多多保重身体！

祝

好！

儿子: 小勇
六月八号

Notes to Text 6

a. The sentence 我一切都很好, meaning '*Everything is fine with me*', is often used in personal letters. The interrogative form of the sentence can be used as a greeting at the beginning of a letter:

(你)近来一切都好吗？

(nǐ) jìnlái yíqiè dōu hǎo ma?

Has everything been going well with you recently?

b. The phrase 多多保重身体 (*take care*) is a very frequently used closing remark in a personal letter, especially when you write to your parents, grandparents or elderly people. In ending a letter, one can also use the following phrases to express the wish to hear from the other person. For example:

等着你的回信。

děngzhe nǐde huíxìn.

Looking forward to your reply.

盼回音。

pàn huíyīn.

Look forward to your reply.

36

有时间请来信谈谈你的近况。

yǒu shíjiān qǐng lái xìn tántan nǐde jìn kuàng.

Please write and let us know how you are, if you have time.

如果有什么事需要我帮忙，请尽管来信。

rúguǒ yǒu shénme shì xūyào wǒ bāngmáng, qǐng jǐnguǎn lái xìn.

If there's anything I can do to help, please do not hesitate to get in touch.

c.　The following expressions are useful when you wish to mention something else in the letter:

对了，还有一件事想告诉你。

duìle, hái yǒu yí jiàn shì xiǎng gàosu nǐ.

Yes, there's something else I want to tell you.

说起 . . .，你能不能 . . . ?

shuōqǐ . . . , nǐ néng bu néng . . . ?

Talking about . . . , can you . . . ?

顺便提一下，. . .

shùnbiàn tí yíxià, . . .

By the way, . . .

Exercises for 3.4

1　The following is a letter with certain information missing. Fill in the missing parts with an appropriate phrase or sentence given in the box on the next page:

小明：

　　你好！

　　好久没有收到你的 ___(1)___ ，不知你是否一切都好？ ___(2)___ ？

　　我有一件大事要告诉你： 我有男朋友了！他叫刘大虎，是个足球运动员。我们是在一个朋友的生日晚会上认识的，最近常常见面，___(3)___ 。我们准备七月去上海玩几天。___(4)___ ，咱们一定要聚一聚。请尽早告诉我你七月份的日程安排。

　　___(5)___ ，我这两天才接上了互联网，可以用电子邮件了。我的电子邮件地址是: lixiaoxia@pek.edu.cn。你给我的电子邮件地址，我不知放到哪里去了。如果方便的话，你先给我发一个吧。这样我们就可以在网上通话了。

　　___(6)___ 。

　　祝好！

友: 晓夏
六月七号

___(7)___ 。

37

(a) 你如果那时候在上海的话

(b) 又: 秀芳生了个小女孩，起名叫荷芝

(c) 上个月寄去的照片是否收到

(d) 希望尽快收到你的回信

(e) 相处得很好

(f) 对了

(g) 来信

2 You have just found a pen-friend in China. Since your first letter to him/her, you have started to learn Chinese. Write another letter to your pen-friend and describe how you find your Chinese class, and perhaps your classmates.

Vocabulary

3.1

近况	jìn kuàng	recent situation
随信寄去	suí xìn jìqu	enclosed are . . .
另	lìng	p.s.
又及	yòují	p.s.

3.2

邮编	yóubiān	postcode
编辑部	biānjì bù	editorial department

3.3

搬	bān	to move
城南	chéng nán	south of the city
少了	shǎo le	to be short of; to be missing
同伴	tóngbàn	companion
春游	chūn yóu	spring outing
约	yuē	to arrange; to invite
城东	chéng dōng	east of the city
孤峰岭	Gūfēng Lǐng	Gufeng Mountain
郁金香	yùjīnxiāng	tulip
风景	fēngjǐng	scenery
优美	yōuměi	beautiful
集合	jíhé	to gather; to get together
康乐	kāng lè	healthy and happy
接受	jiēshòu	to accept
邀约	yāoyuē	invitation
游	yóu	to visit; to tour
带上	dàishang	to bring with
风雨无阻	fēngyǔ wúzǔ	rain or shine
激动不已	jīdòng bùyǐ	to be tremendously excited

客人	kèrén	guest
荣幸	róngxìng	pleasure; honour
机会	jīhuì	opportunity
错过	cuòguò	to miss
准时	zhǔnshí	to be on time; timely
出席	chūxí	to be present; to attend
一游	yì yóu	for a visit
出嫁	chūjià	to get married (for a woman)
婚礼	hūnlǐ	wedding
喜酒	xǐjiǔ	wedding banquet
奉陪	fèngpéi	to accompany
抱歉	bàoqiàn	apologies
代我	dài wǒ	on my behalf; for me
有约	yǒu yuē	to have a prior engagement
邀约	yāoyuē	to invite
辞谢	cíxiè	to decline with regret
务请原谅	wùqǐng yuánliàng	please excuse me; apologies
真不巧	zhēn bùqiǎo	unfortunately
出差	chūchāi	to go on a business trip
聚会	jùhuì	get-together; party
真可惜	zhēn kěxī	what a shame
遗憾	yíhàn	shame that . . . ; pity that . . .
由于	yóuyú	due to
出席	chūxí	to attend
学术会议	xuéshù huìyì	academic conference
庆祝	qìngzhù	to celebrate
晚宴	wǎnyàn	evening banquet
大使馆	dàshǐguǎn	embassy
主厅	zhǔtīng	main hall
举行	jǔxíng	to hold
国庆	guóqìng	National Day
招待会	zhāodàihuì	reception

3.4

想必	xiǎngbì	to reckon
编	biān	to compile
休假	xiūjià	to be on holiday
泰山	Tài Shān	Mount Taishan; Taishan Mountain
日出	rìchū	sunrise
景色	jǐngsè	scenery
独特	dútè	unique
陶醉不已	táozuì bù yǐ	to be completely intoxicated
济南	Jǐ'nán	[a city in China]
有兴致	yǒu xìngzhì	to be interested
不知不觉	bù zhī bù jué	without realising
眉目	méimù	sign of a positive outcome (*lit.* eyebrow and eye)
互联网	hùlián wǎng	Internet

第四单元：通知、小广告及其它
Unit Four: Announcements, small ads and others

This unit deals with another type of concise, short writing. As readers of this type of writing are either the general public or people you do not know very well, the writing is more formal in both sentence structure and wording than the writing in Unit Two.

4.1 通知 Announcements

范文 *1, Text 1*

通知

　　为了丰富我院广大师生员工的业余文化生活，特邀请北京杂技团本周末来我院演出。欢迎大家前来观看。

时间：2001年1月6日(星期六)晚7时整
地点：本院大礼堂
票价：本院师生员工免费，非本院师生员工一元

医学院工会
2001年1月3日

Notes to Text 1

a.　An announcement consists of the title, its main text, the organiser and the date of issue. As announcements in Chinese are mostly about coming events or activities, the text usually explains what the event is and then spells out the time, venue and other relevant information. The title can be general, e.g. 通知; or specific, e.g. 春节联欢会 (*Chinese New Year Party*), 学术报告会 (*Lecture*). An announcement about the coming of a film, play, etc., can also be called 海报. An announcement about a football match or any other kind of ball game can be 球讯.

b. The following expressions are often used in writing a public announcement:

> 为了 (*in order to*), 由于 (*due to*), 特邀请 (*especially invite*),
> 特安排 (*especially arrange*), 欢迎各位/大家 (*welcome everyone*),
> 前来观看/参观/参加 (*come and watch/come for a visit/come to take part*)

c. The character 本 is the formal term for '*this*'. For example: 本周末 (*this weekend*), 本院 (*this college*), 本政府 (*this government*).

d. The term 前来 means exactly the same as 来 except that the former is more formal than the latter. For example:

> 本画廊从一月至三月将举办世界名画展，欢迎大家前来参观。
> **běn huàláng cóng yíyuè zhì sānyuè jiāng jǔbàn shìjiè míng huà zhǎn, huānyíng dàjiā qiánlái cānguān.**
> *This Gallery will hold the World Famous Paintings Exhibition from January to March. Everyone is welcome.*

e. 非 is a formal term for 不是 when placed before a noun. For example:

> 非本校职工不许入内。
> **fēi běn xiào zhígōng bù xǔ rù nèi.**
> *Non-staff members of the college are not allowed to come in.*

Exercise for 4.1

Read Model 1 above again and write a similar announcement on behalf of the Chinese Department stating that a Chinese calligrapher has been invited to teach the overseas students Chinese calligraphy. The purpose of this is to improve the students' handwriting and foster their interest in learning Chinese. You decide on the time and place. Admission: students of the Chinese Department, free, otherwise 5 *Yuan*.

4.2   小广告 Small ads

By small ads, we mean non-commercial, personal advertisements. Here we include those small ads that you are likely to write when you are in a Chinese-speaking community, namely, looking for accommodation, looking for a part-time job, or buying and selling things.

范文 2, *Text 2*

求租

　　因考研究生复习，求租南方大学附近楼房一间。租期一个月。要求有水、电、热水器及电话。联系电话: 5188213。

张文树
2001年12月15日

范文 3, *Text 3*

家教

　　本人是语言学院的美国留学生，愿利用暑假教授英文。收费根据情况商定。联系电话: 86153492。

史约翰
2001年7月15日

范文 4, *Text 4*

急购

　　本人急需一辆24或26英寸女车。联系电话: 6351767。

王兰
2001年9月15日

范文 5, *Text 5*

出售

本人因学完回国，有以下电器出售：
    14寸彩电 - 350 元
    微波炉 - 220 元
    音响 - 200 元

有兴趣者，请尽快与本人联系。电话: 7133056。

         雅岩
         2001年6月25日

Notes to Texts 2–5

a. For small ads, titles are important. You want the reader to know immediately what the ad is about. As for the wording of the title, it is very flexible. For example, when renting accommodation, the ad can also be titled as 租房, 急租. When looking for a job, it can have a general title such as 求职 (*seeking a job*) or a specific title depending on what work you would like to do (e.g. 教钢琴, *teach piano*; 教英文, *teach English*; 看孩子, *baby-sitting*). Another important piece of information to include here is a contact number.

b. Normally, we use the construction '*number + measure word + noun*', for example, 一间楼房 (*one room in a building*), 一个磁盘 (*one disk*). However, in writings such as small ads, the order '*noun + number + measure word*' is usually used, as in 楼房一间 (as in Model 2), and 磁盘一个 (as in Model 6 below).

c. In the above texts, several words have been shortened due to the informal style of writing. Here are the full forms together with the shortened forms in brackets: 女式自行车(女车) ；彩色电视机(彩电).

Exercises for 4.2

1 You are graduating soon, and want to sell the following items: old textbooks, a desk lamp and a bike. Write an ad that includes the details of the items for sale and the price you are asking for them.

2　You are in Beijing for six months on an exchange programme, and you wish to live off campus, either with other students or with a Chinese family. Write an ad specifying your requirements.

4.3　其它 Others

In this section, we shall cover the following notices which do not fall into a single category: Lost and found (including looking for a lost item and looking for the owner of a lost item); receipts (of cash or an item) and written requests for leave.

4.3.1 寻物启事，失物招领 *Lost and found*

范文 6, *Text 6*

寻物启事

　　本人不慎于昨日(五月七号)在计算机房内丢失磁盘一个。磁盘上有本人姓名，盘内有个名为HIS2的重要文件。有拾到者，请与历史系研究生班王洪联系。必有重谢。

电话: 728866
电子邮件: wh16@ghm.pku.cn

范文 7, *Text 7*

招领启事

　　昨晚(七月十号)七点半，本人在工人体育场门口拾到上衣一件，上兜内有现金若干。有丢失者，请速到中山公园办公室认领。

Notes to Texts 6 and 7

a. In Chinese, a distinction is made between notices that look for a lost item and those that look for the owner of a lost item. The former is called 寻物启事, and the latter 失物招领 or 招领启示. However, they share the same format: (i) title, which can be very general, e.g. 寻物启事, 失物招领, or more specific, e.g. 寻自行车, 手表招领; (ii) time and place where the item was lost or found; (iii) detailed description of the item in case of a lost item; but very general description of the item in case of a found item; (iv) contact person, who can be the author of the notice or someone else, and the means of contact.

b. The following expressions are often used in notices looking for lost items: 本人 (*I*), 不慎 (*carelessly*), 有发现者/有拾到者 (*whoever has found it*), 请与 . . . 联系 (*please get in touch with* . . .), 面谢/重谢 (*to thank in person/a handsome reward*).

c. In a notice looking for the owner of a lost item, the following expressions are often used: 本人 (*I*), 在 . . . 拾到 (*found . . . in/at* . . .), 有丢失者 (*whoever has lost it*), 请速到 . . . 认领 (*come to . . . to claim it immediately*).

d. Both the verbs 发现 and 拾到 mean '*have found*' in English. However, while 拾到 is usually followed by an item or cash, 发现 can also be followed by a person, e.g. a missing child.

Exercises for 4.3

1   Fill in the blanks in the following notice:

失物招领

　　本人昨天下午(5月六号)在图书馆一层阅览室＿＿＿笔记本一个，有丢失者请到中文系系办公室＿＿＿。电话分机: 5021。

李维
2001年5月7号

---

2   Suppose you lost your wallet. Write a notice giving details about your wallet and the contents of the wallet, and where and when you lost it.

4.3.2 收据和借条 *Receipts*

范文 8, *Text 8*

收据

今收到王可宁先生捐款叁仟肆佰元整，用于帮助贫困地区儿童教育。
此据。

收款人：王平
2001年5月7日

范文 9, *Text 9*

借条

今借到中文系录音机一台，用完后速还。
此据。

借物人：李勇
2001年8月1日

Notes to Texts 8 and 9

a. A receipt in Chinese must be specified as either 收据, which is written by the recipient of the cash or goods, or 借条, which is written by the borrower of the cash or goods. The format is the same: title (i.e. 收据 or 借条), main body, the signature and the date. Note that before the signature, you need to spell out who you are, i.e. whether you are the recipient or the borrower. If you are the recipient of some money, cash or a cheque, you sign it as 收款人. Normally, people would write receipts only for money but not for items. The borrower of an item would sign it as 借物人 and the borrower of the cash would sign it as 借款人.

b. In writing a receipt or cheque for a sum of money, the normal practice is to write the numbers in a special set of characters in order to avoid any confusion or illegal alteration. The following are the numbers from one to ten and the numbers for 100 and 1,000 in both normal and special forms:

NORMAL	一	二	三	四	五	六	七	八	九	十
SPECIAL	壹	贰	叁	肆	伍	陆	柒	捌	玖	拾

NORMAL	百	千
SPECIAL	佰	仟

c. The term 整 normally means '*whole*' or '*complete*'. But when it is used after an amount of money, it means '*only*'.

d. The phrase 此据 (*this as a proof*) is used only at the end of a receipt, any kind of proof or certificate.

Exercises

1 Professor Wang Ning has donated two volumes on Chinese art to the library of Eastern University. Write a receipt on behalf of the library.

2 You are going on a field trip to Hong Kong, but unfortunately you have not received the subsidy from your home university. The Chinese department where you are studying now has agreed to lend you 3,500 *Yuan* on condition that you return the money in three months' time. Write a receipt as a borrower of this amount.

4.3.3 请假条 *Written request for leave*

范文 *10, Text 10*

请假条

林老师：

　　我因昨晚发烧，今天不能前去上课，请准假一天为盼。附医生证明一张。

　　　　　　　　　　　　　　　　　　二年级学生：林芳
　　　　　　　　　　　　　　　　　　2001年10月5日

47

Notes to Text 10

a. A note asking for a short leave from either one's teacher or one's boss consists of the following four components: (i) title, i.e. 请假条, (ii) form of address, e.g. 王老师, 张经理; (iii) reason for leave; and (iv) signature and date.

b. Phrases often used: 由于 (*due to . . .*), 因(为) (*because . . .*), 不能 (*cannot*), 望准为盼 (*hope the leave can be granted*), 请批准 (*please grant me the leave*), 特此请假 . . . 天/星期/月 (*hence ask for leave for . . . days/weeks/months*).

Exercises for 4.3

1 Fill in the blanks using appropriate words/expressions introduced in this unit (not just in Model 10):

    (a) (an announcement)

       _____庆祝中秋节，今晚七时在礼堂放映电影《梁山伯与祝英台》。

    (b) (a receipt)

       _____张向群房租柒佰捌拾元_____。此_____。

    (c) (a written request for leave)

       _____我患感冒，头疼咳嗽，不能前去上课，_____请假一天，望准_____。

    (d) (lost and found)

       (i) 六月八日下午，_____在中文系图书馆_____钱包_____，内有现金_____。有丢失_____，请速到中文系302号房间_____。

       (ii) 上周六上午(六月十三号)，本人在游泳池_____丢失了一件黑白相间的女式游泳衣。有_____，请与中文系三年级李小明_____。

2 Suppose you are studying in China. Write to Prof. Li, telling him that you are unable to come to school because your father is coming to see you from America and you have to meet him at the airport. You would like to take one day off.

Vocabulary

4.1

丰富	**fēngfù**	to enrich
我(们学)院	**wǒ(men xué)yuàn**	our college
广大	**guǎngdà**	all members of . . .

师生员工	shīshēng yuángōng	students and staff
业余	yèyú	spare time
特邀请	tè yāoqǐng	to specially invite
杂技团	zájì tuán	acrobatic troupe
演出	yǎnchū	to give a performance
前来观看	qiánlái guānkàn	to come and watch
大礼堂	dàlǐtáng	assembly hall
免费	miǎnfèi	free of charge
非	fēi	non
医学院	yīxuéyuàn	medical college
工会	gōnghuì	trade union
联欢会	liánhuānhuì	party
学术报告会	xuéshù bàogàohuì	academic talk
海报	hǎibào	announcement (for a film, concert, etc.)
为了	wèile	in order to
由于	yóuyú	due to
特安排	tè ānpái	to specially arrange
欢迎各位	huānyíng gè wèi	all are welcome
大家	dàjiā	everyone
参观	cānguān	to visit
参加	cānjiā	to take part
画廊	huàláng	art gallery
举办	jǔbàn	to hold
世界	shìjiè	world
名画展	mínghuà zhǎn	famous painting exhibition
球讯	qiúxùn	announcement (for football, and other ball games)

4.2

有兴趣者	yǒu xìngqù zhě	anybody interested
租房	zū fáng	seeking accommodation
急租	jí zū	accommodation needed urgently
求租	qiúzū	seeking accommodation
租期	zū qī	rental period
家教	jiājiào	private tuition
利用	lìyòng	to take advantage of
暑假	shǔjià	summer vacation
收费	shōufèi	fees
商定	shāngdìng	to negotiate
急购	jí gòu	to buy urgently
女车	nǚ chē	woman's bike
出售	chūshòu	for sale
学完	xuéwán	to finish studies
电器	diànqì	electrical appliances
彩电	cǎi diàn	colour TV
微波炉	wēibōlú	microwave oven
音响	yīnxiǎng	hi-fi

4.3.1

不慎	búshèn	carelessly
丢失	diūshī	to lose
磁盘	cípán	disk
计算机房	jìsuànjī fáng	computer room
必有重谢	bì yǒu zhòng xiè	there will be a generous reward
拾到	shídào	to have found; to have picked up
兜	dōu	pocket
若干	ruògān	a certain amount; a certain number
丢失者	diūshī zhě	the person who has lost it
认领	rènlǐng	to claim
失物	shī wù	lost item
招领	zhāolǐng	to look for the owner
寻	xún	to look for
有发现者	yǒu fāxiàn zhě	whoever has found it
有拾到者	yǒu shídào zhě	whoever has found it
与......联系	yǔ . . . liánxì	to contact
面谢	miàn xiè	to thank in person

4.3.2

收据	shōujù	receipt
捐款	juānkuǎn	donation (of money)
叁仟肆佰	sān qiān sì bǎi	three thousand four hundred
整	zhěng	only
此据	cǐ jù	hereby confirm
收款人	shōu kuǎn rén	recipient of cash
借条	jiètiáo	receipt (*lit.* borrowing note)
借物人	jiè wù rén	the borrower of sth.

4.3.3

请假条	qǐngjià tiáo	written request for leave
准假...为盼	zhǔn jià . . . wéi pàn	to hope permission will be given for . . . (duration)
附	fù	attached; enclosed
证明	zhèngmíng	certificate
望准为盼	wàngzhǔn wéipàn	hoping that leave be granted
请批准	qǐng pīzhǔn	please grant me leave
特此请假	tècǐ qǐngjià	hence ask for leave
中秋节	zhōngqiū jié	mid-autumn festival
放映	fàngyìng	to show (a film)

第五单元：正式书信
Unit Five: Formal letters

This unit deals with formal letters – introducing their format and style. As formal letters are often addressed to people whom the writer has never met or does not know well, the style of the writing is formal and some expressions are for writing only. Below we shall cover the following types of formal letters: letters of application, inquiring about job opportunities, requesting information (about university courses), and how to write replies.

5.1 申请信 Letters of application

范文 *1, Text 1*

南海市图书馆馆长先生：

　　从五月二十六日《南海晚报》所登的贵馆广告里，知道你们需要招聘一名图书管理员。我目前是英国金桥大学汉学专业本科四年级学生，今年七月即将毕业。我很热爱图书管理工作，很愿意应聘。

　　从随信寄去的个人简历中，您可以看到，在四年大学学习中，我学习了现代汉语、中国文学、中国历史、中国文化等课程，并都取得了优异成绩。从我的简历中，您还可以看到，我对图书管理这项工作十分感兴趣；在1998年和1999年暑假期间，曾两次在东阳市图书馆做短期工作，掌握了一定的图书分类、编目、登记等工作的经验。目前中国正在继续改革开放，英文书籍材料越来越多。我的母语是英语，同时，也精通汉语。我相信对于贵馆的图书管理工作，我一定能够胜任。

　　按照贵馆广告里所提要求，随信寄去本人简历一份，照片两张，请查收。如蒙录用，定勤勉工作，不负你们的期望。

　　　　　　　此致
敬礼！

　　　　　　　　　　　　　　　　　　Jane Matthew (马玉珍)
　　　　　　　　　　　　　　　　　　2001年5月30日

51

Notes to Text 1

a. In writing a job application letter, the following information is generally required, unless there are specific requirements laid out in the advertisement:

- where you got the information to make this application;
- brief self-introduction;
- relevant personal interests and professional experience that you think can make your application successful, including your qualifications;
- inquiries about the things you are not sure of;
- statement of what extra documents, e.g. CV, you have enclosed.

b. When writing a letter of application, if it is not clear who the letter should be addressed to, the normal practice is to address it to the head of the organisation (if it is a small organisation), the personnel department or the department where the vacancy is. For example, 尊敬的经理先生 (*respected Mr Manager*), 尊敬的人事科科长 (*respected head of the Personnel Department*), 尊敬的销售部主任 (*respected head of the Sales Department*). The term 尊敬的 is most frequently used in front of the recipient. Alternative terms such as 敬爱的 (*dear*) and 亲爱的 (*dear*) are occasionally used. If you know the recipient's surname, suppose it is 王 and he is the manager, you can address him/her as 尊敬的王经理 (*respected Manager Wang*).

c. To show respect for the organisation you would like to work for, the term 贵 (*your*) is used instead of 你们的 in front of it. For example, 贵公司 (*your company*), 贵校 (*your school; your university*), 贵馆 (*your library*), 贵报 (*your newspaper*), 贵国 (*your country*). Please note that once 贵 is used, the noun following it is likely to be shortened.

d. Common closing remarks in formal letters:

此致 敬礼！ *With best wishes.*
祝合作愉快！ *Wishing a pleasant cooperation.*
期待您的早日回复！ *Look forward to hearing from you soon.*

e. The following are some more useful expressions and constructions in writing a job application letter:

最近看到 … … … … 刊登的(招聘)广告，得知 … … … … …
(I've) recently seen the job advertisement in . . . , and hence have learnt that . . .

从 … … … … 的招聘广告中获悉，贵 … … … … …
(I have) learnt from the advertisement advertised in . . . , your . . .

我对 … … … … 非常感兴趣，现给您写信应聘。
I am very interested in . . . , and I am writing to you to apply for this position.

我本人极愿从事此项工作，特写此信应聘。
I myself would very much like to do this job, and therefore am writing to apply for it.

从我的简历中，您不难看出/很容易看到 ... ...。
From my CV, you could easily see that ...

我之所以要申请此项工作，(主要)是因为 ... ...。
The (main) reason I have in applying for this job is that ...

我要申请这项工作的另一个原因是 ... ...。
Another reason I have in applying for this job is that ...

我对做好这项工作充满信心。
I have complete confidence that I can do this job well.

我有能力也有信心做好这项工作。
I have the ability as well as confidence to do the job well.

Exercises for 5.1

1　Rewrite Model 1 and try to use some of the phrases listed in Note (e) above.

2　Apply for one of the following posts. They were advertised in《南海晚报》on September 2, 2001. In your letter, you need to include the following information: where you saw the ad, why you want to apply, your qualifications (if any), your previous experience, your ability to use Chinese, and to ask questions regarding the job.

(1)

香港国际图书出版社
诚聘
中英文翻译

本出版社拟招聘中英文翻译一名。

应聘条件：　大学本科毕业；35岁以下；精通中英文；有一定的笔译经验；能从事电脑中英文文字处理；热爱本职工作；责任心强。

基本待遇：　免费住宿；年薪160,000–210,000港币。

应试方法：　2001年9月30日前寄一寸近照两张，个人简历一份。10月上旬通知面试和笔试时间。

联系人：　香港九龙荣华大街26号，香港国际图书出版社社长丁昌顺先生。

(2)

香港华通银行北京办事处

招聘

本办事处拟招聘两名市场开发人员，35岁以下，大学文化，口才、文才俱佳，有极强的公关能力，能经常出差或长期驻外，懂电脑中英文处理。

以上人员如录用，待遇优厚。应聘者请于9月28日前寄个人简历及照片一张，过期不予考虑。

来信请寄: 北京东亚饭店7层701室，香港华通银行北京办事处人事科。

5.2 求职信 Letters inquiring about job opportunities

范文 2, Text 2

华夏国际贸易公司总经理先生:

我是英国英伦大学汉学专业四年级学生，今年夏天即将毕业。毕业后，我很想去中国的合资企业工作，不知贵公司是否需要?

随信寄去我的简历，上面列有我在大学所学的主要课程。你可以看到，四年来我的各门功课成绩一直名列全班前茅。1998年和1999年夏天，我曾在香港和台湾的几家公司做过推销工作，并得到所在公司的好评。此外，我很喜欢社会活动；我曾是英伦大学国王学院的学生会主席，并多次成功地组织过有关经济、社会、文化等方面的讨论。不仅如此，我还有一定的中英文打字能力，可以用电脑进行中英文字处理。

如果贵公司需要一名推销员，公关人员或者秘书，我相信自己一定能够胜任。

至于待遇，我的要求不高。我愿意拿与公司同类职工一样的工资，并愿意住公司的职工宿舍。

我有信心为贵公司做出贡献。

期待您的早日回复。

此致

敬礼！

John Davies (戴章良)

2001年5月28日

54

Notes to Text 2

a. A letter seeking job opportunities can include some or all of the following information:

- very brief self-introduction;
- purpose of writing this letter;
- your professional abilities and experiences and your personal interests;
- what you can offer and contribute;
- your requirements for pay, travel, etc.

b. Relevant phrases and sentences:

首先请原谅我冒昧给您写信，我是 … … … …
First of all, please excuse me for taking the liberty of writing to you.
  I am . . .

我渴望为/希望去 … … … … 工作
I am very eager to work for . . . /hope to go and work . . .

我的愿望是到 … … … … 工作
My dream is to go and work for . . .

自 … … 以来，我一直 … … … …
Since . . . , I have been . . .

我曾经是/在 … … … …
I once worked as . . . / worked for . . .

我热爱 … 而且也善于 …
I am passionate about . . . and also I am good at . . .

我有 … … … … 的经验
I have experience in . . .

在 … … 方面，我希望能 … … … …
Regarding . . . , I hope I am able to . . .

关于 … … ，我的要求是 … … … …
About . . . , my requirements are . . .

Exercises for 5.2

1   Use some or all of the phrases in Note (b) above to rewrite Model 2.
2   北京华英贸易有限公司 (*Beijing Hua Ying Trading Ltd*) is a China–Britain joint-venture company, and you want to work in that company. Write to the chief manager of the company to see whether he can offer you a job. In your

letter, you have to impress him by presenting yourself as a confident person and a person willing and able to make contribution to his company.

3   Write a genuine letter to a company or an institution you have in mind and see whether they can offer you a job you would like to do.

5.3   索取信息的信 Letters requesting information

范文 3, Text 3

北方大学对外汉语教学中心负责人：

从互联网北方大学的主页上，得知贵中心将于今年暑假举办对外汉语培训班。我对此非常感兴趣，现写信索取入学申请表，以及培训班的学习时间、学费、住宿等详细情况。

我的通讯地址是：　　Mr. Oliver Matthew
　　　　　　　　　　7 New Street
　　　　　　　　　　London NW2 UK
我的电子邮件地址是: omatthew33@hotmail.com
盼望能早日得到您的回信。

此致

敬礼！

Oliver Matthew (孟立吾)
2001年6月26日

Notes to Text 3

a.   When you write a letter of enquiry, you may not be clear who you should write to. It is all right in Chinese to address the letter to 负责人 (*the responsible person* or *the person in charge*) of the department or the organisation you are writing to. For example:

北京中国文化大学研究生部负责人 *The person responsible for Graduate Studies at Beijing Chinese Culture University*

香港东海大学暑期项目负责人 *The person responsible for Summer Programmes at Hong Kong Donghai University*

b.   Relevant phrases and sentences

从朋友处获悉 … … … *(I) have heard from a friend . . .*
据说；听说 … … … *(I) have heard . . .*

56

(我)很高兴得知 … … … *I'm very pleased to hear . . .*

我迫切希望能够参加 … *I am very eager to be able to attend . . .*

这对我是一个很好的学习机会。 *This is a very good learning opportunity for me.*

请尽快将 … … … … 寄给 … *Please send . . . as soon as possible.*

恳切希望贵(处)能尽快把 … … … … 寄给我。 *I sincerely hope that you will send me . . . as soon as possible.*

Exercises for 5.3

1 Try to use the phrases and sentences listed in Note (b) above to rewrite Model 3.

2 You have learned from a friend that 台湾中央大学国语中心 will hold an advanced Mandarin Chinese training course in Taibei next summer. Write to the 国语中心 requesting detailed information about the course, such as the starting date, length, cost, arrangements for accommodation, etc.

5.4 回信 Replies

范文 *4, Text 4*

尊敬的梁国章先生：

　　谢谢您寄来的《鲁迅文学奖学金申请表》和'申请事项'。申请表已填好，随信给您寄去。同时寄去本人像片两张，请查收。

　　关于我的推荐信，请跟以下两位联系索取：

1. 北京西南大街66号，北京中文大学文学研究中心

　　　　邱士泉　教授

2. Professor Richard Johnson
   Department of Chinese
   University of East Valley
   London U.K.

　　恳切希望'鲁迅文学基金会'能对我的申请给以充分的考虑。

　　　　　　此致

敬礼！

　　　　　　　　　　　　Stephan Ogden (司徒凡)
　　　　　　　　　　　　2001年5月6日

Notes to Text 4

a. In reply to letters offering someone a job, a scholarship or a place on an academic programme, the following expressions are often used:

感谢您/谢谢您 … 月 … 号的来信。
Thank you for your letter dated . . .

谢谢您在百忙之中(给我) … … … …
Thank you for . . . (to/for me) while you are so busy.

(我)十分高兴获悉贵公司决定录用我。
(I'm) very pleased to know that your company has decided to appoint me.

(我)十分高兴获悉贵校决定给我提供奖学金。
(I'm) delighted to know that your university has decided to provide me with a scholarship.

(我)十分高兴获悉贵校决定接受我上暑期汉语进修班。
(I'm) very pleased to know that your university has accepted me for the summer Chinese language course.

我非常高兴接受你们的聘用/奖学金。
I am extremely delighted to accept your offer/scholarship.

我会将所需材料准备好，按时去报到。
I will get all the required documents ready and come to register on time.

b. Other relevant phrases and sentences:

随信寄去报名费/申请费 … … … 元/英镑/美元(现金/支票)。
Please find enclosed the registration fee/application fee of . . . Yuan/Pounds Sterling/US Dollars (in cash/cheque).

另用挂号信寄去现金/支票 … … … … 元。
I'm sending. . . . Yuan (in cash/cheque) by registered mail.

以下两位愿作我的推荐人。
The following two people are willing to be my referees.

我的推荐人的地址是/如下：
The addresses of my referees are/are as follows:

Exercises for 5.4

1 You want to apply for a place on a course called 当代中国研究 (*Contemporary China Studies*) in 南方大学. 丛玉玲女士 from 南方大学外事处 (*Foreign Affairs Office of Nanfang University*) has sent you an application form and

asked you to return the completed form as soon as possible. She has also asked you to send her two recent photographs of yourself, the addresses of two referees and $25 registration fee. Now write a reply to her and do what she has asked you to do.

2 You have received the following letter. Write a reply to accept the offer.

XXX先生/小姐:

　　我们十分高兴地通知你,你已被正式聘为本出版社的翻译,合同期为三年,从9月1号开始上班。附上合同两份,请在上面签名,并将其中的一份尽快寄回本社。

　　　　　此致

　　敬礼!

　　　　　　　　　　　　　　　光华出版社人事部主任: 李源
　　　　　　　　　　　　　　　2001年8月1号

Vocabulary

5.1

馆长	guǎnzhǎng	head of the library
所登的	suǒ dēng de	carried; printed (e.g. in newspaper)
招聘	zhāopìn	to recruit; to invite application
图书管理员	túshū guǎnlǐyuán	librarian
本科	běnkē	undergraduate
应聘	yìng pìn	to apply (for a job)
简历	jiǎnlì	curriculum vitae
课程	kèchéng	(academic) course
优异成绩	yōuyì chéngjì	excellent results
短期	duǎn qī	short term
分类	fēnlèi	to classify; to sort out
编目	biānmù	to catalogue
登记	dēngjì	to list; to register
书籍	shūjí	books
母语	mǔyǔ	mother tongue
精通	jīngtōng	to be an expert on; to be good at
胜任	shèngrèn	to be competent
请查收	qǐng cháshōu	please find ...
如蒙录用	rú méng lùyòng	if (I am) employed
定勤勉	dìng qíngmiǎn	will definitely work hard
不负 ... 期望	bú fù ... qīwàng	will not let ... down

此致 敬礼	cǐ zhì jìnglǐ	with best wishes
合作	hézuò	cooperation
期待	qīdài	to look forward to, expect
早日	zǎorì	early; soon
回复	huífù	to reply; a reply
人事科	rénshìkē	personnel department
科长	kēzhǎng	section head
销售部	xiāoshòubù	sales department
主任	zhǔrèn	director
贵	guì	your (polite form)
刊登	kāndēng	to print; to carry (in a newspaper or a magazine)
得知	dézhī	to know
获悉	huòxī	to have heard
极愿	jí yuàn	would very much like
从事	cóngshì	to do; to engage in . . .
之所以 . . .	zhīsuǒyǐ	the reason why
申请	shēnqǐng	to apply
能力	nénglì	ability
出版社	chūbǎnshè	publisher
诚聘	chéngpìn	to sincerely recruit
翻译	fānyì	translator; to translate
拟	nǐ	to intend; to plan
应聘条件	yìngpìn tiáojiàn	requirements for application
一定	yídìng	certain (specific)
笔译	bǐyì	translation
文字处理	wénzì chǔlǐ	word processing; to word-process
热爱	rè'ài	to love
本职工作	běnzhí gōngzuò	one's own job
责任心强	zérèn xīn qiáng	strong sense of responsibility
基本待遇	jīběn dàiyù	basic terms of employment
免费	miǎnfèi	free of charge
住宿	zhùsù	accommodation
年薪	niánxīn	annual salary
应试方法	yìng shì fāngfǎ	method for applying
近照	jìn zhào	recent photograph
上旬	shàngxún	the first half (of a month)
面试	miànshì	interview
笔试	bǐshì	written exam
社长	shèzhǎng	head of a publishing firm
办事处	bànshìchù	office; branch
市场	shìchǎng	marketing; market
开发	kāifā	development
口才	kǒucái	eloquence
文才	wéncái	talent in writing
俱佳	jù jiā	to be good at both
公关	gōngguān	public relations
长期驻外	chángqī zhù wài	to work elsewhere on a long-term basis
优厚	yōuhòu	generous

应聘者	yìngpìnzhě	applicant
过期	guò qī	to be past the deadline
不予考虑	bù yǔ kǎolǜ	will not be considered

5.2

上面列有	shàngman liè yǒu	listed in . . . are
合资企业	hézī qǐyè	joint venture
名列前茅	míng liè qiánmáo	to be among the best
推销	tuīxiāo	marketing
所在公司	suǒ zài gōngsī	the company where one works
好评	hǎopín	high opinion; favourable comments
此外	cǐwài	furthermore; in addition
社会活动	shèhuì huódòng	social activities
学生会	xuéshēng huì	student union
主席	zhǔxí	chairman
组织	zǔzhī	to organise
有关	yǒuguān	relevant
不仅如此	bù jǐn rú cǐ	in addition
一定的	yídìngde	a certain degree of . . .
打字	dǎzì	typing
推销员	tuīxiāo yuán	sales person
秘书	mìshū	secretary
至于	zhìyú	as for
要求	yāoqiú	demands; requirements
拿 . . . 工资	ná . . . gōngzī	to be paid
贡献	gòngxiàn	contribution
冒昧	màomèi	to take the liberty
渴望	kěwàng	to be eager to; to long for

5.3

对外汉语教学	duìwài hànyǔ jiàoxué	teaching Chinese as a foreign language
中心	zhōngxīn	centre
负责人	fùzérén	the person in charge
互联网	yīngtèwǎng	Internet
主页	zhǔyè	home page
短训班	duǎnxùn bān	short training course
索取	suǒqǔ	to obtain
入学申请表	rù xué shēnqǐng biǎo	application form for entering educational establishment
住宿	zhùsù	accommodation
详细情况	xiángxì qíngkuàng	detailed information
通讯地址	tōngxùn dìzhǐ	postal address
电子邮件	diànzǐ yóujiàn	e-mail
迫切	pòqiè	eager; urgent
恳切	kěnqiè	sincerely

5.4

鲁迅	**Lǔ Xùn**	[name of a Chinese writer]
文学	**wénxué**	literature
奖学金	**jiǎngxuéjīn**	scholarship
事项	**shìxiàng**	particulars; relevant items
填好	**tiánhǎo**	to have filled in (forms)
相片	**xiàngpiān**	photo
推荐信	**tuījiàn xìn**	reference letter
联系	**liánxì**	to contact
研究	**yánjiū**	research
给以	**gěiyǐ**	to give
充分的考虑	**chōngfènde kǎolǜ**	full consideration
暑期	**shǔqī**	summer
进修班	**jìnxiū bān**	refresher course
聘用	**pìnyòng**	to employ
报到	**bàodào**	to register
报名费	**bàomíng fèi**	registration fee
申请费	**shēnqǐng fèi**	application fee
挂号信	**guàhào xìn**	registered letter
推荐人	**tuījiàn rén**	referee
聘为	**pìnwéi**	to be employed as
合同期	**hétong qī**	length of contract
为	**wéi**	to be
附上	**fùshang**	attached are/as . . .
合同	**hétong**	contract
百忙之中	**bǎimángzhīzhōng**	amid one's busy life
提供	**tígōng**	to provide

第六单元: 转述
Unit Six: Reporting speech

In this unit, we deal with reporting speech. We look first at some techniques in reporting conversations, and then at techniques in reporting formal speech.

6.1 对话转述 Conversation reporting

范文 *1, Text 1*

(a)
丈夫: 你用我的电脑了吗?
妻子: 我可没用你的电脑。
Reporting: 丈夫问妻子是否用了他的电脑，妻子说她没用。

(b)
王婷: '这个碗怎么碎了? '
张强: '是我不小心把它打碎了。'
Reporting: 张强说是他不小心把那个碗打碎了。

(c)
小方: 你怎么才来? 我都等了你半天了。
小梅: 我昨晚熬夜赶论文，早上睡过了头。实在对不起。
Reporting: 小方埋怨小梅来晚了。小梅抱歉地说她前一天晚上赶论文，早上睡过了头。

(d)
小明: '你什么时候能修好这辆自行车? '
王师傅: '我今天下午肯定能修好。'
Reporting: 王师傅很有把握地说他那天下午肯定能修好小明的自行车。

Notes to Text 1

a.   In reporting, words referring to time and location usually change depending on the context. For example, 今天 changes to 那天 in Model 1d. Below are some more examples.

今天 *today*　　　　　→那天 *that day*
明天 *tomorrow*　　　→第二天 *the following day*
昨天 *yesterday*　　　→前一天 *previous day*
这儿 *here*　　　　　→那儿 *there*

b.   The demonstrative pronoun 这个 sometimes changes to 那个, as shown in Model 1b.

c.   When reporting a yes–no question, add 是否 (*if; whether*) before the verb, and get rid of the question word 吗.

d.   Often you need to describe the speaker's attitude or mood by using appropriate adverbs such as: 很有把握地 (*confidently*), 有信心地 (*confidently*), 无意中 (*unintentionally*), 满不在乎地 (*with a carefree tone*), 失望地 (*disappointedly*), 满脸不高兴地 (*unhappily*), 沮丧地 (*depressed*), 兴高采烈地 (*happily*), 自豪地 (*proudly*).

Exercise for 6.1

Report the following pieces of conversations:
(a)   方华：'我根本没告诉小平这件事。'
(b)   李一建：'我这次考试考得很一般。真让人失望。'
(c)   明雨：'妈妈，我准备明天带我的男朋友回家见你和爸爸。'
(d)   林林：'太好了，妈妈！万万没想到你会来。'
(e)   小王的哥哥：'你用我的手机了吗？'
　　　小王：'没用。'

6.2   正式讲话转述 Formal speech reporting

范文 *2, Text 2*

Transcript of a commercial

'长高乐' —— 冲出矮人世界的良药
　　身材矮小会给许多青少年的事业及爱情带来痛苦。'长高乐'是目前国内外唯一治疗矮身材的良药。25岁以下的男女青少年服用2–4盒后，均可增高7.5–11厘米。社会上曾流传此药有副作用，这是毫无根据的。请消费者认准'良药'牌注册商标，以防假冒。

Reporting the commercial

　　昨晚电视上有一个广告，说有一种药叫‘长高乐’，能使矮人长高。这个广告认为，身材矮小会给青少年的事业及爱情带来痛苦。它声称，‘长高乐’这种药是目前国内外唯一治疗矮身材的良药，并断言，25岁以下的男女青少年服用2–4盒后，都可以增高7.5–11厘米。该广告否认‘长高乐’有副作用。它告诫消费者：为了防止假冒，不要买没有‘良药’牌注册商标的‘长高乐’。

Notes to Text 2

a. To report formal speech, the following reporting words are often used:

指出 (*to point out*), 强调指出 (*to emphasise*), 表示 (*to state*), 重申 (*to reiterate*), 断言 (*to state with certainty*), 认为 (*to think*), 声称 (*to claim*), 宣布 (*to declare*), 提议 (*to propose*), 建议 (*to suggest*), 警告说 (*to warn*), 告诫说 (*to warn*), 解释说 (*to explain*), 透露 (*to reveal*), 暗示 (*to hint*), 承认 (*to admit*), 否认 (*to deny*), 反驳说 (*to reject*), 预料 (*to predict*), 呼吁 (*to call for*), 谴责说 (*to denounce*), 介绍 (*to introduce*), 补充说 (*to add*), 相信 (*to believe*), 解释说 (*to explain*).

b. To avoid repetition when referring to the commercial, 这个广告, 该广告 and 它 are used in the reporting speech.

Exercises for 6.2

1 Choose appropriate reporting words below and fill in the blanks:

　　　　警告说　　强调　　介绍　　声称　　坚信

(a) 在昨天的全校教师大会上，张校长＿＿＿＿＿了鼓励学生多提问、活跃课堂气氛的重要性。

(b) 在今天举行的记者招待会上，海威公司的总经理向大家＿＿＿＿＿了公司近几年的发展情况。

(c) 政府的发言人昨天＿＿＿＿＿＿，雇用非法移民的雇主将受到法律上的惩罚。

(d) 这家公司的经理＿＿＿＿＿新的管理方法会大大提高经济效益。

(e) 那家报纸＿＿＿＿＿有人给政府官员行贿以获取定单。

2 In the following, (a) is a transcript of an interview by a journalist with the mayor of an imaginary city called 西河市 in China, and (b) is a report of the interview. Some words are missing in (b). Read both (a) and (b), and fill in the blanks in (b). After each blank, four reporting words are given in the brackets; choose an appropriate one.

65

(a)

记者： 市长先生，去年一年，西河市的经济情况怎么样？

市长： 西河市的经济情况总起来是好的。全市经济比上一年增长21.8%，出口创汇比上一年增长23.4%。这些可喜现象一方面是由于国家给了我们这个沿海城市一些很优惠的政策，另一方面，也是全体市民共同努力的结果。当然，我们也面临着不少问题；物价上涨，通货膨胀居高不下，市民有意见。在这个问题上，我们有信心、有能力在今后两三年内把通货膨胀率控制在5%以内。

记者： 有些群众反映有的市政府官员接受贿赂，您怎么看这个问题？

市长： 我想我们应该尽快建立市民监督电话，市民一旦发现有政府官员受贿，可以向政府举报。我以前讲过多次，在这儿我再说一遍，人民政府是为人民服务的，所有的政府官员都必须廉洁奉公。如果查出哪一个官员接受贿赂，不管他的职位有多高，我们都将按党纪国法给予严厉惩罚。

记者： 您打算怎样继续发展西河市的经济？

市长： 我们要大力扶持创汇大户，为外商创造良好的投资环境。只要是有利于西河市经济发展的事，我们都愿做最大的努力。市政府大楼位于市中心商业区，也可以考虑出租或者出售。

(b)

　　当被问到西河市去年的经济情况时，西河市市长＿＿＿＿＿＿＿＿（呼吁，认为，强调，重申），去年西河市的经济情况总起来是好的。全市经济比上一年增长21.8%，出口创汇比上一年增长23.4%。他＿＿＿＿＿＿＿（呼吁，指出，强调，透露），这些可喜现象一方面是由于国家给了这个沿海城市一些很优惠的政策，另一方面，也是全体市民共同努力的结果。他＿＿＿＿＿＿＿（重申，承认，提议，断言），市政府也面临着物价上涨，通货膨胀等问题。但是他＿＿＿＿＿＿＿＿＿（介绍，建议，相信，暗示），市政府能在今后两三年内把通货膨胀率控制在5%以内。在谈到政府官员接受贿赂问题的时候，这位市长＿＿＿＿＿＿＿（否认，建议，透露，谴责）尽快建立市民监督电话，使市民能够随时举报受贿的政府官员。他＿＿＿＿＿＿＿＿（解释，反驳，重申，否认），人民政府是为人民服务的，所有的政府官员都必须廉洁奉公。他＿＿＿＿＿＿＿＿（解释，反驳，警告说，承认），如果查出哪一个官员接受贿赂，不管他的职位有多高，都将按党纪国法给予严厉惩罚。在谈到怎样继续发展西河市经济的时候，这位市长＿＿＿＿＿＿＿（断言，表示，解释，反驳），要大力扶持创汇大户，为外商创造良好的投资环境。他＿＿＿＿＿＿＿＿（否认，建议，透露，谴责），市政府愿意考虑出租或者出售市政府大楼。

3 孙铁光, aged 32, was being questioned in court about killing his wife. Report what 孙铁光 said below, using appropriate reporting words. You may start your report with 孙铁光在法庭上… … … .

法官： 孙铁光，是你杀死你妻子的吗？

孙： 是的。

法官： 你为什么要杀死你的妻子？是不是你又爱上了别的女人？

孙： 不，不，我没有爱上别的女人。我过去爱我的妻子，现在仍深深地爱着她。我已经讲过多次，我并没有想杀她；当时我的确是喝醉了，对自己失去了控制。

法官： 但不管怎么说，她是被你杀死的，对吗？

孙： 是的，我愿意为她的死承担一切法律责任。但是如果说我故意杀死我妻子，那是不正确的。

Vocabulary

6.1

是否	shìfǒu	if; whether
电脑	diànnǎo	computer
碗	wǎn	bowl
打碎	dǎsuì	to break into pieces
熬夜	áoyè	to stay up all night
赶	gǎn	to try to finish
论文	lùnwén	thesis; dissertation
睡过了头	shuìguòletóu	overslept
埋怨	mányuàn	to complain
抱歉地	bàoqiànde	apologetically
很有把握地	hěn yǒu bǎwòde	confidently
有信心地	yǒu xìnxīnde	confidently
无意中	wúyì zhōng	unintentionally
满不在乎地	mǎn bú zàihude	nonchalantly
失望地	shīwàngde	disappointedly
满脸不高兴地	mǎn liǎn bù gāoxìngde	unhappily
沮丧地	jǔsàngde	depressed; dejectedly
兴高采烈地	xìnggāo-cǎiliède	happily; in high spirits
自豪地	zìháode	proudly
万万没想到	wàn wàn méi xiǎngdào	completely unexpectedly
手机	shǒujī	mobile phone

6.2

冲出	chōngchū	to break away from
矮人	ǎirén	short people
良药	liángyào	good medicine; effective remedy
身材	shēncái	stature; physique
矮小	ǎixiǎo	small and short
事业	shìyè	career

爱情	àiqíng	love
痛苦	tòngkǔ	pain
国内外	guónèiwài	at home and abroad
唯一	wéiyī	only; unique
治疗	zhìliáo	to cure; treatment
均	jūn	both; all
增高	zēnggāo	to increase the height; to make taller
流传	liúchuán	(the rumour) says; to spread
副作用	fù zuòyòng	side effects
毫无根据	háo wú gēnjù	without grounds; groundless
消费者	xiāofèizhě	consumers
认准	rènzhǔn	to double-check
牌	pái	brand (of product)
注册商标	zhùcè shāngbiāo	trade mark
以防	yǐ fáng	to beware of; in order to prevent
假冒	jiǎmào	imitations
指出	zhǐchū	to point out
强调指出	qíangdiào zhǐchū	to emphasise
表示	biǎoshì	to state
重申	chóngshēn	to reiterate
断言	duànyán	to state with certainty
认为	rènwéi	to think
声称	shēngchēng	to claim
宣布	xuānbù	to declare
提议	tíyì	to propose
建议	jiànyì	to suggest
警告说	jǐnggàoshuō	to warn
告诫说	gàojièshuō	to warn
解释说	jiěshìshuō	to explain
透露	tòulù	to reveal
暗示	ànshì	to hint; to imply
承认	chéngrèn	to admit
否认	fǒurèn	to deny
反驳说	fǎnbóshuō	to reject
预料	yùliào	to predict
呼吁	hūyù	to call for; to appeal
谴责说	qiǎnzéshuō	to denounce
介绍	jièshào	to introduce
补充说	bǔchōngshuō	to add
活跃	huóyuè	to enliven; to liven up
气氛	qìfēn	atmosphere
记者招待会	jìzhě zhāodàihuì	press conference
总经理	zǒngjīnglǐ	general manager
政府	zhèngfǔ	government
发言人	fāyánrén	spokesperson
雇佣	gùyōng	to employ
非法	fēifǎ	illegal
移民	yímín	immigrant

雇主	gùzhǔ	employer
法律	fǎlǜ	law
惩罚	chéngfá	punishment
管理	guǎnlǐ	management
提高	tígāo	to increase; to improve
经济效益	jīngjì xiàoyì	economic efficiency
行贿	xínghuì	to bribe
以	yǐ	in order to
获取	huòqǔ	to obtain
定单	dìngdān	order
总起来	zǒng qǐlái	in general
增长	zēngzhǎng	to increase
出口创汇	chūkǒu chuàng huì	export to gain foreign currency
可喜现象	kěxǐ xiànxiàng	gratifying achievements
沿海城市	yánhǎi chéngshì	coastal city
优惠	yōuhuì	favourable; preferential
政策	zhèngcè	policy
共同努力	gòngtóng nǔlì	joint efforts
面临着	miànlínzhe	to be faced with
物价上涨	wùjià shàngzhǎng	prices rising
通货膨胀	tōnghuò péngzhàng	inflation
控制在 ... 以内	kòngzhì zài ... yǐnèi	control ... within...
贿赂	huìlù	bribe
市民监督	shìmín jiāndū	supervision by citizens
随时举报	suíshí jǔbào	to inform at any time
受贿	shòuhuì	to accept bribes
廉洁奉公	liánjié fènggōng	to fulfil duties honestly
查出	cháchū	to find out
职位	zhíwèi	position
党纪国法	dǎng jì guó fǎ	Party discipline and national law
给予	jǐyǔ	to give
严厉惩罚	yánlì chéngfá	severe punishment
大力扶持	dàlì fúchí	to provide ample support
创汇大户	chuànghuì dàhù	companies and factories which earn large amounts of foreign currency
外商	wàishāng	foreign businessmen
投资环境	tóuzī huánjìng	investment environment
出租	chūzū	for rent
出售	chūshòu	for sale
法庭	fǎtíng	court
法官	fǎguān	judge
杀死	shāsǐ	to kill
爱上	àishang	to fall in love
的确	díquè	indeed
喝醉	hēzuì	drunk
失去	shīqù	to lose
控制	kòngzhì	control
不管怎么说	bùguǎn zěnmeshuō	no matter what you say

愿意	**yuànyì**	willing
承担	**chéngdān**	to bear (responsibility)
责任	**zérèn**	responsibility
故意	**gùyì**	intentionally; deliberately
不正确	**bú zhèngquè**	incorrect

第七单元: 用于举例、换言和总结的连接成分
Unit Seven: Exemplification, reformulation and summary

7.1 举例 Exemplification

范文 *1, Text 1*

---

a. 中国的改革开放同时也带来了一系列副作用，例如： 通货膨胀，贫富不均，犯罪率升高，等等。
b. 亚洲地区有不少文明古国，例如，中国就是一个有五千多年历史的国家。
c. 现在越来越多的人意识到，中国目前腐败现象的根子在领导干部和政府官员本身。拿用公款请客来说吧，老百姓有权动用公款吗？只有那些有权有势的人才有资格动用公款。这一点是显而易见的。

Notes to Text 1

a. 例如 (*for example; such as*), 如 (*such as*) and 象 (*such as*) are usually used to introduce examples represented by some noun phrases, as in '例如：通货膨胀，贫富不均，犯罪率升高，等等。' (*for example, the inflation, the gap between the rich and the poor, rising crime rates, etc.*).

b. 例如 can also introduce a sentence, as in '例如，中国就是一个有五千多年历史的国家。' (*for instance, China is a country with a history of over 5,000 years*).

c. Phrases such as 以 . . . 为例 (*to take . . . as an example*), 拿 . . . 来说/讲 (*to take . . . as an example*), 比方说 (*for example*) are usually followed by sentences, as in '拿用公款请客来说吧，老百姓有权动用公款吗？' (*Take*

71

entertaining guests with public funds as an example. Do ordinary people have the authority to use public funds?). 以 . . . 为例 is more formal than 拿 . . . 来 说/讲 . . . or 比方说.

7.2 换言 Reformulation

范文 2, *Text 2*

> a. 改革开放使人民的物质生活水平得到了很大改善。但仅仅提高物质生活水平是不够的，要'两个文明'一起抓。换句话说，在抓紧物质文明建设的同时，也要抓精神文明建设，提高全国人民的道德水平，在全国建立一个良好的社会秩序。
> b. 教学改革的重点就是要提高教学质量。具体地说，就是要研究教学法，研究学生学习的规律和特点，帮助他们高效率地学好每一门课。

Notes to Text 2

a. 换句话说 (*in other words*) can be replaced with 换言之 (*in other words*), 具体而言 (*specifically speaking*) or 即 (*i.e.*), but these phrases are more formal than 换句话说.

b. Other less formal conjunctions of reformulation include 也就是说 (*that is to say*), 就是说 (*that is*) and 具体地说 (*specifically speaking*).

7.3 总结 Summary

范文 3, *Text 3*

> a. 一九七八年以来，我国的经济形势逐年改善，科学技术迅速发展，人民的生活水平有了很大的提高。总之，改革开放给中华大地带来了一片繁荣景象。
> b. …… …… 我精通汉语，了解中国的文化和历史，并对去中国工作有极大的兴趣。一句话，我坚信我能做好这项工作。

Notes to Text 3

a. The word 总之 (*in short*) is rather formal and can be replaced with 总而言之 (*in short; briefly*), 简(而)言之 (*to put it briefly*).

b. Less formal conjunctions of summary include 总起来说 (*to sum up*), 总括起来说 (*to sum up*), 总的看来 (*generally speaking*), 总的来说 (*generally speaking*), 概括起来说 (*to sum up*) and 一句话 (*in a word*).

Exercises for 7.1–7.3

1 Fill in the following blanks with appropriate conjunctions of exemplification, reformulation and summary:

(a) 我们中国所面临的是一个要'人治'还是要'法治'的问题。_____，我们是要由一个人来治理国家，还是用法律，宪法来治理国家。

(b) 在这次会议上，我们讨论并通过了政府工作报告，制定了一系列有关税务的法律，确定了明年的财政计划。_____，我们圆满完成了为这次会议预定的全部任务。

(c) 在国际人权会议上，一些西方国家，_____，美国、英国、法国等，在人权问题上对中国进行了指责。

(d) 我认为追求美是人的本性。_____，年轻人找对象要找漂亮的，穿衣服也要穿好看的。

(e) 你病好了以后，每天早晨应出去散散步，有时间的话，还应该去游泳，打球。_____，要坚持锻炼身体。

(f) 除了少数民族以外，各地政府都要严格地执行计划生育政策。_____，就是要提倡晚婚、晚育，一对夫妇只生一个孩子。

2 The following is an excerpt from a lecture on Chinese history and some questions and answers after the lecture. Imagine you are the lecturer. Rewrite this part of the lecture on the basis of the questions asked by the students, so that students next year can understand you better.

毛泽东在中国的历史上是一个伟大的人物，但他也犯过不少错误。我个人认为他的一生应该是错误与成绩三七开。我们不能只看到他的成绩，而忽视了他对中国人民所犯下的错误。我们也不能因为他犯过很多错误，而把他的功绩抹掉。

学生甲：老师，您在这一段中所讲的中心意思是什么？

（Hint: Is the student asking for examples, reformulation or a summary?）

教师：我所讲的中心意思是对毛泽东的一生要进行客观的、一分为二的评价。

学生乙：老师，您说的'三七开'是什么意思？

（Hint: Is the student asking for examples, reformulation or a summary?）

教师：我的意思是毛泽东的一生错误应该占30%，成绩占70%。

学生丙：您谈到毛泽东犯过不少错误。他主要犯过哪些错误？

（Hint: Is the student asking for examples, reformulation or a summary?）

教师：一九五八年的'大跃进'和一九六六年至一九七六年的'文化大革命'就是他的两个很严重错误。由于'大跃进'，农业生产遭到严重破坏，成千上万的农民被饿死。文化大革命期间，毛泽东号召红卫兵起来造反，中国的工业、农业、经济几乎完全瘫痪，许多知识分子被迫害致死。

Vocabulary

7.1

改革开放	**gǎigé kāifàng**	reform and opening up
一系列	**yíxìliè**	a series
副作用	**fùzuòyòng**	side effect
通货膨胀	**tōnghuò péngzhàng**	inflation
贫富不均	**pín fù bù jūn**	gap between the rich and the poor
犯罪率	**fànzuì lǜ**	crime rate
文明	**wénmíng**	civilisation
意识到	**yìshidào**	to have realised
腐败	**fǔbài**	corruption
现象	**xiànxiàng**	phenomenon
根子	**gēnzi**	root
领导干部	**lǐngdǎo gànbù**	leading cadre
政府官员	**zhèngfǔ guānyuán**	government official
公款	**gōng kuǎn**	public funds
动用	**dòngyòng**	to use
有权有势	**yǒu quán yǒu shì**	the powerful and influential
有资格	**yǒu zīgé**	to be qualified
显而易见	**xiǎn ér yì jiàn**	obvious

7.2

物质	**wùzhì**	material
改善	**gǎishàn**	to improve
仅仅	**jǐnjǐn**	only
提高	**tígāo**	to raise; to improve
抓	**zhuā**	to pay attention to
抓紧	**zhuājǐn**	to pay special attention to
物质文明	**wùzhì wénmíng**	material civilisation
建设	**jiànshè**	construction
精神文明	**jīngshén wénmíng**	spiritual civilisation
道德	**dàodé**	morality; moral
建立	**jiànlì**	to establish
秩序	**zhìxù**	order
教学	**jiàoxué**	teaching
重点	**zhòngdiǎn**	focus
质量	**zhìliàng**	quality
具体地	**jùtǐde**	specifically
高效率	**gāoxiàolǜ**	high efficiency

7.3

经济形势	**jīngjì xíngshì**	economic situation
逐年改善	**zhúnián gǎishàn**	to improve year by year

科学技术	kēxué jìshù	science and technology
迅速发展	xùnsù fāzhǎn	to develop rapidly
繁荣景象	fánróng jǐngxiàng	scene of prosperity; prosperity
精通	jīngtōng	to have a good command of
极大的	jídàde	enormous; great
坚信	jiānxìn	to believe strongly
人治	rén zhì	to rule by people
面临	miànlín	to be faced with
法治	fǎ zhì	to rule by law
治理	zhìlǐ	to run; to govern
宪法	xiànfǎ	constitution
通过	tōngguò	to pass
政府	zhèngfǔ	government
工作报告	gōngzuò bàogào	working report
制定	zhìdìng	to formulate; to draw up
税务	shuìwù	taxation
确定	quèdìng	to determine; to decide on
财政	cáizhèng	fiscal; financial
圆满	yuánmǎn	successfully
预定的	yùdìngde	predetermined; scheduled
任务	rènwù	task
人权	rén quán	human rights
指责	zhǐzé	to accuse; to criticise
追求	zhuīqiú	to pursue; to seek
本性	běnxìng	nature
坚持	jiānchí	to adhere to; to stick to
少数民族	shǎoshù mínzú	ethnic minority; minority nationality
严格	yángé	strictly
执行	zhíxíng	to implement
计划生育	jìhuà shēngyù	family planning
政策	zhèngcè	policy
提倡	tíchàng	to advocate
晚婚	wǎn hūn	to marry late
晚育	wǎn yù	to have children late
犯	fàn	to make (mistake)
三七开	sān qī kāi	to divide into 30% and 70%
忽视	hūshì	to neglect; to overlook
功绩	gōngjì	achievement; contribution
抹掉	mǒdiào	to erase
客观	kèguān	objective
一分为二	yì fēn wéi èr	looking at both sides of the coin
占	zhàn	to constitute; to make up
大跃进	dàyuèjìn	Great Leap Forward
至	zhì	to
文化大革命	wénhuà dàgémìng	Cultural Revolution
遭到	zāodào	to suffer from
破坏	pòhuài	damage; destruction
成千上万	chéng qiān shàng wàn	thousands and thousands

期间	qījiān	period
号召	hàozhào	to call on; to summon
红卫兵	hóngwèibīng	Red Guard
造反	zàofǎn	to rebel
几乎	jīhū	almost
瘫痪	tānhuàn	to paralyse
知识分子	zhīshi fènzǐ	intellectual
迫害	pòhài	to purge; a purge
致死	zhì sǐ	to cause death

第八单元: 比较与对比，明喻与暗喻

Unit Eight: Comparison and contrast, simile and metaphor

Comparisons and contrasts are used to present similarities and differences between two entities, and simile and metaphor are used to draw an analogy between two entities, i.e. to use one entity to explain the other in order to help people understand better what is being talked about. These are very useful techniques in both academic writing and writing about daily life.

8.1 比较与对比 Comparison and contrast

范文 *1, Text 1*

a. 虽然美国和英国都是民主国家，但是两个国家的政治制度却不完全一样。美国的国家元首是总统，美国总统每四年选举一次。美国的国会分众议院和参议院；众议院每两年选举一次，参议院的三分之一席位每六年选举一次。美国总统是国家的最高政治领导人，但他不是议会成员。美国有宪法。而英国却不同。英国的国家元首是女王，她不需要选举。英国的议会分上议院和下议院；下议院至少每五年选举一次，上议院不用选举。英国首相是国家的最高政治领导人，他/她也是议会的成员。英国没有宪法。

b. 第二次世界大战期间，欧洲人民和亚洲人民都蒙受了巨大的灾难。德国和意大利法西斯侵占了大片东西欧国家的领土。同样，日本法西斯也将中国，朝鲜等亚洲国家的领土归为己有。德意侵略者在欧洲到处烧杀掠夺，使欧洲各国人民付出巨大牺牲。日本军队在亚洲的所作所为与德意侵略者毫无区别；他们强奸妇女，杀害老人，儿童以及无辜，把亚洲各国人民视为奴隶。1944年欧洲各国人民在美国等国的大力协助下，对德意侵略者发动了猛烈反攻。与欧洲人民一样，亚洲人民在美国和前苏联等国的支持帮助下也对日本军队进行反击。德意日终于在1945年宣布投降。

Notes to Text 1

a. You can use one of the following two ways to make contrasts and comparisons. One is to write all the main points about one of the subjects to be compared, and then go on to write all the main points about the other subject, as in (i) below. Model 1a is arranged in this way.

(i)
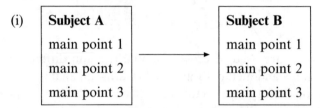

The other way is to take each point in turn from both of the subjects and to contrast them immediately, as illustrated in (ii). Model 1b is arranged in this way.

(ii)
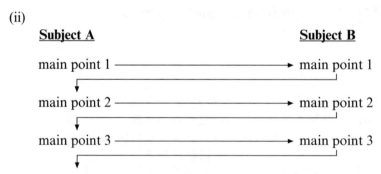

b. Phrases like 不完全一样 (*not completely the same*) and 而 . . . 却不同 (*but . . . is different*) are often used in making contrasts. Other similar phrases include:

但(是) . . . 却不同	*but . . . is different*
可(是) . . . 却截然相反	*but . . . is just the opposite*
然而 . . . 却完全不一样	*but . . . is completely different*
与/跟 . . . 不同的是 . . .	*what is different from . . . is . . .*
A 与 B 不同的是 A . . . 而 B . . .	*the difference between A and B is that A . . . but/while B . . .*

c. Phrases like 同样 (*similarly*), 与...毫无区别 (*to be no different at all from* ...) and 与...一样 (*the same as*...) are often used in comparisons. Similar phrases include the following:

与/跟...完全相同	*completely the same as*...
与/跟...并无区别	*to be no different from*...
与/跟...完全一样	*completely the same as*...
与/跟...类似/相似	*similar to*...

Exercises for 8.1

1 Read the phrases in Notes b and c again, and try to complete the following sentences:

 (a) 篮球运动员_____足球运动员_____是前者一般身材非常高大而后者需要有很快的奔跑速度。

 (b) 我家乡的天气_____这儿非常_____，夏天最高温度通常不超过二十八摄氏度。

 (c) 张太太性格活泼、开朗。而张先生的性格_____，他很内向，跟不熟悉的人说话还常常脸红。

 (d) 我认为'电脑'这个词_____'计算机'这个词的意思_____，两者都可以翻译成'computer'。

2 Rewrite the passages in Model 1a and Model 1b, so that they correspond to the different ways of arranging contrasts and comparisons in (i) or (ii) in Note a. The following is a hint for rewriting Model 1a.

美国与英国在政治制度上的对比:

A. 美国	**B. 英国**
1. 国家元首 = 总统	1. 国家元首 = 女王
2. 总统四年选一次	2. 女王不需要选举
3. 国会: 众议院 – 两年选一次	3. 议会: 上议院 – 不用选
参议院 – 1/3席位六年选一次	下议院 – 五年选一次
4. 总统 = 最高政治领导人	4. 首相 = 最高政治领导人
5. 总统 ≠ 议会议员	5. 首相 = 议会议员
6. 有宪法	6. 无宪法

3 Write a short essay on each of the following topics. Do the work in two stages. First make two lists of main points about the two subjects to be compared or contrasted, and then write the essay.

 (a) 中国人和英国人吃饭的习惯

 (b) 我的中学生活和我的大学生活

 (c) 我的父母

8.2 明喻与暗喻 Simile and metaphor

范文 2, Text 2

> a. 漓江的水真绿，绿得仿佛是一块无瑕的翡翠。
> b. 小王打起球来，像小老虎一般，跑得快，冲得猛。
> c. 我来到她的卧室时，她穿着一件白纱裙子，简直如同一位美丽的天使。这时我的心里就像燃烧起一把热火………………。
> d. 稻子熟了，黄澄澄的，跟铺了一地金子似的。
> e. 他们简直是些吸血鬼，老百姓的钱都进了他们的腰包。
> f. 虽然我们现在面临着许多困难，但这只是黎明前的黑暗。
> g. 我醒来的时候，我的周围已经变成了一片血海。
> h. 现在她终于明白，她跟刘永涛的关系已经成了一个梦。

Notes to Text 2

a. To make a simile between two entities, one can use the pattern '*A + simile word + B* (. . .)'. Sentences in Model 2a-c above are of this type. The following are some words and phrases which are often used in similes.

好像	*to be like; to seem*
好比	*to be just like; can be compared to*
就像	*to be just like*
如	*to be like; as; as if*
如同	*to be like; as*
仿佛	*as if; to seem*
好似	*to be like; to seem*
像/同 . . . 一样	*to be like . . .*
仿佛 . . . 似的	*as if . . . ; to be like . . .*
跟 . . . 似的	*to be just like . . .*
同/跟/像 . . . 一般	*to be just like . . .*
恰似 . . .	*to be exactly like . . .*

b. Sentences in Model 2e-h above are examples of metaphor. Metaphor does not require those words used for simile. The analogy drawn between the two entities is implied in the sentence. The pattern used in metaphor is usually '*A* + 是/成了/变成了 + *B*'.

c. Metaphor is not only more economical (in that it does not require words like 象, 仿佛, etc.), but it is also more powerful in convincing people. In the following, we can see that the sentences in (b) are weaker than those in (a).

(i)

    (a)   车是他的命，他知道怎样爱护。
          The rickshaw was his life, and he knew how to take care of it.

    (b)   车像他的命，他知道怎样爱护。
          The rickshaw was like his life, and he knew how to take care of it.

(ii)

    (a)   他是一本活字典，有不知道的字或者词，我总是去问他。
          He is a walking dictionary. When I have words I don't know, I always go to ask him.

    (b)   他像一本活字典，有不知道的字或者词，我总是去问他。
          He is like a walking dictionary. When I have words I don't know, I always go to ask him.

Exercises for 8.2

1   Read the following sentences and underline the use of simile and metaphor:

    (a)   这个城市的马路真像提包上的拉链，今天挖开，说是要搞下水道；刚刚填好，明天又挖开，说是要安地下电缆。

    (b)   我们的事业就好比飞奔向前的火车。理想就如同火车头，纪律恰似铁轨。火车呼啸飞奔，一是靠车头的强大引力，二是靠两条铁轨的规范作用。

    (c)   啊！黄河，你是我们民族的摇篮。

    (d)   我们到达天安门的时候，那里已经变成了旗的海洋。

2   Use your imagination and try to use simile or metaphor to make the following sentences more vivid. '_____' indicates where you may like to use the simile or metaphor.

    (a)   他从地里回来的时候，满头大汗，被汗水湿透了的衣服紧紧贴在他的身上。_____

    (b)   她的眼泪 *像雨滴* _____不停地流出来，有的落在床上，有的落在地上。

    (c)   上海的南京路到处都是身穿各种高档时装的中国男女，有穿中式的，有穿西式的，大家都在向人们显示自己漂亮的服装和优美的身材。_____。

    (d)   他一心想发财，满脑子里都是钱，白天想钱，晚上做梦也想钱。 *对他来说 钱就是上帝。* _____。

    (e)   他每天都期待着见到他的女朋友。如果有一天他没见到她，他会吃不下饭，睡不着觉，更不会有心思上课学习。_____。

Vocabulary

8.1

民主	mínzhǔ	democratic
政治	zhèngzhì	political
制度	zhìdù	system
国家元首	guójiā yuánshǒu	head of state
总统	zǒngtǒng	president
选举	xuǎnjǔ	election
国会	Guóhuì	Congress
众议院	Zhòngyìyuàn	House of Representatives
参议院	Cānyìyuàn	Senate
领导人	lǐngdǎorén	leader
成员	chéngyuán	member
宪法	xiànfǎ	constitution
女王	nǚwáng	queen
议会	yìhuì	parliament
上议院	Shàngyìyuàn	House of Lords
下议院	Xiàyìyuàn	House of Commons
首相	shǒuxiàng	prime minister
欧洲	Ōuzhōu	Europe
亚洲	Yàzhōu	Asia
蒙受	méngshòu	to suffer; to sustain
灾难	zāinàn	disaster; catastrophe
法西斯	fǎxīsī	fascist
侵占	qīnzhàn	to invade and occupy
领土	lǐngtǔ	territory
朝鲜	Cháoxiǎn	(North) Korea
归为己有	guī wéi jǐ yǒu	to take as one's own
侵略者	qīnlüèzhě	invader
烧杀掠夺	shāo shā lüèduó	to burn, to kill and to rob
饱受战争磨难	bǎo shòu zhànzhēng mónàn	to suffer a great deal from the hardship of the war
所作所为	suǒzuò suǒwéi	behaviour
毫无区别	háo wú qūbié	no difference at all
强奸	qiángjiān	to rape
杀害	shāhài	to kill
无辜	wúgū	innocent; innocent person
视为	shìwéi	to treat as; to regard as
奴隶	núlì	slave
协助	xiézhù	assistance
发动	fādòng	to launch
猛烈	měngliè	vigorous; fierce
反攻	fǎngōng	counter-attack
前苏联	qián Sūlián	the former Soviet Union
终于	zhōngyú	finally; at last
宣布	xuānbù	to announce

投降	tóuxiáng	surrender
截然相反	jiérán xiāngfǎn	completely the opposite
然而	rán'ér	however; but
类似	lèisì	similar
相似	xiāngsì	similar; alike
前者	qiánzhě	the former
后者	hòuzhě	the latter
奔跑	bēnpǎo	to run
速度	sùdù	speed; pace
超过	chāoguò	surpass; exceed
摄氏度	shèshìdù	degree centigrade; Celsius
性格	xìnggé	nature; disposition; temperament
活泼	huópo	lively; vivacious
开朗	kāilǎng	open and clear; sanguine
内向	nèixiàng	introverted
两者	liǎngzhě	both

8.2

明喻	míngyù	simile
暗喻	ànyù	metaphor
漓江	Líjiāng	Li River
仿佛	fǎngfú	to seem; as if
无瑕	wú xiá	flawless
翡翠	fěicuì	jadeite
老虎	lǎohǔ	tiger
冲	chōng	to rush; to dash
猛	měng	fierce; vigorous
白纱	bái shā	white gauze
简直	jiǎnzhí	simply
如同	rútóng	like; as
天使	tiānshǐ	angel
燃烧	ránshāo	to burn
稻子	dàozi	rice; paddy
熟	shú	ripe
黄澄澄	huángdēngdēng	glistening yellow; golden
铺	pū	to pave; to surface
跟...似的	gēn...shìde	to be just like ...
金子	jīnzi	gold
吸血鬼	xīxuèguǐ	bloodsucker; vampire
腰包	yāobāo	purse; pocket
面临	miànlín	to be faced with; to be confronted with
黎明	límíng	dawn; daybreak
黑暗	hēi'àn	dark
周围	zhōuwéi	surroundings; around
血海	xuèhǎi	sea of blood
梦	mèng	dream

好比	hǎobǐ	to be just like; can be compared to
好似	hǎosì	to be like; to seem
爱护	àihù	to take good care of
活字典	huó zìdiǎn	walking dictionary
提包	tíbāo	handbag
拉链	lāliàn	zipper; zip fastener
挖	wā	to dig
下水道	xiàshuǐdào	sewer
填好	tiánhǎo	to fill in
安	ān	to fix; to install; to lay
地下电缆	dìxià diànlǎn	underground electric cable
事业	shìyè	cause; undertaking
飞奔	fēibēn	to dash
理想	lǐxiǎng	ideal
火车头	huǒchētóu	locomotive
纪律	jìlǜ	discipline
恰似	qiàsì	exactly like
铁轨	tiěguǐ	rail track
呼啸	hūxiào	to whistle; to whizz
靠	kào	to rely on; to depend on
引力	yǐnlì	pulling power; traction force
规范作用	guīfàn zuòyòng	regulating function
民族	mínzú	nation
摇篮	yáolán	cradle
旗	qí	flag; banner
湿透	shītòu	wet through; to get soaked
贴	tiē	stick
落	luò	to fall; to drop
高档	gāodàng	high-grade; superior quality
时装	shízhuāng	fashionable clothes; fashions
显示	xiǎnshì	to show; to display; to demonstrate
优美	yōuměi	graceful
发财	fā cái	to get rich; to make a fortune
期待	qīdài	to expect; to look forward to
心思	xīnsi	mood; state of mind

第九单元： 步骤、过程和发展
Unit Nine: Procedure, process and development

9.1 步骤与过程 Procedure and process

范文 *1, Text 1*

> 你会炒豆芽吗？首先要把豆芽、葱丝和肉丝准备好。然后把油倒进锅里，放在炉子上烧热。油烧热以后，先把肉丝放进锅里，稍后，再把豆芽、葱丝放进锅里。接着往锅里放一点儿盐，随后，不停地翻弄锅里的菜。接下来，往锅里放一点儿醋。最后，再往锅里放一点儿香油就行了。你可以让你的朋友们尝尝这个菜，他们一定会喜欢。

Notes to Text 1

a. In describing procedures and processes, the following expressions are often useful:

首先	*first of all; to begin with*	先	*first*
然后	*then; after that; afterwards*	接下来	*following that*
…以后	*after …*	…之后	*after …*
随后	*soon afterwards*	接着	*following that*
最后	*finally*		

b. To indicate intervals, one can use the following words and phrases:

稍过片刻	*after a short while; after a moment*
稍后	*after a short while; after a little while*
过一会儿	*after a while*
过…分钟	*after … minutes*

c. In '先把肉丝放进锅里，稍后，再把豆芽、葱丝放进锅里。' the word 再 is used to indicate that the action of 把豆芽、葱丝放进锅里 takes place after

85

the action of 把肉丝放进锅里 has been completed. In this case, it should be translated as '*then*'. Here is another example: 很多人喜欢先喝酒，再吃主食 (*Many people prefer to drink first, then have the main course*).

Exercises for 9.1

1 Rearrange the following sentences in a logical way, and then use the words and phrases in Notes a and b above to write a cohesive passage on the basis of the following sentences. You may start your passage with '结婚的那一天，...'

   (a) 新娘跟着新郎去见他的父母，新娘要称他们为爸爸、妈妈。

   (b) 新郎把新娘接到他父母的家。

   (c) 新郎坐专车去新娘家。称新娘的父母为爸爸，妈妈。

   (d) 年轻人都去新房闹'洞房'。一般要闹到夜里十一，二点钟。

   (e) 大家去饭店跟客人们一起吃饭。新郎和新娘要向他们自己的父母以及客人们敬酒。客人们也向新郎、新娘敬酒。

   (f) 到了新郎父母的家，在门口要放鞭炮，欢迎新娘。

2 Describe the procedure, step by step, for making coffee with milk and sugar. You should start the procedure from the time when you fill the kettle with tap water. The following words are useful for the description:

水龙头 (*tap*), 灌 (*to fill*), 水壶 (*kettle*), 开关 (*switch*), 把 . . . 打开 (*to switch on*), 烧开 (*to boil*), 倒 (*to pour*), 小勺儿 (*tea-spoon*), 一点儿 (*a little*), 搅 (*to stir; to mix*).

9.2 过去事物的发展过程 Past development process

范文 2, *Text 2*

> ### 我们俩的相爱过程
>
> 　　最早的时候，我们只是一般的同学关系。见面打个招呼，没有很多的交往。不久，我发现她是一个非常美丽而又善良的姑娘。此后，我们的交往日趋增多，经常一起去图书馆、电影院。很快，我意识到自己已经深深地爱上了她。有一次，我在还她书的时候，在书中夹了一封信，表达了我对她的爱慕之心。接着，我接到她的电话，说我信中讲的话也是她想要对我说的话。顿时，我全身热血沸腾。稍后，我们便把这件事告诉了我们各自的父母，并得到了他们的默许。接下来，我们在同学中间公开了我们之间的关系。最后，我们在毕业后的第二年结婚了。现在我们已经有了一个儿子和一个女儿。

Notes to Text 2

a. To indicate the beginning of a past process, one can use the following words and phrases:

最早的时候， 开始的时候， 最初， 起先， 起初

b. To show events in a sequential order in a past process, the following words and phrases are often useful:

此后	*after this; since then*	后来	*afterwards; later*
...以后	*after ...*	...之后	*after ...*
从那以后	*since then; after that*	接着	*following that*
接下来	*following that*	随后	*following that*
最后	*finally*		

c. Sometimes, one needs to indicate the immediacy of one action or event following another, or a short interval between two actions or events. To describe vividly such immediacy or intervals, one can use the following words and phrases:

不久	*before long; soon after*
不一会儿	*before long; not long after that*
不多时	*very soon; before long*
很快	*very soon*
片刻	*instantly; in an instant*
顷刻之间	*in a moment*
刹那间	*in an instant; instantly*
顿时	*immediately; at once*

Exercises for 9.2

1 Fill in the following blanks with the appropriate words in Notes a, b and c above:

(a) _____，是德国先开始采用夏时制的。_____，法国、意大利、英国等国也都先后仿效。

(b) 中国的改革已经进行了十几年了。_____，农村实行承包责任制，调动了农民的积极性。_____，在城市允许个体经营，让一部分人先富起来。_____，发生了'六·四'事件，中国政府减慢了改革的步伐。一九九二年春天，邓小平去深圳视察，并号召全国加速改革。_____，中国政府决定把长期以来中国实行的计划经济改变成市场经济。_____，中国政府又在一些大城市建立了一些股票市场。

(c) _____，他觉得自己是大学教授，做生意赚钱不是他应该做的事情。_____，爱人和孩子都劝他，说现在物价上涨得这么厉害，只靠工资是绝对不够的。_____，他看到他的同事们也一个接一个地辞职做生意去了。_____，他也决定'下海'赚钱。

(d) _____，这里是一片很平的农田，_____ 一些单位在这儿盖起
了住宅楼。_____，一家家小饭馆儿，小商店在这儿开了张。从那
_____，这儿的人和车辆越来越多。_____，这儿建起了超市、
电影院、购物中心，变成了热闹的商业区。

2   Write a passage describing the personnel changes in your department or school
that have taken place since you began to study there. Or write a passage
describing the changes in your city or neighbourhood since you moved there.

9.3 论点的展开 Developing an argument

范文 3, *Text 3*

> 我认为海外华人去大陆投资做生意利大于弊。首先中国大陆是个巨大
> 的潜在市场，那里人口众多。随着近十几年来生活水平的提高，人们的购
> 买力逐年增长，在那里做生意，赚钱的机会是很多的。其次，那里的劳动
> 力便宜，生产成本与西方相比要低得多。除此之外，大陆政府为海外投资
> 者制定了许多免税、减税的优惠政策，很有吸引力。不仅如此，大陆还制
> 定了一系列保护投资者的法律，使海外投资者能够有一种安全感，较放心
> 地在大陆投资。更重要的是，我们都是中国人，在大陆投资没有语言障
> 碍。再说我们了解中国的人情，这对很快建立起我们的关系网是极其重要
> 的。我认为最吸引人的是，目前世界经济的发展中心正在向亚太地区转
> 移。西方各国正面临着严重的经济萧条，而中国的经济迅速发展。世界经
> 济发展的变化毫无疑问会给去中国的投资者增强很多信心。
> 当然，去中国投资也会有许多令人头疼，让人心烦的问题。……

Notes to Text 3

a. When presenting one's point of view or reasons in support of an argument,
it is possible to list them by using ordinal numbers such as 第一 (*firstly*),
第二 (*secondly*), 第三 (*thirdly*), etc. However, it is more forceful to list them
in the way that reasons for investing in mainland China are presented in
Model 3, that is, by using the following words and phrases:

首先	*first of all*
其次	*secondly*
除此之外	*besides*
不仅如此	*not only that; moreover*
更…的是…	*what is more … is …*
再说	*furthermore*
最…的是…	*what is most … is …*

b. The phrases 更 . . . 的是 . . . and 最 . . . 的是 . . . are usually used in the following pattern:

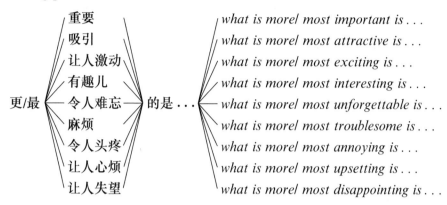

	重要	*what is more/ most important is . . .*
	吸引	*what is more/ most attractive is . . .*
	让人激动	*what is more/ most exciting is . . .*
	有趣儿	*what is more/ most interesting is . . .*
更/最	令人难忘 的是 . . .	*what is more/ most unforgettable is . . .*
	麻烦	*what is more/ most troublesome is . . .*
	令人头疼	*what is more/ most annoying is . . .*
	让人心烦	*what is more/ most upsetting is . . .*
	让人失望	*what is more/ most disappointing is . . .*

c. The phrase 不仅如此 requires the use of 还 in the following sentence, as in '不仅如此，大陆还制定了一系列 . . .' (*moreover, the mainland also set up a series of . . .*).

d. Other words which can be used to present points of view, reasons or arguments include 此外 (*besides; in addition; moreover*), 而且 (*also*) and 另外 (*in addition; moreover; besides*).

Exercises for 9.3

1 Fill in the blanks in the following letter with appropriate conjunctions to help to establish a cohesive structure for the letter.

道明兄：

你好！生活、学习一定都很顺利吧？

最近，我在学习中遇到了很多问题。一直想找你聊聊，可知道你很忙，只好以笔代口了。_____，我们所学的每一门课我都有不少问题，可不知应先解决哪些。_____，我发现汉字越来越难，远远不如一年级的时候那么容易记了。_____，每一门课的老师都给我们布置很多作业。_____，辅导课的老师_____让我们翻译一些很难的文章。我真觉得有点儿招架不了了。_____，我夜里失眠，睡不着觉，而白天上课却没精神，总想睡觉。_____，我对自己能学好汉语几乎失去了信心。

道明兄，你能抽时间跟我聊聊吗？

多谢！

德民
2001年2月12日

2   A friend of yours is thinking of applying to your school/university to study Chinese and has written to you for advice about your school/university. Write him/her a positive letter, telling him/her the advantages of studying Chinese at your school/university. You may provide him/her with information about your teachers, the teaching materials, the library, the computing facilities, the campus, the accommodation, the city, the weather, etc. It is better to make a list of the advantages before you start to write.

9.4 发展趋势 Developmental trend

范文 4, Text 4

a. 虽然近来含酒精饮料的销量急剧上升，但据警察局的统计，在过去三个月里，因酒后驾车造成的交通事故比却去年同期下降了百分之十六。

b. 我市今年一月到六月的进口额基本持平，出口创汇额有所增长，预计今年下半年的出口创汇将比上半年增加60,000,000美元。

c. 这所中学的学生考试不及格率已从1998年的6%降低到今年的0.4%。每年考入高等院校的学生比例也在稳步增长。

d. 东阳村农民的收入近年来继续呈上升趋势。从1995到2001年，全村平均个人收入从每年480元迅速增加到每年6800元。

e. 虽然上个月来我们餐馆的用餐人数有明显的增加，但我们上个月的营业收入却有少量的下降。

Notes to Text 4

a.   In describing a developmental trend, it is often necessary to use verbs such as those listed in (A) below, and to use adverbs such as those listed in (B) below to modify the verbs, as in '急剧上升', '基本持平', '有所增长', '稳步增长', '迅速增加'.

(A) verbs

减少	*to decrease*	下降	*to fall; to drop*
降低	*to drop*	下跌	*to fall; to drop*
跌落	*to fall; to slump*	增加	*to increase*
增长	*to increase; to rise; to grow*	升高	*to rise; to go up*
上升	*to rise; to go up*	持平	*to be level; to level up*

(B) adverbs

迅速(地)	*rapidly*	很快(地)	*quickly*
急剧(地)	*dramatically*	慢慢(地)	*slowly*
缓慢(地)	*slowly*	逐渐(地)	*gradually*
渐渐(地)	*gradually*	逐步(地)	*step by step; progressively*

稳步(地)	*steadily*	持续(地)	*continuously*
不断(地)	*continuously; unceasingly*		
少量	*in a small amount*		
有一定(的)	*to a certain degree; somewhat*		
有所	*to a certain degree; somewhat*		
基本(上)	*on the whole*		

b. To indicate the amount, the percentage or the number by which an entity or a phenomenon has changed, one can use the pattern:

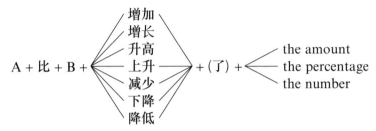

c. The following pattern is useful in presenting a development from one specific point to another:

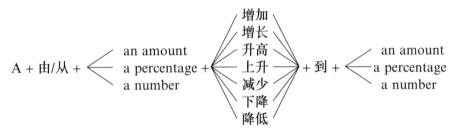

as in '全村平均个人收入从每年480元迅速增加到每年6800元' (*The average per capita income of the whole village increased rapidly from 480 yuan to 6800 yuan*).

d. 呈上升趋势 (*to show a rising tendency*) is a useful phrase, and its opposite is 呈下降趋势 (*to show a falling tendency*).

e. Words such as 增加, 上升, 下降, and 减少 can also be used as nouns, and they can be modified by adjectives, as in '明显的增加' (*clear increase*) and '少量的下降' (*slight fall*).

Exercises for 9.4

1 The information in the graph below will help you complete the following paragraph about the numbers of visitors to Nanling Botanic Garden, Xishan Zoo and Beidao Park. Write out the paragraph, replacing each letter (A) and (B) with an appropriate word from the lists (A) and (B) in Note a and replacing (C) with the correct number from the graph.

以下图表显示了自1990年到1998年参观游览南岭植物园、西山动物园和北岛公园的人次。除了1992年到1995年这段时间以外，西山动物园一直是人们最喜欢去的地方。1990年有近（C ＿＿）人次参观了西山动物园。虽然在接下来的三年里，参观人次（B ＿＿）（A ＿＿），但是从1993年到1997年，参观人次却（B ＿＿）（A ＿＿）。1997年，西山动物园新开设了儿童动物园，这使得参观人次在一年内由（C ＿＿）（B ＿＿）（A ＿＿）到（C ＿＿）。而南岭植物园的情况却不同：1991年植物园新建了一个餐馆，在这之后的两年里，参观植物园的人次从（C ＿＿）（B ＿＿）（A ＿＿）到（C ＿＿），但从1993年开始，参观人次（B ＿＿）（A ＿＿），一直（A ＿＿）到1998年的（C ＿＿）。也许北岛公园是最没意思的地方了：1990年参观人次只有（C ＿＿），从1990年到1992年只有（B ＿＿）（A ＿＿）。在1992年到1994年期间，参观人次基本（A ＿＿）。1995年北岛公园开始在公园内的昆明湖上举办游艇活动，参观游览北岛公园的人次（B ＿＿）（A ＿＿），1996年（A ＿＿）到（C ＿＿），但是自从那时起，参观人次却在（B ＿＿）（A ＿＿）。

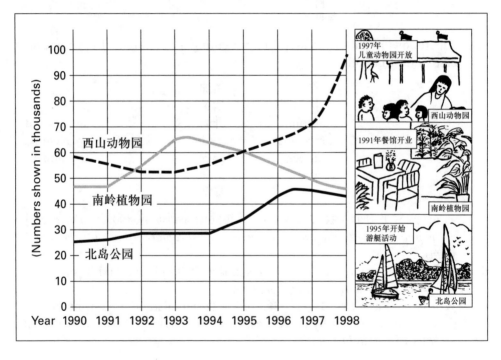

2 Answer the following questions about the graph on the next page, and then write a description of the graph concerning the number of visitors to the Exhibition Centre, the Museum and the Art Gallery. You should comment on the reasons for each increase or decrease in numbers.

(a) 图表提供了有关哪些地方的信息？

(b) 人们最喜欢去哪个地方？

(c) 1998年初参观那个地方的人次是多少？

(d) 为什么1996年参观那个地方的人次急剧增加？

(e) 1990年参观人次最少的是哪个地方？

(f) 1992年以后，参观那个地方的人次的情况如何？

(g) 1998年参观人次最少的是哪个地方？

(h) 1995年参观博物馆的人次与1990年参观博物馆的人次比较，情况如何？

(i) 1995年以后的情况如何？

(j) 在什么时候参观美术馆的人次和参观博物馆的人次一样多？

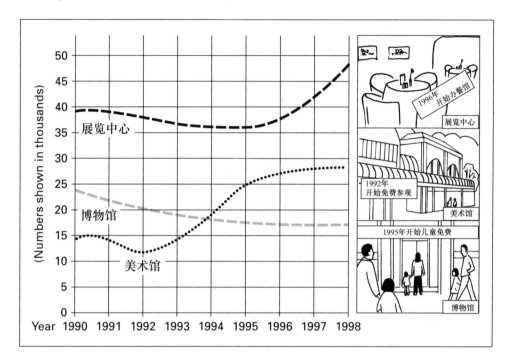

3 Write an essay about the number of foreign tourists who visited Dong'an City, Wutai City and Fangzhou City, and make comments on the increases in numbers and on the reasons for the increases.

年份	去东安市的 外国游客	去五台市的 外国游客	去方州市的 外国游客
1995	5,400	1,600	6,900
1996	5,800	1,500	10,200*
1997	6,000	1,900	12,300
1998	10,200*	2,200	12,500
1999	11,000	2,800*	13,000
2000	13,000	3,000	12,800
2001	14,800	2,900	13,400

* 从1999年开始有从北京到五台市的直飞航班。1996年从北京到方州市的飞机票降价30%。
1998年东安市在北京开设旅游办事处，为游客代办机票、车票、住宿等等。

Vocabulary

9.1

炒	chǎo	to stir-fry
葱丝	cōngsī	sliced spring onion
油	yóu	cooking oil
倒	dào	to pour
锅	guō	pan; wok
炉子	lúzi	cooker
烧热	shāorè	to heat up
盐	yán	salt
翻弄	fānnòng	to stir
醋	cù	vinegar
香油	xiāngyóu	sesame oil
尝尝	chángchang	to have a taste; to try
专车	zhuānchē	special car
闹洞房	nào dòngfáng	to hold house-warming activities in the bridal chamber
敬酒	jìngjiǔ	to offer a toast
放鞭炮	fàng biānpào	to set off firecrackers

9.2

打招呼	dǎ zhāohu	to greet
交往	jiāowǎng	contact
善良	shànliáng	kind-hearted; kind
日趋	rìqū	day by day
夹	jiā	to put in between; to insert
表达	biǎodá	to express
爱慕	àimù	admiration; affection
热血沸腾	rèxuè fèiténg	extremely excited (*lit.* hot blood boiling)
默许	mòxǔ	consent
采用	cǎiyòng	to adopt
夏时制	xiàshí zhì	summer time
仿效	fǎngxiào	to emulate; to imitate
实行	shíxíng	to implement
承包责任制	chéngbāo zérèn zhì	contract and responsibility system
调动	diàodòng	to boost; to arouse
积极性	jījíxìng	enthusiasm
允许	yǔnxǔ	to permit; to allow
个体经营	gètǐ jīngyíng	individual business; private business
减慢	jiǎnmàn	to slow down
改革	gǎigé	reform
步伐	bùfá	step; pace
深圳	Shēnzhèn	[name of a city in China]
视察	shìchá	to inspect

号召	hàozhào	to call upon
加速	jiāsù	to speed up
计划经济	jìhuà jīngjì	planned economy
市场经济	shìchǎng jīngjì	market economy
建立	jiànlì	to establish
股票市场	gǔpiào shìchǎng	stock market
做生意	zuò shēngyi	to do business
赚钱	zhuàn qián	to make money
劝	quàn	to urge; to try to persuade; to discourage
物价	wùjià	price
上涨	shàngzhǎng	to rise; a rise
绝对	juéduì	absolutely
同事	tóngshì	colleague
一个接一个	yíge jiē yíge	one by one
辞职	cízhí	to resign; to quit
下海	xiàhǎi	to go into business
农田	nóngtián	farmland
盖	gài	to build
住宅楼	zhùzhái lóu	residential buildings
购物中心	gòuwù zhōngxīn	shopping centre
商业区	shāngyè qū	commercial district

9.3

海外华人	hǎiwài huárén	overseas Chinese
投资	tóuzī	to invest
利大于弊	lì dà yú bì	advantages outnumber disadvantages
潜在	qiánzài	potential
购买力	gòumǎilì	purchasing power
逐年	zhúnián	year by year
劳动力	láodònglì	labour force
制定	zhìdìng	to formulate; to draw up
免税	miǎnshuì	tax exemption; tax-free
减税	jiǎnshuì	tax reduction
优惠	yōuhuì	preferential
政策	zhèngcè	policy
吸引力	xīyǐn lì	attractive; attraction
一系列	yíxìliè	a series
保护	bǎohù	to protect
障碍	zhàng'ài	barrier; obstacle
人情	rén qíng	human relationship
关系网	guānxì wǎng	network
亚太地区	Yà-Tài dìqū	Asian Pacific Region
转移	zhuǎnyí	to shift; to move
面临	miànlín	to be faced with
经济萧条	jīngjì xiāotiáo	economic recession
毫无疑问	háowú yíwèn	without doubt
增强	zēngqiáng	to strengthen

心烦	**xīnfán**	upsetting; disturbing; troublesome
以笔代口	**yǐ bǐ dài kǒu**	to write a letter instead of talking
布置	**bùzhì**	to assign (homework)
招架不了	**zhāojià bùliǎo**	to be unable to cope
失眠	**shīmián**	to be unable to sleep
没精神	**méi jīngshen**	to have no energy
抽时间	**chōu shíjiān**	to find time

9.4

含酒精	**hán jiǔjīng**	to contain alcohol
销量	**xiāoliàng**	amount of sales; sales volume
急剧	**jíjù**	dramatically
上升	**shàngshēng**	to increase
造成	**zàochéng**	to cause
交通事故	**jiāotōng shìgù**	traffic accident
同期	**tóngqī**	the same period
下降	**xiàjiàng**	to decrease
进口额	**jìnkǒu'é**	imports; import volume
持平	**chípíng**	to be level; to be flat
出口创汇额	**chūkǒu chuàng huì é**	export earnings
预计	**yùjì**	it is predicted
不及格率	**bù jígé lǜ**	failure rate
稳步	**wěnbù**	steadily
呈	**chéng**	to show; to display
趋势	**qūshì**	trend; tendency
明显	**míngxiǎn**	obvious; clear
营业收入	**yíngyè shōurù**	business income; trading income
参观	**cānguān**	to visit; visiting
游览	**yóulǎn**	to visit
南岭植物园	**Nánlǐng Zhíwùyuán**	Nanling Botanic Garden
西山动物园	**Xīshān Dòngwùyuán**	Xishan Zoo
北岛公园	**Běidǎo Gōngyuán**	Beidao Park
开设	**kāishè**	to open
期间	**qījiān**	period
举办	**jǔbàn**	to hold; to run (an event)
游艇	**yóutǐng**	boating; boat
直飞航班	**zhífēi hángbān**	direct flight
代办	**dàibàn**	to do (something for somebody)

第十单元: 对人外貌的描写
Unit Ten: Descriptions of people's physical attributes

Comprehensive descriptions of people's physical attributes employ a large portion of the propositional language available in Chinese, and to attempt a full summary in this section would be unrealistic. This unit covers only commonly used descriptions of a person's physical attributes, such as hair, eyes, facial shape, other facial features, build, height, etc.

10.1 头发 Hair

范文 1, Text 1

a. 我第一次见到他的时候，他的头发乌黑发亮。但十几年不见，他已满头银发，成了一个白发苍苍的老人。而且他也已经开始谢顶了。

b. 她那披肩的长发是金黄色的，并且有点儿鬈，虽然有点儿蓬乱，但具有一种自然的魅力。

Notes to Text 1

a. In English, the verb '*to have*' is often used in the description of hair, as in '*she has curly hair*'. However, the Chinese equivalent 有 is usually not used. In this case, you can say '她是鬈头发' or '她的头发有点儿鬈'.

b. When talking about the colour of the hair, you often need to use the pattern '... 是 ... 的', as in '他的头发是金黄色的' (*His hair is blond*). However, when you describe the hair metaphorically, this pattern is not necessary, and you can simply use the structure 'someone's hair + an adjective', as in '他的头发乌黑' (*His hair is dark and shiny*), or '她的头发苍白' (*Her hair is grey*).

c. When you use an adjective to modify the noun 头发, it is stylistically more elegant to use an adjective which has more than one syllable. For example, instead of '白的头发' (*grey hair*), it is better to say '灰白的头发' (*grey hair*) or '花白的头发' (*grey hair*).

Exercises for 10.1

1 Put the following phrases into appropriate places below, and pay attention to the sentence structure in which the phrases can be used. Some phrases can be used more than once and each place may have more than one phrase suitable for it.

白发苍苍	满头银发	头发乌润	头发油亮	头发光洁
头发蓬乱	披头散发	头发稀疏	秃顶	谢顶

(a) 我的旁边坐着一位_____的老太太。
(b) 他_____，穿着一件T恤衫，肩上还背着一个书包。
(c) 虽然张教授已经_____，但是看上去身体还很健康。
(d) 她丈夫只有三十出头，可却已_____。
(e) 他进来的时候，_____，后面还跟了一个女孩子。

2 Put the following phrases into appropriate places below, and pay attention to the sentence structure in which the phrases can be used. There may be more than one phrase suitable for one place, and some phrases may be suitable for more than one place.

花白的头发	灰白的头发	金黄的头发	卷曲的头发
波浪式的头发	乌黑的头发	披肩的长发	齐耳的短发
细长的小辫			

(a) 她那_____似乎能显示出她的朝气和个性。
(b) 从他那_____，也许你能猜出他的年龄。
(c) 她一头_____，走到哪里都很引人注意。
(d) 我记得那时你扎着两根_____。
(e) 王先生五十多岁，一头_____。

3 Make a sentence or sentences, describing the hair of a person around you and ask your classmates to guess whom you are describing.

4 Describe the hair of your parents and grandparents.

10.2 胡子 Beard

范文 *2, Text 2*

a. 那个留着小胡子的人是谁?
b. 他那络腮胡也已花白。
c. 他爷爷留着山羊胡，而他爸爸却留着八字胡。

Notes to Text 2

a. In English, we can say '*he is growing a moustache*'. The counterpart of '*grow*' in Chinese is 留, as in '他留着八字胡'.

b. Here are other expressions in the same category: 大胡子 (*big beard*), 小胡子 (*small beard*), 络腮胡 (*full beard*), 连鬓胡 (*whiskers; side-burns*), 山羊胡 (*goatee*), 八字胡 (*a moustache*).

10.3 眼睛 Eyes

范文 *3, Text 3*

a. 他那双浓眉大眼向我投来亲切的目光，使我忘了孤独。
b. 她是单眼皮，眼睛也不大，但总是充满着热情。
c. 从他那敏锐的目光中，我知道他是一个很有知识的学者。

Notes to Text 3

a. In Model 3a, '浓眉大眼' (*bushy eyebrows and big eyes*) is used as subject. It can also be used as object, as in '我喜欢他那双浓眉大眼', as modifier, as in '他是一个浓眉大眼的小伙子', or as predicate, as in '那个小伙子浓眉大眼'. Other phrases which have similar functions include '细眉细眼' (*fine eyebrows and eyes*), '近视眼' (*short-sighted*), '远视眼' (*long-sighted*), '单眼皮' (*single eyelid*), '双眼皮' (*double eyelids*).

b. 向 somebody 投来/去 ... 的目光 means *to glance at somebody*, as in '我向她投去同情的目光' (*I gave her a sympathetic look*).

99

c. The phrase 充满着 or 充满了 is often preceded by words such as 眼睛 or 目光 to mean that '*the eyes are full of* . . .', as in '她的目光里充满了悲伤' (*Her eyes are full of sadness*). Here are some more examples:

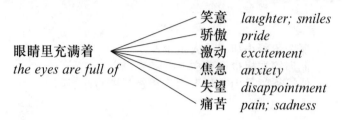

眼睛里充满着
the eyes are full of

笑意 *laughter; smiles*
骄傲 *pride*
激动 *excitement*
焦急 *anxiety*
失望 *disappointment*
痛苦 *pain; sadness*

Exercises for 10.2 and 10.3

1 Put a tick beside the words below which you think are positive, a cross beside the words which you think are negative, and a circle beside the words which you think are neutral.

明亮的	有神的	敏锐的	严肃的	热情的	亲切的
冷酷的	试探的	含笑的	乌黑的	亮晶晶的	凶狠的
迟钝的	痴呆的	信任的			

2 Place the adjectives above into two separate lists, those that can modify 眼睛 and those that can modify 目光. Many of the adjectives can go in both lists.

3 Make two sentences, describing the eyes of two people you know.

10.4 鼻子 Nose

范文 4, Text 4

> a. 她那俊俏笔挺的鼻子使得她那张文静的脸显得更加秀丽。
> b. 虽然这个男孩儿的鼻子有点儿扁平，但他却很逗人喜爱。

Notes to Text 4

a. When a personal possessive pronoun is used to indicate whose nose is being referred to, it is often stylistically better to put a demonstrative 这 or 那 after the pronoun, as in '她那俊俏笔挺的鼻子' (*her pretty and straight nose*). This rule also applies to descriptions of other personal physical attributes, as in '她那文静的脸' (*her gentle and quiet face*).

b.　　Here are other descriptions of the nose:

高鼻子 *high nose*　　　　　　　　尖鼻子 *pointed nose*
鹰钩鼻子 *Roman nose; aquiline nose*　　挺直的鼻子 *straight nose*
扁平的鼻子 *flat nose*

10.5　嘴和牙 Mouth and teeth

范文 5, *Text 5*

> a. 她的嘴唇略微有点儿厚，可是线条很美。张口时，会露出一排整齐的牙齿。
> b. 她那红红的嘴唇包着洁白的牙齿，笑的时候，就像一朵盛开的鲜花，非常迷人。

Notes to Text 5

a.　　线条 here means lines of the mouth.
b.　　'张口时，会露出 . . .' can be translated as '*When she opens her mouth, it reveals . . .*'
c.　　排 is usually used as a measure word for a row of teeth.
d.　　Here are other descriptions of the mouth and teeth:

樱桃小嘴 *a small cherry mouth*　　厚厚的嘴唇 *thick lips*
薄薄的嘴唇 *thin lips*　　　　　　嘴唇苍白 *the lips are pale*
唇无血色 *the lips are pallid*　　　嘴唇发紫 *the lips have become pale*
整齐的牙齿 *even teeth*　　　　　洁白的牙齿 *white teeth*
稀疏的牙齿 *gapped teeth*　　　　不整齐的牙齿 *uneven teeth*
发黄的牙齿 *yellow teeth*

10.6　面容 Face

范文 6, *Text 6*

> a. 他，长脸，大眼，棕红色的皮肤，英俊的脸上带有一种男性的刚毅。
> b. 她变得老多了，那憔悴的脸上布满了皱纹。
> c. 她的脸是鸭蛋形的，加上一双明亮的眼睛和笔挺的鼻子，显得格外眉清目秀。

Notes to Text 6

a. The adjective 英俊的 (*handsome*) is usually used to describe a man rather than a woman.

b. 鸭蛋形的(脸) or 鸭蛋脸 (*oval face*) are usually used to describe a woman.

c. Below are two groups of descriptions; one is for physical features of the face and the other is for facial expressions.

(a) Descriptions of physical features of the face:

圆(圆的)脸	长(长的)脸 ✗	苹果脸 ✗	四方脸 ✗ ✓
瓜子脸 ✓	鸭蛋脸 ⃝	五官端正 ⃝	眉清目秀 ✓
扁平的脸 ⃝	苍白的脸 ✗	蜡黄的脸 ✗	红润的脸 ✗
英俊的脸 ✓	清秀的脸 ✓	秀丽的脸 ✗	憔悴的脸
刚毅的脸 ✗	布满皱纹的脸 ✗	清瘦的脸 ✗	削瘦的脸 ✗
俊秀的脸 ✓	丑陋的脸 ✗	熟悉的面孔 ✓	
陌生的面孔 ✗	脸上刻着一道道皱纹 ✗		

(b) Descriptions of facial expressions:

When angry or unhappy:
板着脸 *to keep a straight face*, 绷着脸 *to pull a long face*,
拉长了脸 *to pull a long face*, 脸色铁青 *the face turns livid*

When happy or pleased:
满脸笑容 *the face is full of smiles*, 眉开眼笑 *to beam with joy*,
眉飞色舞 *to be enraptured with dancing eyebrows and radiant face*,
喜笑颜开 *to light up with pleasure*, 满面春风 *radiant with happiness*

When happy but casual and relaxed:
脸上笑嘻嘻的 *beaming; smiling broadly*

When in good mood and good health:
神采奕奕 *glowing with health and radiating vigour*,
容光焕发 *one's face glows with health*, 满面红光 *glowing with health*

When embarrassed:
满脸羞愧 *to look ashamed*, 脸上红一阵白一阵 *to turn red and then turn pale*, 面红耳赤 *to be red in the face*

When in difficult situations:
愁眉苦脸 *to have a worried look*, 愁容满面 *to look extremely worried*,
满脸愁云 *to look extremely worried*

When unpleasantly shocked:
脸刷地一下白了 *to suddenly turn pale*, 面无血色 *the face is pale*,
面如土色 *to turn deadly pale*, 面色苍白 *the face is extremely pale*

When shocked and embarrassed:
脸腾地一下红了 *the face suddenly turns red*

When being unfriendly and cold:
脸上冷冰冰的 *the attitude is cold and unfriendly*, 脸上阴森森的 *to look unfriendly and cold*

When being suspicious:
满脸疑惑 *to look dubious*

When being worked up:
面红耳赤 *to be red in the face*

When being ill or malnourished:
面如土色 *to turn deadly pale*, 面黄肌瘦 *sallow and emaciated*,
面色苍白 *the face is extremely pale*, 脸色蜡黄 *the face is sallow*,
面无血色 *the face is pale*

When courageously facing a dangerous situation:
面不改色 *to remain calm*

When grinning cheekily:
嬉皮笑脸 *to grin cheekily*

Exercises for 10.4–10.6

1   Look at the descriptions in Note 6c (a) again, and put a tick beside the words which you think are positive, a cross beside the words which you think are negative and a circle beside the words which you think are neutral.

2   Fill in the blanks below using the phrases in Note 6c (b) above. For some blanks, more than one phrase is suitable.

(a)   当警察来告诉她她的儿子偷了别人的东西时，她 *面无血色* 不知道该说什么好。

(b)   我刚才听说李老师和他的妻子离婚了。怪不得这几天他很少跟别人讲话，整天 *脸上阴森森的。*

(c)   王教授给我们上课时总是 _____，同学们都特别喜欢上他的课。 *脸上笑嘻嘻的。*

(d)   当警察告诉她她丈夫出了车祸时，她 *面色苍白*，很快就昏倒了。

(e)   我走进房间，看见 *满脸愁云* 的老奶奶躺在病床上。这时，我忍不住哭了起来。

(f)   他常常不交作业。老师批评他，可是他却 *满脸笑容*，好象他没有做错什么事一样。

(g)   你知道这几天他为什么整天 *眉开眼笑* 吗？他跟他女朋友订婚了。

(h)   我只在他房间里呆了两分钟。他 _____，一看就知道他还在恨我。 *拉长了脸*

103

General writing practice 10.1

1 Read the following three paragraphs. Each paragraph describes one of the pictures on the next page. Which person is being described in each paragraph?

A. 他有一张长脸，高高的鼻子，略微有点儿尖。他的头发乌黑，但很短。他留着八字胡，戴着一副近视眼镜，显得眼睛不大。他那紧闭着的两片嘴唇让人觉得他十分严肃。

B. 她的脸圆圆的。虽然她鼻子有点儿扁平，但她那双有神的大眼睛总是放射出亲切温柔的目光。她那波浪式的头发伴随着一张笑容可掬的面容，使人一看就知道她是一个非常可爱的女性。

C. 他的脸有点儿长方形，有很浓密的络腮胡子。头发油亮光洁，牙齿洁白而整齐。高高的鼻梁两边是一双浓眉大眼，从那儿你可以看到他那含笑的目光。

2 Write three paragraphs about the three remaining pictures.

3 Now write a similar paragraph describing a friend of yours, a member of your family or anyone you know.

10.7 身材 Stature

范文 7, *Text 7*

> a. 他那魁梧的身材，站在前面，好像一座铁塔。
> b. 她身材苗条，健美，充满活力，如同春天早晨一棵亭亭玉立的小树。
> c. 一个二十来岁的人走进来，他身材既矮又胖，丝毫没有青年人的蓬勃朝气。
> d. 他身高两米，体重九十公斤，现在是一个篮球俱乐部的职业篮球运动员。

Notes to Text 7

a. In describing someone's stature, you can say 他那 + adjective + 的身村, as in '他那魁梧的身材' (*his strapping figure*), or you can say 他身材 + adjective, as in '她身材苗条' (*She is slim*).

b. In describing someone's height or weight in English, it is often necessary to use verbs like '*be*' or '*weigh*'. However, in Chinese, no verb is required. Sometimes, we can use the verb 有 to add a sense of estimate to the sentence, as in '他身高(有)两米' (*He is (about) two metres tall*) and '他体重(有)九十公斤' (*His weight is (about) 90 kilograms*).

1 冯杰

2 丛乐森

3 史丽安

4 孙德龙

5 林培芬

6 宋之东

c. Here are other descriptions of stature:

身材高大 *his/her stature is big and tall*
身材矮小 *his/her stature is short and small*
身材粗壮 *his/her stature is sturdy*
身材瘦弱 *his/her stature is thin and weak*
身材苗条 *his/her stature is slim*
修长的身材 *tall and slim build*
丰满的身材 *a robust stature*
魁梧的身材 *powerfully built*
粗胖的身材 *burly*
消瘦的身材 *thin build*
匀称的身材 *well-proportioned stature*
中等身材 *medium build*

10.8 年龄 Age

范文 8, Text 8

a. 他那红润的脸上总是充满了笑容，而且皱纹极少，不认识他的人根本不会相信他已进入'花甲'之年了。
b. 这个人看上去四十岁出头，两条弯弯的眉毛下有一双机灵的眼睛。

Notes to Text 8

a. In describing someone's age in English, we often have to use the verb '*be*', as in '*she is over 70*', or '*he is 18 this year*'. However, in the description of one's age in Chinese, the Chinese equivalent of '*be*' is not used, as in '他今年十八岁'. Sometimes, it is possible to use the verb 有 in describing the age in Chinese, which adds a sense of estimate to the description, as in '她有七十多岁' (*She is more than 70 years old*).

b. '花甲' 之年 here refers to the age of 60. Other similar expressions include '而立' 之年 and '不惑' 之年. The former stands for the age of 30 when a man should stand on his own feet, and the latter for the age of 40 when a man should no longer be misled. These expressions derive from ancient Chinese philosophy. For this kind of expression, it is often necessary to use verbs like (已) 进入, and (已) 到 (了), as in '他已进入 "花甲" 之年' (*He has reached the age of 60*) .

c. When describing someone's age approximately, we can employ phrases which precede the age expression (pre-modifier), or phrases that come after the age expression (post-modifier).

Pre-modifiers include: 大约 (*about*), 接近 (*nearly*), 将近 (*nearly*), 差不多 (*almost*).

Post-modifiers include: 左右 (*or so*), 出头 (*over*), 来岁 (*about*), 多岁 (*over*), 上下 (*or so*).

d. Below are other descriptions of age:

大约有十岁左右 *about ten years old*
十七，八岁 *17 or 18 years old*
二十出头 *over 20*
接近三十了 *nearly 30*
三十来岁 *about 30 years old*
已进入 '而立' 之年 *already 30 years old*
已到 '不惑' 之年 *already 40 years old*
已过 '花甲' 之年 *already passed the age of 60*

General writing practice 10.2

1 Using the following as a guideline, write separate letters about each of the four people in the pictures on the next page. In your letters, give detailed descriptions of the four people.

亲爱的纪书丰:

因为我得陪我妈妈去医院看病，下星期一我不能去火车站接你，非常抱歉。我的邻居(李毕德/王丽珍/宋华玲/丁思兴)答应代我去车站接你。由于你从来没有见过(他/她)，下面我把(他/她)的样子给你描述一下。

(Now give a detailed description of one neighbour)

我已经把你的样子告诉了我的邻居，希望你们在火车站都能认出对方来。

祝你旅途愉快！下星期一见。

吴天明
2001年1月12日

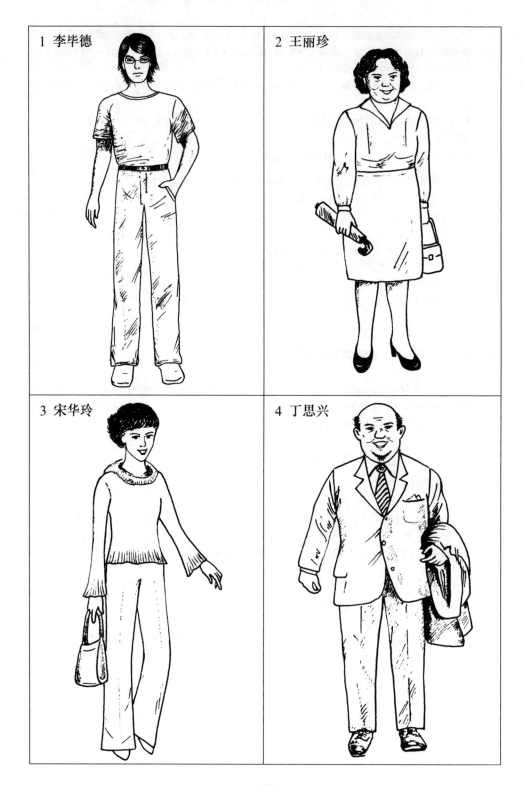

1 李毕德

2 王丽珍

3 宋华玲

4 丁思兴

2   Imagine that you have been asked to meet a visitor whom you have never
    seen before. Write a letter to him, arranging a time and a place to meet. In
    your letter, you should describe what you look like and how you will be
    dressed.

Vocabulary

外貌	wàimào	physical appearance

10.1

乌黑发亮	wūhēi fāliàng	dark and shiny
银发	yínfà	grey hair
谢顶	xièdǐng	bald
披肩长发	pījiān cháng fà	shoulder-length hair
金黄	jīnhuáng	blond; golden
鬈曲	quánqū	curly
魅力	mèilì	charm
灰白	huībái	grey
花白	huābái	grey
乌润	wūrùn	dark and glossy
油亮	yóuliàng	glossy; sleek
光洁	guāngjié	shiny and neat
蓬乱	péngluàn	dishevelled
披头散发	pītóu sǎnfà	with dishevelled hair; with hair in disarray
稀疏	xīshū	thinning; sparse
秃顶	tūdǐng	bald
T恤衫	tìxùshān	T-shirt
波浪式的	bōlàngshìde	wavy
齐耳	qí'ěr	trimmed to the ears
细长	xìcháng	thin and long
小辫	xiǎobiàn	short braid; pigtail
朝气	zhāoqì	vigour; vitality
个性	gèxìng	character
扎着	zhāzhe	to be wearing

10.2

留着	liúzhe	to be growing; to have (a beard)
八字胡	bāzihú	moustache
络腮胡	luòsāihú	full beard
连鬓胡	liánbìnhú	whiskers; side-burns
山羊胡	shānyánghú	goatee

10.3

浓眉大眼	nóngméi dàyǎn	heavy eyebrows and big eyes; heavy features
投	tóu	to cast; to throw
孤独	gūdú	loneliness; lonely
单眼皮	dān yǎnpí	single eyelid
充满	chōngmǎn	to be full of
敏锐	mǐnruì	sharp
学者	xuézhě	scholar
细眉细眼	xì méi xì yǎn	fine eyebrows and narrow eyes
近视眼	jìnshìyǎn	short-sighted
远视眼	yuǎnshìyǎn	long-sighted
双眼皮	shuāng yǎnpí	double eyelids
同情	tóngqíng	sympathy
悲伤	bēishāng	sadness
焦急	jiāojí	anxiety; worry
失望	shīwàng	disappointment
痛苦	tòngkǔ	pain; agony; misery
有神	yǒushén	piercing
冷酷	lěngkù	unfeeling; callous
试探的	shìtànde	probing
含笑	hánxiào	smiling
亮晶晶	liàngjīngjīng	glistening; shiny
凶狠	xiōnghěn	vicious
迟钝	chídùn	slow
痴呆	chīdāi	dull-witted
信任的	xìnrènde	trusting

10.4

俊俏	jùnqiào	pretty; charming
笔挺	bǐtǐng	straight
文静	wénjìng	gentle and quiet
秀丽	xiùlì	beautiful; pretty
逗人喜爱	dòu rén xǐ'ài	amusing; lovable
尖鼻子	jiān bízi	pointed nose
鹰钩鼻子	yīnggōu bízi	Roman nose; aquiline nose
挺直的鼻子	tǐngzhíde bízi	straight nose
扁平的鼻子	biǎnpíngde bízi	flat nose

10.5

嘴唇	zuǐchún	lip
略微	lüèwēi	slightly; a little
线条	xiàntiáo	lines
露出	lùchū	to reveal

盛开	**shèngkāi**	blossoming; blooming
迷人	**mírén**	enchanting; charming; fascinating
樱桃	**yīngtáo**	cherry
苍白	**cāngbái**	pale; pallid; wan
唇无血色	**chún wú xuěsè**	the lips are pallid
发紫	**fā zǐ**	to turn blue
洁白	**jiébái**	clean and white
发黄	**fā huáng**	to become yellow

10.6

棕红色	**zōnghóngsè**	brown
皮肤	**pífū**	skin
英俊	**yīngjùn**	handsome
刚毅	**gāngyì**	fortitude; steadfast; resolute
憔悴	**qiáocuì**	wan and sallow; thin and pallid
布满了皱纹	**bùmǎnle zhòuwén**	full of wrinkles
鸭蛋脸	**yādàn liǎn**	oval face
眉清目秀	**méiqīng mùxiù**	to have delicate features
四方脸	**sìfāng liǎn**	square face
瓜子脸	**guāzǐ liǎn**	oval face
五官端正	**wǔguān duānzhèng**	to have regular features
蜡黄	**làhuáng**	sallow; waxy yellow
红润	**hóngrùn**	ruddy; rosy
清秀	**qīngxiù**	delicate and pretty
清瘦	**qīngshòu**	thin; lean
削瘦	**xiāoshòu**	emaciated; thin
俊秀	**jùnxiù**	pretty; of delicate beauty
丑陋	**chǒulòu**	ugly
陌生	**mòshēng**	strange; unfamiliar
刻着	**kèzhe**	to be carved; to be engraved (used metaphorically here)
道	**dào**	(a measure word for wrinkles)
板着脸	**bǎnzhe liǎn**	to have a stern expression
绷着脸	**běngzhe liǎn**	to look displeased; to pull a long face
拉长了脸	**lāchángle liǎn**	to pull a long face
脸色铁青	**liǎnsè tiěqīng**	the face turns livid/angry
眉开眼笑	**méikāi yǎnxiào**	to beam with joy; to be all smiles
眉飞色舞	**méifēi sèwǔ**	enraptured with dancing eyebrows and radiant face; to be pleased with oneself
喜笑颜开	**xǐxiào yánkāi**	to light up with pleasure; to be wreathed in smiles
满面春风	**mǎn miàn chūnfēng**	beaming with satisfaction; radiant with happiness
笑嘻嘻	**xiàoxīxī**	beaming; smiling broadly
神采奕奕	**shéncǎi yìyì**	glowing with health
容光焕发	**róngguāng huànfà**	face glows with health
满脸羞愧	**mǎn liǎn xiūkuì**	to look ashamed

红一阵白一阵	**hóng yízhèn bái yízhèn**	to turn red and then pale
面红耳赤	**miàn hóng ěr chì**	to be red in the face; to flush with embarrassment
愁眉苦脸	**chóuméi kǔliǎn**	to have a worried look
愁容满面	**chóuróng mǎnmiàn**	to look extremely worried
满脸愁云	**mǎnliǎn chóuyún**	to look extremely worried
刷地一下白了	**shuāde yíxià báile**	to suddenly turn pale
面如土色	**miàn rú tǔsè**	to turn deadly pale
腾地一下红了	**tēngde yíxià hóngle**	to suddenly turn red
冷冰冰的	**lěngbīngbīng de**	cold and unfriendly
阴森森的	**yīnsēnsēn de**	cold and unfriendly; forbidding
满脸疑惑	**mǎnliǎn yíhuò**	to look unconvinced; to seem to have doubts
面黄肌瘦	**miàn huáng jī shòu**	sallow and emaciated; thin and haggard
面不改色	**miàn bù gǎi sè**	to remain calm; not to change colour
嬉皮笑脸	**xīpí xiàoliǎn**	grinning cheekily; smiling
车祸	**chē huò**	traffic accident
昏倒	**hūndǎo**	to faint
忍不住	**rěnbúzhù**	cannot help (doing something)
伴随	**bànsuí**	to accompany
笑容可掬	**xiàoróng kějū**	to be radiant with smiles
浓密	**nóngmì**	thick; dense

10.7

魁梧	**kuíwǔ**	big and strong; powerfully-built
铁塔	**tiě tǎ**	iron tower
苗条	**miáotiao**	slender; slim
健美	**jiànměi**	vigorous and graceful; strong and handsome
活力	**huólì**	vitality; vigour; energy
亭亭玉立	**tíngtíngyùlì**	slim and graceful
丝毫	**sīháo**	the slightest amount/degree
蓬勃朝气	**péngbó zhāoqì**	youthful and vigorous
粗壮	**cūzhuàng**	sturdy; strong
修长	**xiūcháng**	tall and slim; slender
丰满	**fēngmǎn**	robust; bulky
匀称	**yúnchèn**	well-proportioned
中等	**zhōngděng**	medium

10.8

弯弯的	**wānwānde**	bent
机灵	**jīling**	clever; intelligent
抱歉	**bàoqiàn**	to be sorry; to apologise
旅途	**lǚtú**	journey

第十一单元：对人心态的描写
Unit Eleven: Descriptions of people's emotional attributes

The need to describe people's emotional attributes arises fairly frequently, although most people do not usually need to write long descriptions of their emotional attributes. The correct use of short but appropriate phrases and sentences can often achieve the purpose. This unit deals with descriptions of one's emotional attributes, such as happiness, sadness, depression, horror, anger, etc.

11.1 喜爱 Liking

范文 1, Text 1

a. 他爱好长跑，每天清晨坚持锻炼，一年四季风雨无阻。
b. 吴天明从小酷爱文学，特别是对老舍的小说，简直是爱不释手。
c. 多么好的朋友啊！当他知道我要去访问那个边远的地区时，便忍痛割爱，把他那小巧玲珑的移动电话借给了我。
d. 老李两口子特别宠爱他们的那个小孙女。
e. 自从王志强爱上了张玉雪，他们俩情意绵绵，整天难舍难分。

Notes to Text 1

a. The verb 酷爱 usually takes a noun referring to a hobby or something abstract as its object. Similar verbs include 爱好, 喜爱, and 热爱. These words can be used as nouns as well. In this case, the word usually appears in the pattern of 对 . . . 的喜爱, as in '她表现出对网球的十分喜爱'.

b. The phrase '爱不释手' means 'to caress admiringly'. When the object is indicated, it appears before the phrase and is preceded by the preposition 对, as

113

in the pattern of '对 something 爱不释手'. This requirement of the use of 对 also applies to other phrases, such as '忍痛割爱' (*to part with what one treasures*), '朝思暮想' (*to yearn for . . . day and night*), '情意绵绵' (*to have endless affection for . . .*), '情深似海' (*to love . . . as deep as the ocean*), etc.

c. The verb 宠爱 (*to dote on*) refers to the love shown to children by parents and grandparents or to junior by senior. The verb 疼爱 (*to love dearly*) can also be used in a similar way. To express one's respect and admiration for someone senior or superior to oneself, the verbs such as 爱慕 (*to adore; to admire*), 爱戴 (*to love and esteem*) are often used. These words can be used as nouns as well. In this case, the word usually appears in the pattern of 对 . . . 的爱慕, as in '她的话表达了她对那位英雄的爱慕' (*Her speech expressed her admiration for that hero*).

Exercises for 11.1

Fill in the blanks with appropriate phrases from those listed below:

爱好   热爱   朝思暮想   情意绵绵   情深似海   爱戴

1 各国人民都_____和平，反对战争。
2 她对在美国读书的丈夫_____，整天吃不下饭，睡不着觉。
3 他们一家人对我_____，将来我一定要好好报答他们。
4 从他的话中，你可以听出他对他以前的那个女朋友仍然_____。
5 他的_____是绘画。
6 他知识渊博，教学认真，热情周到，深受学生们的_____。

11.2 快乐 Being happy

范文 *2, Text 2*

> a. 听到这个消息，她开心地笑了。
> b. 王老师讲完那个笑话以后，学生们都笑得直不起腰来。
> c. 看到自己丢失的护照和钱被警察找回来了，那位英国老人又惊又喜。
> d. 当我接到了剑桥大学的录取通知书时，我们全家人喜出望外，都过来向我表示祝贺。

Notes to Text 2

a. Adverbs of manner such as 开心地, 高兴地, 快活地, etc. are normally used before the verb to indicate that someone does something in a happy manner, as in '他开心地笑了' (*He laughed with joy*), '孩子们高兴地跑出去' (*The children ran out happily*).

b. To describe the degree of someone's happiness, one can use '得 + a phrase/ clause' as a degree complement. The degree complement occurs after the verb, as in '学生们都笑得直不起腰来' (*The students all killed themselves laughing; The students all laughed so much that they couldn't hold their backs straight*), '我高兴得跳了起来' (*I was so happy that I jumped up*).

c. Stylistically, it is often better to use a four-character phrase than a two-character phrase to describe someone's happiness, as in '老人又惊又喜' (*The old man was surprised and pleased*) in comparison with '老人很惊喜' (*The old man was surprised and pleased*).

Exercises for 11.2

1   Put the following phrases in the appropriate blanks below. Please note that some of the phrases require the use of 地 or 得.

    眼泪都流出来了，不好意思，喊了起来，乐开了花，兴高采烈

(a) 知道自己考试得了第一，马小玉＿＿＿＿＿＿＿回到家，把这个好消息告诉了她的父母。

(b) 今年又获得了大丰收，农民们心里＿＿＿＿＿＿＿。

(c) 这个相声把一些观众笑＿＿＿＿＿＿＿。

(d) 她的同屋问她'你爱上王海涛了吗?'，她＿＿＿＿＿＿笑了。

(e) 一看到自己得了大奖，他就兴奋＿＿＿＿＿＿'我得奖了！我得奖了！'。

2   Combine the following into six four-character phrases, and then make a sentence with each of them.

    惊喜，心花，欣喜，喜笑，万分，怒放，喜出，颜开，望外，若狂

3   Imagine that a family has won £2,000,000 in a National Lottery Draw (国家六合彩抽奖). Write a short essay describing the excitement and the joy of the family members.

11.3   伤心与悲痛 Sorrow and grief

范文 3, *Text 3*

a. 他母亲的逝世使他很悲伤。

b. 当意识到再也见不到自己心爱的女儿了，他们夫妻两人抱头痛哭。

c. 看到自己的丈夫在一旁哭泣，王淑华的泪水像断了线的珠子似的掉了下来。

Notes to Text 3

a. To express the cause and the resultative state of the sadness and grief, one can use the pattern 'the noun indicating the cause + 使 + somebody + 很 + 悲伤/悲痛/伤心/痛心/痛苦/'.

b. '抱头痛哭' means *'to cry on each other's shoulders'*. Other descriptions of crying include '默默的哭泣' (*to weep quietly*), '失声痛哭' (*to burst out crying loudly*), '放声大哭' (*to cry loudly*) '泣不成声' (*to choke with sobs*).

c. '泪水像断了线的珠子似的掉了下来' means *'Tears dropped like pearls falling from a broken string'*. Other descriptions of tears include '眼里充满了泪水' (*The eyes are full of tears*), '泪如泉涌' (*Tears well up like water from of a spring*), '泪水夺眶而出' (*Tears well from one's eyes*).

Exercises for 11.3

Use the expressions you have learned to write a paragraph describing each of the following pictures.

Picture 1:

Picture 2:

11.4 忧愁 Being sad and depressed

范文 *4, Text 4*

a. 爸爸的病情使全家人都很忧愁。
b. 最近李树青感到很沮丧,因为他的学习成绩总是很差。
c. 看到总经理那忧心忡忡的样子,大家都为公司的前途担心。
d. 他看上去愁眉苦脸,可能他遇到了什么不愉快的事情。

Notes to Text 4

a. To express the cause of sadness and depression and the resultative state, one can use the pattern 'the noun indicating the cause + 使 + somebody + 很 + 忧虑 (*worried; concerned*) / 忧伤 (*distressed*) / 苦恼 (*vexed; worried*) / 苦闷 (*depressed*)' or 'the noun indicating the cause + 使 + somebody + 愁眉不展 (*to have a worried frown*) / 愁眉苦脸 (*to have a worried look*)'.

b. In the English sentence '*She is depressed*', the link verb '*is*' is required, but the Chinese counterpart 是 is not used in a Chinese sentence of this type, as in '她很沮丧' (*She is depressed*). However, one can use the verb 感到 or 觉得 in this type of sentence, as in '她觉得很沮丧 (*depressed*) / 很苦恼 (*vexed; worried*) / 很烦恼 (*vexed; worried*)'.

c. In the phrase '那忧心忡忡的样子', 忧心忡忡的 is used as a modifier with the noun 样子 meaning '*the look of being down-hearted*'. Other phrases can also be used in the same way, as in '烦闷 (*unhappy; worried*) / 的/唉声叹气 (*sighing in despair*) / 的/闷闷不乐 (*depressed*) 的 + 样子'.

Exercises for 11.4

1 Put an appropriate phrase in each blank in the sentences below. You may need to use 很 and 的 in filling some blanks.
   (a) 自从失业以后，爸爸整天_____。这使得全家人也_____。
   (b) 我故意装出_____样子，让他们以为我_____。
   (c) 虽然她女儿的手术很成功，但刘秀华还是觉得_____，因为她担心她女儿会从此成了残废。
   (d) 她这几天看上去_____，也许她失恋了。

2 Write a short paragraph describing someone's depression. This person can be someone you know or someone imaginary. In your writing, state what caused the depression, how s/he felt during that time and what his/her appearance was like, and try to use words such as 使, 感到, 看上去, 样子.

11.5 惊恐 Being terrified and panic-stricken

范文 *5, Text 5*

a. 夜里她一个人往家走时，确实感到很恐惧。
b. 听到这个消息，他心惊胆颤。
c. 从她那惊慌的样子，我意识到一定发生了什么事。
d. 被警察抓住后，那个小偷吓得面无血色。

Notes to Text 5

a. 感到 in Model 5a is optional, as in '她(感到)很恐惧 (*frightened*) / 很害怕 (*scared*) / 很惊慌 (*panic-stricken*) / 很恐慌 (*terror-stricken*)'.

b. '他心惊胆战' means '*He is trembling with fear*'. We can also optionally use 感到 in this kind of sentence, as in '他(感到)心惊肉跳 (*He is twitching with anxiety*) / 惊恐万状 (*He is in a total panic*) / 大惊失色 (*He turns pale with fright*)'.

c. In '她那惊慌的样子', 惊慌的 is a modifier used with 样子. Other phrases can also be used in this way, as in '恐惧的/害怕的/心惊胆战的/惊恐万状的 + 样子'.

d. 得 used after a verb can introduce a degree complement, as '吓得面无血色', meaning '*so frightened that one turns pale*'. Other examples include '吓得心惊肉跳', '吓得惊恐万状', '吓得大惊失色', '吓得两腿哆嗦' (*so frightened that one's legs start to tremble*), '吓得说不出话来' (*so frightened that one loses one's power of speech*), '吓得出了一身冷汗' (*so frightened that one breaks out in a cold sweat*).

Exercises for 11.5

1 Put an appropriate phrase in each blank in the sentences below. You may need to use 很 and 的 in filling some blanks.

(a) 突然一声枪响，把那两个人吓得_____。

(b) 我当时没有注意到她那_____面孔。

(c) 昨天夜里的那个奇怪的电话使玛丽感到_____，她一夜没睡着觉。

(d) 听到敲门声，马铁民_____，他以为警察来抓他了。

2 Make four sentences using the following words to describe that someone is terrified.

(a) 吓得　(b) 感到　(c) 样子　(d) 觉得

11.6　生气与愤怒 Being angry and indignant

范文 *6, Text 6*

a. 他对这个决定感到非常气愤，你看他坐在那儿气得脸红脖子粗。

b. 总经理发火的时候，大家都不敢说话。

c. 当听说我把他的宝马汽车撞坏了，我爸爸勃然大怒。

d. 看到由于医院的医疗事故自己的儿子成了残废，李大伟气得两眼冒金星。

Notes to Text 6

a. Chinese uses the preposition 对 to introduce the cause of the anger, as in '他对这个决定感到非常气愤' (*He is furious about the decision*). Here the verb 感到 is optional and the adverb 非常 can be replaced with 很. Other words such as 生气 (*angry*), 恼火 (*annoyed*) can also be used in this pattern, as in 'somebody 对 . . . (感到)很 + 生气/恼火'.

b. 气 (*angry*) can be used alone (without 生) when it is followed by 得, which introduces a degree complement, as in '气得脸红脖子粗' (*so angry that one's face becomes red, to get red in the face from anger*) and '气得两眼冒金星' (*so angry that one sees red*). Here 脸红脖子粗 and 两眼冒金星 are clauses used as degree complements. Other examples include '气得脸一阵红一阵白' (*so angry that one's face becomes red for a while and pale for a while*) and '气得肺都炸了' (*so angry that one feels as if one's chest were about to explode*).

c. '勃然大怒' means '*to fly into a rage*'. Other similar phrases include '火冒三丈' (*to flare up*) and '大发雷霆' (*to be furious*). This kind of four-character phrase cannot be used with degree adverbs such as 很 and 非常.

Exercises for 11.6

1 Fill in the blanks below with appropriate phrases of anger and indignation.
  (a) 在这笔生意中，我们公司损失了二十五万元。总经理听了后_____ __，决定开除那两个负责这笔生意的人。
  (b) 当知道他在吸毒时，他的父亲气得_____，他母亲气得_____。
  (c) 王教授对自己的学生不努力学习十分_____，他把他的学生叫来批评了一顿。

2 Imagine that a young man has been caught by the police for stealing other people's cars, and that his parents, his elder sister and his girlfriend have just learned the news. Write a short paragraph describing the angry feelings of his family members and his girlfriend. Try to use some four-character phrases, 对, 非常, 很 and 得 in your description.

11.7 懊悔 Feeling remorse and regret

范文 7, Text 7

a. 小李后悔没有把这件事早点儿告诉他的女朋友。
b. 那个小伙子对自己过去的所作所为感到很懊悔。
c. 她越想越觉得后悔莫及。

Notes to Text 7

a. In Model 7a, 后悔 is used as a verb. The sentence means '*Xiao Li regrets not having told this matter to his girlfriend earlier*'. Other similar verbs, such as 懊悔 (*to feel remorse and regret*) and 悔恨 (*to be bitterly remorseful*), can also be used in this kind of sentence.

b. The preposition 对 is used to introduce what one feels regret for, as in '对自己过去的所作所为感到很懊悔' (*to feel regret for one's own past behaviour*). The verb 感到 can be replaced with 觉得, but both 感到 and 觉得 are optional here.

c. '后悔莫及' means '*too late to repent*'. Other words can also be used in the same way, as in '感到 + 惭愧 (*ashamed*) / 内疚 (*full of compunction; guilty*) / 羞愧 (*ashamed*)'.

Exercises for 11.7

1 Fill in the following blanks with appropriate words of remorse and regret.

    (a) 他对那件事一点儿也不_____。

    (b) 老王这些天一直在_____上个星期没有去医院看看他的母亲。

    (c) 李教授知道小王对那个试验没有成功十分_____，就走过去安慰他，让他不要感到_____。

2 Make a sentence with each the following phrases.

    后悔莫及，后悔，懊悔，惭愧，内疚

3 Interview four people around you and ask them what they feel regret for. Then write a paragraph on the basis of the information you collect from the interviews.

11.8　思念 Missing and longing for

范文 8, *Text 8*

a. 在英国留学的日子里，李祖光十分挂念他的妻子和他五岁的女儿。

b. 她朗诵的这首诗表达了她对家人的思念。

c. 他对当一名流行歌手朝思暮想，渴望有一天他能在热烈的掌声中为他的歌迷们演唱。

d. 你对他的期望不能太高，应该现实一点儿。

Notes to Text 8

a. Adverbs of degree, such as 十分, 非常, 特别 and 很, are often used to modify verbs with the meaning of *missing* and *longing for*, as in '非常 + 思念 (*long for*) / 想念 (*miss*) / 怀念 (*cherish the memory of*) / 惦念 (*keep thinking of; worry about*) / 挂念 (*miss; worry about*) . . .'.

b. Many verbs with the meaning of *missing* and *longing for* can also be used as nouns. In this case, what one misses or longs for is introduced by the preposition 对, as in '她对家人的思念' (*her longing for her family members*). The pattern is 'somebody + 对 + . . . + 的思念/想念/怀念/惦念/挂念'.

c. '对当一名流行歌手朝思暮想' means '*to yearn to be a pop singer day and night*'. Other four-character phrases can also be used in this pattern, as in '对 somebody/something 无比思念' (*to miss somebody/something very much*) and '对 somebody/something 终生难忘' (*will never forget somebody/something as long as one lives*).

d. 渴望 (*to long for; to long to*) can be a verb as well as a noun, and so can 盼望 (*to look forward to*), 期望 (*to hope; to expect*), 期待 (*to look forward to; to expect*). When used as verbs, they usually appear in the pattern 'Somebody + 渴望/盼望/期望/期待 + verb phrase', as in '我 + 渴望/盼望/期望/期待 + 见到她'. When used as nouns, they usually appear in the pattern 'Somebody + 对 + somebody else/something + 的 + 渴望/盼望/期望/期待', as in '他对成功的渴望/盼望/期望/期待'.

Exercises for 11.8

1 In the following sentences, the words 怀念, 挂念, 期待 are used as verbs. Turn them into nouns and make the necessary changes to the sentences.
    (a) 他画的这幅画表明他十分怀念自己家乡。
    (b) 那个老农民期待他儿子娶一个漂亮的媳妇，早点儿给他生个孙子。
    (c) 她从来没有表露她非常挂念她的女儿。

2 In the following sentences, the words 思念, 惦念, 期望 are used as nouns. Turn them into verbs and make the necessary changes to the sentences.
    (a) 我对他的期望是在这次比赛中拿冠军。
    (b) 大家都意识到他对他母亲的思念。
    (c) 这封家信说明了父母对女儿的惦念。

3 Form three four-character phrases with the words below and then make a sentence with each of the three phrases.

思念   朝思   终生   暮想   难忘   无比

Vocabulary

11.1

清晨	qīngchén	early morning
坚持	jiānchí	without fail
风雨无阻	fēng yǔ wú zǔ	rain or shine
酷爱	kù'ài	to love ardently; to be terribly fond of
老舍	Lǎo Shě	[name of a well-known Chinese writer]
简直	jiǎnzhí	simply
爱不释手	ài bú shìshǒu	cannot put down
边远	biānyuǎn	remote
忍痛割爱	rěn tòng gē ài	to part with what one treasures
小巧玲珑	xiǎoqiǎo línglóng	small and exquisite
移动电话	yídòng diànhuà	mobile phone
宠爱	chǒng'ài	to dote on
情意绵绵	qíngyì miánmián	endless affection goes on and on
难舍难分	nán shě nán fēn	to be loath to part from each other
朝思暮想	zhāo sī mù xiǎng	to yearn for . . . day and night
情深似海	qíng shēn sì hǎi	to love . . . as deeply as the ocean
疼爱	téng'ài	to love dearly
爱慕	àimù	to adore; to admire
爱戴	àidài	to love and esteem
报答	bàodá	to repay
绘画	huìhuà	painting; drawing
渊博	yuānbó	broad and profound
周到	zhōudào	thoughtful; considerate

11.2

开心地	kāixīnde	happily
直不起腰来	zhí bù qǐ yāo lai	couldn't hold one's back straight
护照	hùzhào	passport
录取通知书	lùqǔ tōngzhīshū	admission letter
喜出望外	xǐ chū wàng wài	to be overjoyed
乐开了花	lèkāile huā	to be filled with joy
兴高采烈	xìnggāocǎiliè	greatly delighted; in high spirits
丰收	fēngshōu	rich harvest
惊喜万分	jīngxǐ wànfēn	to be pleasantly surprised
心花怒放	xīnhuā nùfàng	to burst with joy; to be wild with joy
欣喜若狂	xīnxǐ ruòkuáng	to be wild with joy
喜笑颜开	xǐxiàoyánkāi	to be wreathed in smiles
国家六合彩抽奖	guójiā liùhécǎi chōujiǎng	national lottery draw

11.3

悲痛	**bēitòng**	grief; painfully sad
逝世	**shìshì**	to pass away
悲伤	**bēishāng**	sad; sorrowful
意识到	**yìshìdào**	to realise
抱头痛哭	**bàotóu tòngkū**	to cry on each other's shoulder
哭泣	**kūqì**	to cry; to weep
珠子	**zhūzi**	pearl
默默地	**mòmòde**	quietly; silently
失声痛哭	**shīshēng tòngkū**	to burst out crying loudly
放声大哭	**fàngshēng dàkū**	to cry loudly
泣不成声	**qì bù chéngshēng**	to choke with sobs
泪如泉涌	**lèi rú quán yǒng**	tears well up like water out of a spring
泪水夺眶而出	**lèishuǐ duókuàng ér chū**	tears well from one's eyes

11.4

忧愁	**yōuchóu**	sad and depressed
沮丧	**jǔsàng**	dejected; depressed
忧心忡忡	**yōuxīn chōngchōng**	to be downhearted
前途	**qiántú**	future; prospect
愁眉苦脸	**chóuméi kǔliǎn**	to have a worried look
忧虑	**yōulǜ**	worried; concerned
忧伤	**yōushāng**	distressed
苦恼	**kǔnǎo**	vexed; worried
苦闷	**kǔmèn**	depressed
愁眉不展	**chóuméi bù zhǎn**	to have a worried frown
烦恼	**fánnǎo**	vexed; worried
烦闷	**fánmèn**	unhappy; worried
唉声叹气	**āishēngtànqì**	to sigh in despair
闷闷不乐	**mènmèn bú lè**	depressed
残废	**cánfèi**	crippled; disabled
失恋	**shīliàn**	to be disappointed in love; to be broken-hearted

11.5

惊恐	**jīngkǒng**	terrified and panic-stricken
恐惧	**kǒngjù**	frightened
心惊胆战	**xīnjīngdǎnzhàn**	to tremble with fear; to shake with fright
惊慌	**jīnghuāng**	panic-stricken
恐慌	**kǒnghuāng**	terror-stricken
心惊肉跳	**xīnjīng ròutiào**	to twitch with anxiety
惊恐万状	**jīngkǒng wànzhuàng**	to be in total panic

大惊失色	**dàjīng shīsè**	to turn pale with fright
哆嗦	**duōsuo**	to tremble
面孔	**miànkǒng**	face

11.6

愤怒	**fènnù**	indignant
气愤	**qìfèn**	furious
脸红脖子粗	**liǎn hóng bózi cū**	one's face becomes red
宝马汽车	**bǎomǎ qìchē**	BMW (car)
勃然大怒	**bórán dànù**	to fly into a rage
医疗事故	**yīliáo shìgù**	medical negligence
两眼冒金星	**liǎng yǎn mào jīnxīng**	to see red; eyes flash
恼火	**nǎohuǒ**	annoyed
肺	**fèi**	chest; lung
炸	**zhà**	to explode
火冒三丈	**huǒ mào sānzhàng**	to flare up
大发雷霆	**dàfā léitíng**	to be furious; to explode with fury
笔	**bǐ**	(a measure word for a business deal)
生意	**shēngyi**	business; deal
开除	**kāichú**	to expel; to fire; to dismiss
吸毒	**xīdú**	to take drugs

11.7

懊悔	**àohuǐ**	to feel remorse and regret
后悔	**hòuhuǐ**	to regret
所作所为	**suǒ zuò suǒ wéi**	behaviour
后悔莫及	**hòuhuǐ mò jí**	too late to repent; to be sorry afterwards
悔恨	**huǐhèn**	(to be) bitterly remorseful
惭愧	**cánkuì**	(to be) ashamed
内疚	**nèijiù**	to feel guilty
羞愧	**xiūkuì**	(to be) ashamed
安慰	**ānwèi**	to comfort

11.8

思念	**sīniàn**	to miss and long for
挂念	**guàniàn**	to miss; to worry about
朗诵	**lǎngsòng**	to recite (poetry); to give a reading
流行歌手	**liúxíng gēshǒu**	pop singer
渴望	**kěwàng**	to long for/to; to yearn for/to
掌声	**zhǎngshēng**	clapping; applause
歌迷	**gēmí**	fan of a singer/singers
期望	**qīwàng**	to hope; to expect
想念	**xiǎngniàn**	to miss

怀念	huáiniàn	to cherish the memory of
惦念	diànniàn	to keep thinking of; to worry about
无比思念	wúbǐ sīniàn	to miss . . . very much
终生难忘	zhōngshēng nánwàng	will never forget as long as one lives
盼望	pànwàng	to look forward to
期待	qīdài	to look forward to; to expect
娶	qǔ	to marry (a woman)
媳妇	xífù	daughter-in-law; wife
表露	biǎolù	to show; to reveal

第十二单元：对人的性格和品德的描写

Unit Twelve: Descriptions of people's disposition and moral attributes

One often needs to describe other people's, or one's own, disposition and moral attributes. Good descriptions of this type can make your writing attractive and help readers form a vivid image in their mind of the person you are describing. In this unit, we deal with attributes such as being lively, humorous, reserved, clever, honest, etc.

12.1 活泼与幽默 Being lively and humorous

范文 *1, Text 1*

---

a. 他在学校里很活跃，能歌善舞，而且还是学校足球队的守门员。
b. 她是个天真活泼的女孩子，她男朋友是个幽默风趣的电视节目主持人。
c. 李教授非常诙谐，讲话时常常妙语连珠。
d. 王克朋见到女孩子就做鬼脸，出洋相，还喜欢耍贫嘴，常常引得女孩子哈哈大笑。

Notes to Text 1

a. 天真活泼 (*vivacious*) is often used to describe young people, especially girls. Other similar phrases include 天真烂漫 (*unaffected*) and 天真无邪 (*simple and unaffected*).

b. 幽默风趣 (*humorous and witty*) can also be put the other way round, as in 风趣幽默.

c. 妙语连珠 (*one witty remark after another*) can be replaced with 妙趣横生 (*full of wit and humour*).

d. 出洋相 (*to make an exhibition of oneself*) and 耍贫嘴 (*to be garrulous*) usually have negative connotations, but 做鬼脸 (*to pull a face*) has a neutral connotation.

Exercises for 12.1

1 Rewrite the following sentences and describe the following people with the opposite characters.

    (a) 刘明礼在我们班里不爱说不爱笑，性格很死板。

    (b) 大家都认为他的演讲十分乏味，缺少幽默感。

    (c) 他上中学的时候，既不参加文艺活动也不参加体育活动，别人都说他很孤僻。

2 Write a short paragraph using the following phrases to describe three people you know.

    天真活泼，活跃，能歌善舞，诙谐，风趣幽默，妙趣横生，妙语连珠

12.2　热情与乐观 Being warm and optimistic

范文 *2, Text 2*

a. 我们的邻居老王夫妇是四川人。他们两人都非常热情好客。
b. 那几个英国学生发现中国人非常友好，而且有些中国人也很慷慨。
c. 她妈妈性格很开朗，对一切事情都很乐观。
d. 他很自信，对这次考试充满了信心。

Notes to Text 2

a. 慷慨 and 大方 are synonyms, meaning generous, but the former is more formal than the latter. One can also put them together to form a four-character expression.

b. What one is optimistic about has to be introduced by the preposition 对, as in '对一切事情都很乐观' (*be optimistic about everything*).

c. Similarly, 对 has to be used in '对这次考试充满了信心' (*be very confident about this examination*).

128

Exercises for 12.2

1   Pair each of the following phrases with its opposite.

无忧无虑，缺乏信心，冷淡，慷慨，自馁，悲观，热情，大方，狭窄，
自信，吝啬，乐观，多愁善感，充满信心，开朗，小气

2   Fill in each of the following blanks with an appropriate phrase chosen from
the above.
- (a)   在他自馁的时候，张教授及时地帮助他树立了_____。
- (b)   爷爷对自己很_____，但对有困难的人却很慷慨。
- (c)   对这个公司的前途，有的人很乐观，可有的人十分_____。
- (d)   他以前心胸狭窄，如今_____多了。
- (e)   她对她的上司好像总是很热情，而对她的同事却总是那么_____。
- (f)   有些学生过生日，为了不让别人说自己_____，就花很多钱请客。
         这不是大方，而是浪费。
- (g)   年轻的时候，他整天无忧无虑，现在他老了，变得越来越_____。

3   Write a short paragraph to describe three people you know using the words
and phrases in Exercise 1 above.

12.3   拘谨与谦虚 Being reserved and modest

范文 3, Text 3

a. 她性格内向，见了人总是很拘谨，很腼腆。
b. 当我把钱递到她手里时，她尴尬地笑了。
c. 他是一个谨小慎微，胆小怕事的人。
d. 因为李教授总是谦虚谨慎，平易近人，所以大家都很尊重他。
e. 他那彬彬有礼的样子使人觉得他受过良好的教育。

Notes to Text 3

a.   尴尬 (*embarrassed, awkward*) can be used as an adverb as in '他尴尬地笑了'.
Other adjectives such as 不好意思 (*embarrassed*), 拘束 (*cautious; reserved*)
and 腼腆 (*shy*) can also be used in the same way, as in '他不好意思/拘谨/
腼腆地笑了'.

b.   彬彬有礼 (*refined and courteous*) can be used as a modifier with a noun, as in
'彬彬有礼的样子'. Other phrases such as 谨小慎微 (*overcautious*) and 胆小
怕事 (*timid*) can also be used in the same way, as in '谨小慎微/胆小怕事的
样子'.

Exercises for 12.3

1 Form five four-character phrases with the words below:

彬彬　谦虚　近人　谨小　怕事　平易　慎微　谨慎　胆小　有礼

2 Draw a line between a word in Column A and its opposite in Column B.

A	B
内向	大方
腼腆	骄傲
虚心	外向
拘谨	放肆
谦虚	自满

3 Fill in each blank below with an appropriate word chosen from the words in Exercise 2 above.

(a) 他原来见到生人显得很_____，现在他变得大方多了。

(b) 我和我哥哥的性格完全相反，我很_____，而我哥哥却非常外向。

(c) 有的人很有学问，但很_____；有的人没什么学问，但很骄傲。

(d) 丁贵生在学校很_____，可在家里非常放肆。

(e) 李大伟每次考试都得第一，但他并不自满，仍然那么_____。

4 Write a paragraph to describe three people you know using the words and phrases in Exercises 1 and 2 above.

12.4　聪明与诚实 Being clever and honest

范文 4, Text 4

> a. 这个学生不但聪明机灵而且诚实可靠，将来一定会很成功。
>
> b. 我们公司的人个个精明强干，而且能文能武的人也不少。
>
> c. 李教授是个忠厚老实的人，他从来都是言行一致，表里如一。
>
> d. 那个人装出心地善良的样子，其实他是想骗那位老太太的钱。

Notes to Text 4

a. Phrases such as 聪明机灵 (*bright and smart*), 诚实可靠 (*honest and reliable*), 精明强干 (*intelligent and capable*), 能文能武 (*to be cultured in both polite and brave; to be able to wield both the pen and the gun*), etc., can be used both as a predicate, as in '他言行一致，表里如一' (*He is as good as his word, and* *consistent in thought and deed*), and as a modifier, as in '忠厚老实的人' (*a kind and honest person*).

b. 心地善良 (*kindhearted*) can be used as a modifier as in '心地善良的样子' (*to look kindhearted*).

Exercises for 12.4

1 Form six four-character phrases with the words below:

如一	言行	勇敢	表里	实实	光明
精明	一致	正大	机智	强干	老老

2 Pair the following words with their opposite meanings:

狡猾	聪明	迟钝	诚实	凶恶	机灵
敏锐	虚伪	愚蠢	善良	老实	愚笨

3 Fill in each of the following blanks with an appropriate word chosen from the words in Exercise 2.
 (a) 为了赚钱，那个狡猾的商人常常欺骗_____的顾客。
 (b) 许多_____的人很难识别出凶恶的敌人。
 (c) 没想到_____的小李竟干了这么一件愚蠢的事。
 (d) 要做一个_____的人，不要做一个虚伪的人。
 (e) 刘教授观察问题十分_____，相比之下，我就迟钝多了。
 (f) 有的人看上去很愚笨，而实际上却非常_____。

4 Write a paragraph to describe three people you know using the words and phrases in Exercises 1 and 2 above.

Vocabulary

12.1

活泼	**huópo**	lively
幽默	**yōumò**	humorous
能歌善舞	**néng gē shàn wǔ**	good at both singing and dancing
守门员	**shǒuményuán**	goalkeeper
天真活泼	**tiānzhēn huópo**	vivacious
风趣	**fēngqù**	witty
主持人	**zhǔchírén**	presenter
诙谐	**huīxié**	humorous; jocular
妙语连珠	**miàoyǔ liánzhū**	one witty remark after another
做鬼脸	**zuò guǐliǎn**	to pull a face

出洋相	chū yángxiàng	to make an exhibition of oneself
耍贫嘴	shuǎ pínzuǐ	to be garrulous
天真烂漫	tiānzhēn lànmàn	unaffected
天真无邪	tiānzhēn wúxié	artless
妙趣横生	miàoqù héngshēng	full of wit and humour
性格	xìnggé	nature; disposition; temperament
死板	sǐbǎn	inflexible; rigid
乏味	fá wèi	dull; uninteresting
缺少	quēshǎo	to lack; to be short of
孤僻	gūpì	unsociable and eccentric

12.2

乐观	lèguān	optimistic
好客	hàokè	hospitable
慷慨	kāngkǎi	generous
开朗	kāilǎng	cheerful
大方	dàfang	generous
无忧无虑	wú yōu wú lǜ	carefree
缺乏	quēfá	to lack; to be short of
冷淡	lěngdàn	cold; indifferent
自馁	zìněi	to lose confidence; to be discouraged
悲观	bēiguān	pessimistic
心胸狭窄	xīnxiōng xiázhǎi	narrow-minded
吝啬	lìnsè	stingy; mean; miserly
多愁善感	duō chóu shàn gǎn	gloomy
小气	xiǎoqi	stingy; mean; miserly
树立	shùlì	to establish; to set up
上司	shàngsi	boss; superior
浪费	làngfèi	waste

12.3

拘谨	jūjǐn	cautious; reserved
谦虚	qiānxū	modest
内向	nèixiàng	introverted
腼腆	miǎntiǎn	shy; bashful
尴尬	gāngà	embarrassed; awkward
谨小慎微	jǐnxiǎo shènwēi	overcautious
胆小怕事	dǎnxiǎo pàshì	timid
谦虚谨慎	qiānxū jǐnshèn	modest and prudent
平易近人	píngyìjìnrén	amiable and approachable
尊重	zūnzhòng	to respect
彬彬有礼	bīnbīn yǒulǐ	refined and courteous
外向	wàixiàng	extroverted
放肆	fàngsì	unrestrained; reckless
自满	zìmǎn	complacent; self-satisfied
学问	xuéwèn	knowledge; learning; scholarship

12.4

诚实	chéngshí	honest
机灵	jīling	clever; smart
可靠	kěkào	reliable
精明强干	jīngmíng qiánggàn	intelligent and capable
能文能武	néng wén néng wǔ	to be both cultured and brave; to be able to wield both the pen and the gun
忠厚老实	zhōnghòu lǎoshi	kind and honest
言行一致	yánxíng yízhì	to be as good as one's word
表里如一	biǎo lǐ rúyī	to be consistent in thought and deed
心地善良	xīndì shànliáng	kindhearted
老老实实	lǎolǎo shíshí	honestly; conscientiously; in earnest
光明正大	guāngmíng zhèngdà	open and above board; just and honourable
机智勇敢	jīzhì yǒnggǎn	clever and resourceful
狡猾	jiǎohuá	cunning; sly; crafty
愚笨	yúbèn	foolish; stupid; clumsy
赚钱	zhuàn qián	to make money
欺骗	qīpiàn	to deceive; to cheat
识别	shíbié	to distinguish; to detect; to recognise

第十三单元: 对人动作的描写
Unit Thirteen: Descriptions of people's movements and actions

There is a commonly occurring need to describe people's movements and actions. Such descriptions may be needed in writing narratives, reports, instructions or even letters. Since it is difficult to include descriptions of all detailed body movements, we focus in this unit on the descriptions of walking, running, seeing, speaking and listening.

13.1 走 Walking

范文 1, Text 1

> a. 许多老人喜欢在傍晚的时候到海边去散步。
> b. 李明在总经理办公室的门口徘徊了很长一段时间,最后迈着沉重的步伐走了进去。
> c. 他的腿可能受伤了,你看他走起路来摇摇晃晃的。
> d. 当他在热烈的掌声中走上讲台时,他的脚步显得非常从容。

Notes to Text 1

a. 散步 can be replaced with 溜达 (*stroll*) or 闲逛 (*stroll*), but 散步 is more formal.

b. Here 徘徊 (*to pace up and down*) can be replaced with 走过来走过去 or simply 走来走去, although the former is rather formal and the latter two are quite colloquial.

c. In the pattern '迈着 . . . 的步伐' (*walk with . . . strides/steps*), the word 步伐 can be modified by various adjectives, as in '迈着 + 沉重' (*heavy*) / 矫健 (*vigorous*) / 坚定 (*resolute*) / 犹豫 (*hesitant*) + 的步伐'.

d. In '他走起路来摇摇晃晃的', the phrase 摇摇晃晃 (*with tottering steps*) can be structurally replaced with 东倒西歪 (*staggering along*), 一瘸一拐 (*limping along*), 步履蹒跚 (*stumbling along*).

e. In '他的脚步显得非常从容', the word 从容 (*calm*) can be structurally replaced with other adjectives, as in '他的脚步显得很 + 沉重/坚定/犹豫'.

Exercises for 13.1

1 Write sentences using the pattern 迈着 . . . 的步伐, in describing the manner in which the following people walked, in the contexts below.

   (a) Lao Li walked out of the general manager's office after being told that he had been made redundant.

   (b) When he walked onto the tennis court, he seemed to be full of energy. It was clear that he would win the match.

   (c) When she walked to her boyfriend's flat, she was not sure whether he would like to see her any more.

   (d) They were very confident they would win the case when they walked into the court.

2 Try to complete the following sentences and describe how these people walked on the basis of the information given.

   (a) 那个人＿＿＿＿＿＿＿＿＿＿，显然他喝醉了。

   (b) 我爷爷上个星期在医院做了一个手术。虽然现在他＿＿＿＿＿＿＿＿＿，但是他不让别人扶他。

   (c) 昨天李明踢足球的时候，把脚伤了，所以今天他＿＿＿＿＿＿＿＿＿。

3 Try to complete the following sentences and describe how these people walked by using the pattern '. . . 的脚步显得 . . .'.

   (a) 在去李教授葬礼的路上，大家＿＿＿＿＿＿＿＿＿。

   (b) 虽然她后来承认她心里确实很紧张，但当她走到女王跟前时，她＿＿＿＿＿＿＿＿＿。

13.2 跑 Running

范文 *2, Text 2*

a. 一听到枪响，那几个罪犯撒腿就跑。

b. 医院来电话告诉王老师她儿子出了车祸。王老师一接到电话，扭头就往医院跑。到医院时，她已经跑得上气不接下气了。

c. 我非常喜欢非洲的长跑运动员，他们跑起来像一只只小鹿。

Notes to Text 2

a. In Model 2a, the character '一' corresponds to the character '就' to mean '*as soon as*'. The phrase 撒腿就跑 means '*to run off at once*'. If necessary, the direction can be indicated in this kind of four-character phrase by inserting the phrase '往/向 . . .' between '就' and '跑', as in '扭头就往医院跑' (*to turn round immediately and start running towards the hospital*) in Model 2b and '拔腿就往家跑' (*to start running home at once*).

b. The word 得 used immediately after 跑 can introduce a complement of degree, as in '跑得上气不接下气' (*to run so much that one becomes out of breath*). Another example is '跑得气喘吁吁' (*to run so much that one pants hard*).

c. In describing someone's running speed, it is quite common in Chinese to compare a person with an animal, as in '他们跑起来像一只只鹿' (*They run like deer*). Other examples include '他们跑起来像插上了翅膀' (*They run as if they had wings*), '她跑得比兔子还快' (*She runs even faster than a rabbit*), '他跑起来像只乌龟' (*He runs like a tortoise*).

Exercises for 13.2

1 Try to form five set phrases with the words below:

就跑	上气	气喘	像插上了	拔腿	下气
吁吁	扭头	翅膀	不接	就跑	

2 Try to complete the following sentences on the basis of the information given.

(a) 他下了公共汽车，一看手表，再过一分钟他女朋友乘坐的火车就要到站了，他_____。

(b) 我同屋是全国大学生运动会的百米冠军，他跑起来_____。

(c) 小偷在前面跑，警察在后面追，警察和小偷都已经跑_____。

(d) 这个城市的交通问题很严重。上下班时间，马路上的汽车跑起来_____ _____，比走路还慢。

13.3 看 Seeing

范文 3, Text 3

a. 他在我旁边坐下以后就一直盯着我手上戴的结婚戒指，这使我感到非常不舒服。

b. 那个人一进门我就觉得他面熟。我不住地打量他，可就是想不起以前在哪儿见过。

c. 他凝视着墙上挂着的那张母亲的遗像，眼前浮现出母亲生前的笑容。

d. 对于是否购买私人住房，大多数人都还在观望，他们不知道政府的购房政策是否会变。

e. 他们到达那儿以后，仔细观察了那里的地形和环境。

Notes to Text 3

a. The verb 盯 (*to gaze at*) here can be replaced with 看 (*to look; to see*) but not with 瞧 (*to look; to see*). 盯 has the meaning of fixing one's eyes on something, but 瞧 does not. It is possible to say 看一看 and 瞧一瞧, but it is incorrect to say 盯一盯. 看 can be used in both written and spoken Chinese, but 瞧 is usually used in spoken Chinese.

b. The verb 打量 (*to look (someone) up and down; to size up*) here can be replaced by the verb 端详 (*to look (someone) up and down; to scrutinize*). The former focuses on someone's outward appearance and the latter indicates more detailed observation. 打量 can be used for observing human beings as well as objects, but 端详 is usually used for observing human beings.

c. The verb 凝视 (*to stare at*) can sometimes be used interchangeably with the verb 注视 (*to look attentively at*). The former indicates the lengthy focus of one's vision on somebody or something, the latter puts more emphasis on one's attention to somebody or something. 注视 is used more widely than 凝视. For example, 注视, but not 凝视, can be used for observing something abstract, as in '注视形势的发展' (*to look closely at the development of the situation*).

d. The verb 观望 (*to look on from the sidelines; to wait and see*) is often confused with verbs such as 旁观 (*to view as an onlooker*), 观看 (*to watch*), 看望 (*to call on; to visit*), 探望 (*to visit*). 观望 implies hesitant and undecided feelings; 旁观 emphasises the non-involvement of the onlooker, and 观看 means to see something on purpose. 看望 and 探望 are usually used for the situations of visiting patients, elderly people, relatives, friends, etc.

e. The verb 观察 (*to observe; to watch*) should not be confused with the verb 视察 (*to inspect*). The former means to observe something carefully. The person who performs the action of 观察 can be someone junior or someone senior, but the person performing the action of 视察 must be someone senior.

Exercises for 13.3

1 Fill in the following brackets with appropriate characters.

(c) ( )
( ) ⟩ 望
( )

(d) ( )
( ) ⟩ 察

2 Fill in the blanks below with the following words:

看望　　瞧　　视察　　注视　　打量　　观看

(a) 在我们校长的陪同下，教育部长_____了我们学校新建的科研基地。
(b) 我去那个公司面试的那一天，一进门，公司总经理先上下_____了我一番，然后开始用中文问我问题。
(c) 虽然王教授已经退休多年，但是他以前的学生还经常来_____他。
(d) 访问北京的最后那天晚上，代表团去首都剧院_____了精彩的杂技表演。
(e) 通过闭路电视，警察一直在_____着那个人在广场上的活动情况。
(f) 我姐姐指着李大伟对我说：'你_____那个小伙子，长得多帅啊！'。

13.4　听 Listening

范文 4, Text 4

a. 教育部决定召开全国大学校长会议，倾听各大学对教育部工作的意见。
b. 那次秘密会议的第二天他们才发现有人窃听了会议的情况。
c. 因为他不听从教练的指挥，所以他被那个足球俱乐部开除了。
d. 昨天晚上李老师给大家讲了他去西藏旅行的经历，大家听得着了迷，让他今天晚上继续讲。

Notes to Text 4

a. 倾听 (*to listen attentively to*) is usually used in situations where senior or elderly people listen to junior or young people. In situations where junior or young people listen to senior or elderly people, the verb 聆听 is usually used. 倾听 and 聆听 often take words such as 'somebody's 意见/建议/看法, etc.' as their object. It is wrong to say '倾听/聆听 somebody'.

b. The verb 窃听 (*eavesdrop; bug*) refers to the action of listening by means of some listening device. The first character 窃 (*stealthily*) indicates the nature of the listening. There are other words which have the same pattern of word formation, such as 偷听 (*to listen secretly to*), 旁听 (*to listen as a visitor or as a participant at a meeting or in a school class*), and 探听 (*to fish for information; to try to find out*).

c. The verb 听从 (*to listen and obey; to listen and comply with*) should not be confused with the verb 听候 (*to wait for*). The former gives emphasis to the obedience, while the latter indicates the actions of waiting for something and then complying with it. The objects these verbs take are usually 'someone's 指示/决定/建议/安排 . . .'.

d. In '听得着了迷' (*to listen and become spellbound*), 得 introduces a complement of degree 着了迷. Similar phrases include '听得津津有味' (*to listen with great interest*), '听得睡着了' (*to have fallen asleep while listening*).

Exercises for 13.4

1 Fill in the blanks below with the following phrases:

   倾听   聆听   偷听   旁听   听候   听从

   (a) 饭店的服务员很有礼貌地站在那儿，随时_____顾客的吩咐。
   (b) _____别人的私下谈话是不道德的行为。
   (c) 很多政府官员官僚作风严重，从来不愿意_____群众的意见。
   (d) 在军队里，士兵必须_____上级的命令。
   (e) 新的法律允许十八岁以上的成年人去法庭_____。
   (f) 学生们_____了那位著名哲学家的演讲后，都感到收获很大。

2 Write two short paragraphs on the basis of the two pictures below. Use 听得津津有味, 听得睡着了 and 听得打呵欠了 to describe the audience's reactions.

Picture A:

Picture B:

13.5 说 Speaking

范文 5, *Text 5*

a. 他们谈话谈了一个多小时，连饭都忘了吃。
b. 王老师正在教室里给学生们讲解一个数学定理。
c. 最近很多市民都在谈论失业工人的问题。
d. 他好象对国际关系问题很感兴趣，经常跟别人辩论美中关系问题，英中关系问题，英美关系问题等等。

Notes to Text 5

a. When there is an adverbial phrase indicating the length of time or a 得 introducing a complement after 谈话, the verb 谈 has to be reduplicated as in '谈话谈了一个多小时' (*chatted for over an hour*) and '谈话谈得很高兴' (*chatted happily*). Other verbs such as 说话 and 讲话 also follow the same pattern. However, 谈话, 说话 and 讲话 are not the same semantically. Although 谈话 and 说话 are sometimes interchangeable as in '他在跟她谈话/说话' (*He is talking with her*), 谈话 generally means an exchange of words while 说话 most often refers to one-way expression like the English word *speak*. 谈话 can be used formally as in a one-to-one discussion between a boss and an employee or between a teacher and a student. 讲话 can sometimes be used interchangeably with 说话 as in '我气得一个星期没有跟他讲话/说话' (*I was so angry that I didn't speak to him for a week*), but for a meeting or other formal situations, 讲话, rather than 说话, has to be used as in 我在会上讲了话 (*I made a speech at the meeting*). 谈话 and 讲话, but not 说话, can also be used as nouns as in 他的谈话/讲话很幽默 (*His talk/speech is very humorous*).

b. 讲解 (*to explain*) is sometimes used interchangeably with 讲授 (*to lecture*), but the former focuses on the explanation and the latter on imparting the knowledge. The object of 讲解 is usually rather specific such as 一道化学题 (*a chemistry question*), 这个汉字的用法 (*the usage of the character*), etc., but the object of 讲授 can be one of a number of nouns referring to some general knowledge such as 中国历史, 法语语法, etc. Note that 讲解 and 讲授 should not be confused with 讲演, which means '*to make a speech*'.

c. Here 谈论 (*to talk about*) can be replaced with 议论 (*to comment on; to talk about*). The former merely refers to the action of talking about something or somebody, but the latter often alludes to the action of commenting on the rights and wrongs of something or somebody. In formal situations, it is possible to use 讨论 (*to discuss*), which refers to the action of exchanging ideas or talking over something.

d. 辩论 and 争论 both imply debate and argument, but 辩论 suggests debate as an analytical exercise while 争论 suggests a contentious argument. It is important that a distinction be made between 辩论 and 争论 on the one hand and 争吵 on the other. 辩论 and 争论 have neutral connotations but 争吵 means '*to quarrel*' or '*to squabble*' and has a negative connotation. 辩论, 争论 and 争吵 can all be used as nouns.

Exercises for 13.5

1   Fill in the blanks below with appropriate characters.

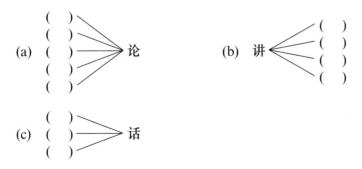

2   Fill in the blanks below with appropriate words. For some blanks, more than one word is possible. Not every word below needs to be used.

议论，讲演，谈话，辩论，说话，讲话，争论，讲授，谈论，争吵，讨论，讲解

(a)   这几天公司的人都在悄悄地_____李大伟用公款出国旅游的事，公司也准备开会_____这个问题。

(b)   去年他来我们系给我们_____了机器翻译的技术和知识。

(c)   为了一个玩具汽车，哥哥和弟弟两个人昨天_____了一个晚上。后来妈妈把他们两人都批评了一顿。

(d)   大家都觉得今天上午马先生在会上的_____特别感动人。

(e)   下班之前我接到电话说总经理要跟我_____，我立刻就觉得紧张起来了。

(f)   就这个问题，他们两个人_____了近三个小时，可是最后谁也没有说服谁。

Vocabulary

13.1

徘徊	**páihuái**	to pace up and down
步伐	**bùfá**	stride; step
摇摇晃晃	**yáoyáohuànghuàng**	with tottering steps
从容	**cóngróng**	calm
溜达	**liūda**	to stroll
闲逛	**xiánguàng**	to stroll
矫健	**jiǎojiàn**	vigorous
犹豫	**yóuyù**	hesitant
东倒西歪	**dōng dǎo xī wāi**	staggering along
一瘸一拐	**yìqué yìguǎi**	limping along
步履蹒跚	**bùlǚ pánshān**	stumbling along; walking haltingly
葬礼	**zànglǐ**	funeral

13.2

撒腿就跑	**sātuǐ jiù pǎo**	to run off at once; to flee
扭头	**niǔtóu**	to turn around
上气不接下气	**shàngqì bù jiē xiàqì**	to become out of breath
气喘吁吁	**qìchuǎn xūxū**	to pant hard
翅膀	**chìbǎng**	wing
兔子	**tùzi**	rabbit

| 乌龟 | wūguī | tortoise |
| 冠军 | guànjūn | champion |

13.3

盯	dīng	to gaze at
戒指	jièzhi	ring
打量	dǎliàng	to look someone up and down; to size up
凝视	níngshì	to stare at
遗像	yíxiàng	a portrait of a deceased person
浮现	fúxiàn	to appear before one's eyes; to materialise
观望	guānwàng	to look on from the sidelines; to wait and see
观察	guānchá	to observe; to watch
地形	dìxíng	topography; terrain
端详	duānxiáng	to look someone up and down; to scrutinize
注视	zhùshì	to look attentively at
旁观	pángguān	to view as an onlooker
探望	tànwàng	to visit
视察	shìchá	to inspect
科研基地	kēyán jīdì	scientific research centre
面试	miànshì	interview
一番	yìfān	(a verbal measure word)
精彩	jīngcǎi	brilliant; wonderful; splendid
杂技	zájì	acrobatics
闭路电视	bìlù diànshì	close-circuit television
帅	shuài	handsome

13.4

教育部	jiàoyùbù	Ministry of Education
倾听	qīngtīng	to listen attentively to
秘密	mìmì	secret
窃听	qiètīng	to eavesdrop; to bug
听从	tīngcóng	to listen and obey; to listen and comply with
教练	jiàoliàn	coach; trainer
指挥	zhǐhuī	order; direction
开除	kāichú	to expel; to fire
西藏	Xīzàng	Tibet
着了迷	zháolemí	to become spellbound
聆听	língtīng	to listen attentively to
偷听	tōutīng	to listen secretly to
旁听	pángtīng	to listen as a visitor (at a meeting or in a school class)
探听	tàntīng	to fish for information; to try to find out
听候	tīnghòu	to wait for
津津有味	jīnjīnyǒuwèi	with great interest

143

随时	suíshí	at any time; at all times
吩咐	fēnfu	to tell; to instruct
不道德	bú dàodé	immoral
官僚作风	guānliáo zuòfēng	bureaucratic way of working
上级	shàngjí	higher authorities
允许	yǔnxǔ	to allow; to permit
成年人	chéngniánrén	adult
法庭	fǎtíng	court
哲学家	zhéxuéjiā	philosopher
收获	shōuhuò	gain; benefit
打呵欠	dǎ hāqian	to yawn

13.5

讲解	jiǎngjiě	to explain
辩论	biànlùn	to debate; to argue
讲授	jiǎngshòu	to lecture
讲演	jiǎngyǎn	to make a speech
争论	zhēnglùn	to argue; to dispute
争吵	zhēngchǎo	to quarrel; to squabble
悄悄地	qiāoqiāode	quietly
公款	gōngkuǎn	public funds
玩具	wánjù	toy
说服	shuōfú	to convince

第十四单元： 对地点和天气的描写
Unit Fourteen: Descriptions of places and the weather

14.1 东西南北 East, west, south and north

范文 *1, Text 1*

---

a. 剑桥和牛津都在英国的南部，离伦敦不远，剑桥在伦敦的北边，而牛津在伦敦的西北边。

b. 青岛地处华东地区，是一个美丽的海滨城市。它位于上海的北边，北京的东南边。

c. 这个城市在市区以北五十公里的地方建了一个新机场，距离老机场二十六公里。

Notes to Text 1

a. It is important to make a distinction between 在...南部 and 在...南边. The former means '*in the south/southern part of...*', and the latter '*to the south of...*'. These rules also apply to 东部/西部/北部/中部 and 东边/西边/北边/东南边/西南边/东北边/西北边.

b. 华东 stands for East China. West China, South China and North China are 华西, 华南, 华北 respectively.

c. Both 地处 (*to be located in; to be situated in*) and 位于 (*to be located in; to be situated in*) can be used in the description of something being in a certain area or a certain location, as in '地处/位于华东地区' (*to be located in East China*). However, when talking about something being in a particular direction in relation to somewhere else, only 位于, and not 地处, can be used, as

---

in '位于上海的北边' (*to be situated to the north of Shanghai*). 地处 and 位于 are usually used in formal writings. In informal writings, they can simply be replaced with 在.

d. In '在市区以北五十公里的地方', the phrase 市区以北五十公里的 (*fifty kilometres to the north of the city*) is a modifier modifying 地方. Here the character 以 can be treated as the equivalent of the English preposition *to*. Note here that in English, the distance, e.g. *fifty kilometres*, appears before the directional phrase, e.g. *fifty kilometres to the north of . . .*, but in Chinese the order is just the opposite; 五十公里 appears after · · · 以北.

e. In '距离老机场二十六公里' (*twenty-six kilometres from the old airport*), 距离 can be replaced with 离 in informal situations.

Exercises for 14.1

1 Use the following and other necessary expressions to complete the descriptive sentences below about the map of 鱼山中学的校园. (Please see next page for the map)

在 · · · 边， 在 · · · 部， 地处， 位于， 距离

(a) 鱼山中学_____这个城市的南部，_____市中心5公里。
(b) 这所中学有一个现代化的体育场，_____校园的_____。
(c) 体育场的_____是网球场。
(d) 学生宿舍_____校园的_____。
(e) 为了方便师生们的生活，学校开办了一个小卖部。小卖部_____网球场的_____，_____学生宿舍的_____。

2 Now follow the sentences in Exercise 1 and try to describe the locations of the other facilities in the map of 鱼山中学的校园.

3 Write a similar description of the campus where you are studying. Start your description by indicating the location of the campus in the city and its distance to the closest supermarket.

14.2 位置 Location

范文 *2, Text 2*

a. 在马路的拐角站着一个人，他好像是迷了路。
b. 有两个老人坐在桌子旁边，一边喝茶一边聊天。
c. 在中山广场的左边矗立着一座大厦，有六十八层，看上去非常宏伟壮丽。
d. 我们公司的办公大楼坐落在繁华的商业区，离火车站步行大约半个小时。
e. 百货商店的对面是一家新开的超级市场。

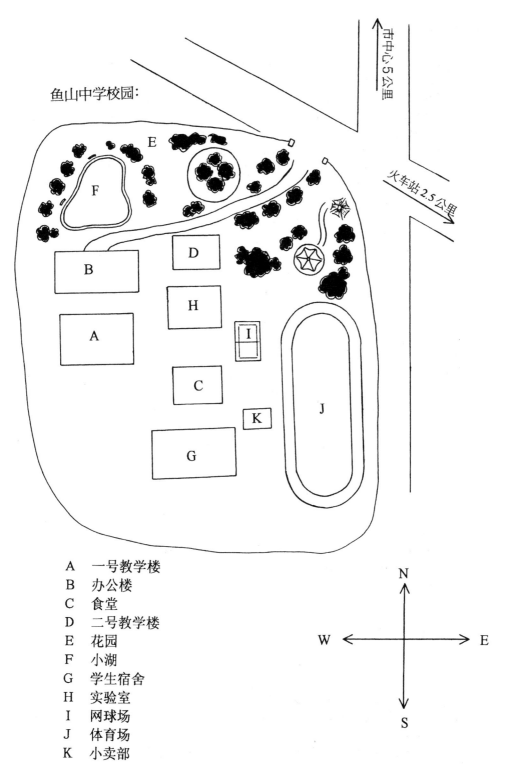

鱼山中学校园：

A 一号教学楼
B 办公楼
C 食堂
D 二号教学楼
E 花园
F 小湖
G 学生宿舍
H 实验室
I 网球场
J 体育场
K 小卖部

Notes to Text 2

a. In a description indicating that there is something or somebody in a certain place, it is important to make a distinction between the known information and the new information. In general, the location in the phrase 在 · · · should be information known to the people involved in the communication, as in '在马路的拐角' (*at the street corner*), '在桌子旁边' (*by the table*), '在中山广场的左边' (*on the left of Zhongshan Square*). The new information is usually given after the verb, as in '站着一个人' (*stands a person*) '矗立着一座大厦' (*stands a large building*). The new information can also appear before the verb. However, in that case it has to be introduced by 有, followed by the verb without 着 and then by the phrase of location, as in '有两个老人坐在桌子旁边' (*There are two old people sitting by the table*). It is possible to change the sentences in Model 2a and 2c into this pattern, as in '有一个人站在马路的拐角' (*There is a person standing on the street corner*), '有一座大厦矗立在中山广场的左边' (*There is a large building standing to the left of Zhongshan Square*).

b. 矗立 (*to stand tall and upright*) can be replaced with 耸立 (*to tower aloft*), both of which are used for high buildings and mountains. They cannot be used for people.

c. The verb 坐落 (*to be located, to be situated*) is only used for buildings, and it is usually used in formal situations. It can be omitted, as in '我们公司的办公大楼在繁华的商业区' (*Our company's office building is in the busy commercial district*).

d. In describing the distance between two places, one can use the structure 'Place A + 离 + Place B + · · · 米/公里/英里' or the structure 'Place A + 离 + Place B + manner of movement + time needed' as in ' · · · 离火车站步行大约半个小时' (. . . *is about half an hour's walk from the train station*). Other examples include '开车二十分钟' (*20 minutes' drive*) and '骑自行车一刻钟' (*15 minutes' by bike*).

e. When the verb 是 is used, the phrase of location does not have to be introduced by the preposition 在, as in '百货商店的对面是 . . .' (*opposite the department store is . . .*) in Model 2e.

Exercises for 14.2

1 Convert the following sentences introduced by 有 into sentences with the new information appearing after the verb + 着.

(a) 有一群孩子坐在小河边，又说又笑。

(b) 有两座高楼耸立在火车站的西侧，一座是邮电大楼，一座是和平宾馆。

(c) 走进他的房间，你会看到有很多中国山水画挂在四周的墙上。

2 Convert the following sentences with the verb + 着 into sentences introduced by 有.

(a) 在八关山的山腰矗立着一座电视塔，电视台就在八关山的山脚下。

(b) 在她的桌子上放着很多书，有中文的，也有英文的。

(c) 我记得当时在他家门口停着两辆崭新的德国奔驰汽车。

3 Complete the description of the town section shown below using appropriate expressions such as 左边, 右边, 对面, 中间.

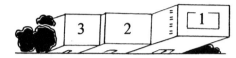

1　百货大楼
2　电影院
3　广东餐馆
4　超级市场
5　药店
6　书店

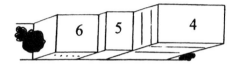

　　在这条街上有百货大楼，电影院，药店，超级市场，广东餐馆，书店。从百货大楼出来，你的＿＿＿＿就是超级市场。药店在超级市场的＿＿＿＿。药店的＿＿＿＿是一家书店。站在书店门口，你可以看到＿＿＿＿是一家广东餐馆，广东餐馆和百货大楼＿＿＿＿是电影院。

4 Use the verb 位于, 坐落, 矗立 or 耸立 to describe the locations of your university, your university library, the highest building in your locality and their distances to the coach station.

5 Write a short essay describing the locations of some main buildings and institutions in your home town and their distances from each other.

14.3　建筑物 Buildings

范文 3, Text 3

a. 以前这个区是一片破旧的平房，可是最近几年这儿建起了很多楼房，在靠海边的地方，还盖了不少别墅。

b. 她住在一幢日本式的二层楼里。那是一座红砖房，典雅美观，造型非常别致。

c. 那是一座有六百多年历史的古代建筑。以前它显得有些破旧简陋，可是最近这座古代建筑装饰一新，看上去非常宏伟壮丽。

d. 由香港商人投资兴建的这座八十六层大楼，富丽堂皇，巍然屹立在五四广场的东边。

Notes to Text 3

a.   Buildings can be classified as:

平房   *one-storey house; bungalow*
别墅   *villa*
瓦房   *tile-roofed house*
红砖房   *red-brick house*
楼房   *building with two or more storeys*
公寓大楼   *apartment building*
大楼   *multi-storey building*
大厦   *tall building*

Nowadays 大厦 is often used as a name of a tall building, as in 国际大厦 (*International Building*).

b.   幢 and 座 are measure words usually used for buildings, as in 一幢二层楼 (*a two-storey building*) and 一座红砖房 (*a red-brick house*).

c.   日本式的 means '*garden with a Japanese style*'. Other examples include '中国式的花园' (*a Chinese style garden*), and '英国式的建筑' (*an English style building*).

d.   有 . . . 历史 can be used as a modifier as in '那是一座有六百多年历史的古代建筑' (*That is an ancient building with a history of over 600 years*). It can also be used as a predicate as in '这座现代建筑只有五十多年的历史' (*This modern building has a history of only 50 years*). In the former, 的 is usually required after 历史, and in the latter before 历史.

e.   There are many words and phrases which can be used to describe buildings. Here are just some of them:

宏伟   *magnificent; grand*   高大   *tall*
壮丽   *magnificent; majestic*   壮观   *magnificent*
豪华   *luxurious; sumptuous*   别致   *unique*
破旧   *old and shabby; worn-out*   简陋   *simple and crude; shabby*
巍然屹立   *to tower imposingly*
富丽堂皇   *sumptuous; gorgeous; splendid*
宏伟壮丽   *magnificent and majestic*
典雅美观   *elegant and artistic*
古色古香   *in a traditional style*
别具一格   *with a unique style*
造型别致   *uniquely designed; unusual design*
结构精巧   *exquisitely constructed*
装饰一新   *re-decorated/renovated*
历史悠久   *with a long history*
破旧简陋   *shabby and basic*
普普通通   *ordinary*

Exercises for 14.3

1 Complete the following sentences with appropriate words and phrases.

(a) 在山脚下有一个＿＿＿＿＿＿＿＿＿＿的庙宇，据说有一千多年＿＿＿＿＿＿＿＿＿＿了。

(b) 最近在这个城市的东部建了一个＿＿＿＿＿＿＿＿＿＿古香的博物馆，占地面积不大，但是＿＿＿＿＿＿＿＿＿别致，结构＿＿＿＿＿＿＿＿＿。

(c) 看到万里长城如此＿＿＿＿＿＿＿＿＿，学生们都显得很激动。

(d) 东城那些＿＿＿＿＿＿＿＿＿的平房与西城新建的＿＿＿＿＿＿＿＿＿别墅形成了一个鲜明的对比。

(e) 市政府大楼是一＿＿＿＿＿＿＿＿＿＿德国＿＿＿＿＿＿＿＿＿的建筑。

2 Make a list of six buildings of different types in your town, and then write a short essay giving a description of them.

14.4 天空 The sky

范文 4, Text 4

a. 早晨我们出发的时候，阳光灿烂。可是不到半个小时就开始乌云翻滚，接着便下起了瓢泼大雨。

b. 这是一个天气晴朗的下午，天空中飘着几朵白云，张先生夫妇漫步走在河边的小路上，欣赏着大自然的美丽。

c. 李大伟抬头看了看阴沉沉的天空，心情觉得更加沉重了。

d. 起床之后，刘太太把窗帘拉开。这时红彤彤的太阳正从海面上慢慢升起，不一会儿，房间里就充满了温暖的阳光。

e. 在迷人的月光下，张立勇和他的女朋友坐在静悄悄的花园里。他俩谁也不说话，只是不停地看着满天星斗闪闪发光。

Notes to Text 4

a. '天气晴朗' (*it is a sunny day*), '阳光灿烂' (*the sun is bright*) and '乌云翻滚' (*dark clouds are rolling in*) can be sentences themselves, and they are often preceded by an adverbial clause of time, as in '八点的时候，天气晴朗/阳光灿烂/乌云翻滚'. Other set phrases, such as '晴空万里' (*it is a clear and boundless sky*), '满天白云' (*the sky is full of white clouds*) '满天乌云' (*the sky is full of dark clouds*), '云开雾散' (*the clouds roll away and the mists disperse*), etc., can also be used in the same way. These phrases are often used as modifiers as well, as in '一个天气晴朗的下午'.

b. Here 朵 is a measure word for the noun 云. And the verb 飘 is often used with 云 to mean '*to float*'.

151

c. Apart from 阴沉沉的 (*cloudy*), other phrases can also be used to modify 天空, such as 蓝蓝的 (*blue*) and 灰蒙蒙的 (*grey*). These phrases are often used as predicates also, as in '天空 + 阴沉沉的/灰蒙蒙的/蓝蓝的'.

d. 红彤彤的 (*red*), 火红的 (*flaming*), 鲜红的 (*bright red*) and 火辣辣的 (*scorching*) are often used to modify 太阳, and 温暖的 (*warm*), 明媚的 (*bright and beautiful*), 灿烂的 (*brilliant*) and 微弱的 (*faint; weak*) are often used to modify 阳光.

e. Adjectives like 迷人 (*enchanting*), 朦胧 (*dim; hazy*), 明亮 (*bright*), 柔和 (*soft*), 明媚 (*bright and beautiful*), 微弱 (*faint; weak*), 阴冷 (*gloomy and cold*) can be used both as modifiers and as predicates to describe 月光, as in '迷人/朦胧/明亮/柔和 + 的月光' and '今晚月光很 + 明媚/微弱/阴冷'.

f. The noun 星星 is often modified by adjectives, as in '闪闪发光 (*sparkling; glittering*) / 闪光 (*sparkling; glittering*) / 亮晶晶 (*glittering; sparkling*) / 明亮 (*bright*) + 的星星'.

Exercises for 14.4

1 Form five four-character phrases with the words below:

灿烂　雾散　晴朗　晴空　云开　翻滚　万里　乌云　阳光　天气

2 Try to complete the following sentences with appropriate words and phrases.
(a) 天渐渐地黑下来了，天空布满了＿＿＿＿＿＿的星星。
(b) 村民们望着那＿＿＿＿＿＿的太阳，都盼望这高温天气尽快结束。
(c) 今天又是一个＿＿＿＿＿的日子，蓝蓝的天空中只有几＿＿＿＿＿白云从远处的山顶上慢慢＿＿＿＿＿过。
(d) 中秋节那天晚上，我们坐在＿＿＿＿＿的月光下，一边吃月饼一边赏月，大家玩得都很开心。
(e) 水面上倒映着天空中＿＿＿＿＿的星星。
(f) 那＿＿＿＿＿的天空让人觉得十分不舒服。

3 Write a short paragraph to describe the sky today and tonight.

14.5　风，雨，雪 Wind, rain and snow

范文 5, *Text 5*

a. 早晨天气预报说今天夜里会有台风。果然，傍晚的时候刮起了大风，不一会儿便下起了倾盆大雨。
b. 从昨天夜里起，天一直在下着鹅毛大雪，外面已经变成了一个银装世界。
c. 洁白的雪花在空中飘来飘去，整个大地一片白茫茫。
d. 李老师冒着狂风暴雨开车把每一个学生都送回了家。

Notes to Text 5

a. The verb 刮 (*to blow*) usually takes words indicating wind as its object, as in '刮 + 大风 (*gale; strong wind*) / 寒风 (*cold wind*) / 台风 (*typhoon*) / 飓风 (*hurricane*)'.

b. Words indicating rain are often used with the verb 下 (*to fall; to descend*), as in '下 + 大雨 (*heavy rain*) / 阵雨 (*shower*) / 毛毛雨 (*drizzle*) / 暴雨 (*torrential rain*) / 倾盆大雨 (*heavy downpour*) / 瓢泼大雨 (*to bucket down with rain*)'.

c. The verb 下 is also often used with words indicating snow, as in '下 + 雪 (*snow*) / 小雪 (*light snow*) / 大雪 (*heavy snow*) / 鹅毛大雪 (*heavy snow in big flakes*)'.

d. The verb 飘 (*to float*) is often used to indicate the way that 雪花 (*snowflakes*) fall, as in '在空中飘来飘去' (*to float in the sky*). Other similar phrases include '满天飞扬' (*to fill the sky*), '满天飞舞' (*to dance in the air*).

e. The verbs 刮, 下, 飘 are often attached with the character 起, as in '天 + 刮起大风' (*it starts to blow heavily*) / 下起大雨 (*it starts to rain heavily*) / 飘起雪花 (*it starts to snow*)', or with the character 着, as in '天 + 刮着大风 (*it is blowing heavily*) / 下着大雨 (*it is raining heavily*) / 飘着雪花 (*it is snowing*)'. Here the character 起 implies that a new state has started, while the character 着 indicates an ongoing state.

f. 狂风暴雨 (*a violent storm*) is a noun phrase and can be replaced with 暴风骤雨 (*a violent storm*). They are often used as objects of verbs or prepositions such as 冒着 . . . (*braving . . .*), 顶着 . . . (*heading into . . .*), 不顾 (*ignoring*), and 在 . . . 中 (*in . . .*).

Exercises for 14.5

1 List as many Chinese words or phrases as you can which have the meaning of raining.

2 List as many Chinese words or phrases as you can which have the meaning of wind.

3 Fill in the following blanks with appropriate words. For some blanks, more than one word is possible.

   (a) 上个星期天，小张和他的同学们不顾_____坚持要去爬山，爬到山顶时，雨停了，太阳出来了。

   (b) 这几天天气非常糟糕。今天早晨起床的时候外面_____着毛毛雨，过了一会儿满天便_____起了白白的雪花，到了下午又_____起了十级台风。

   (c) 我快走到家的时候，忽然下起了_____大雨，我到家的时候，全身都湿透了。

   (d) 雪花还在满天_____，白_____的雪地上只有几只小鸟在寻找食物。

4 Write a short paragraph to describe stormy weather you have experienced or a storm you can imagine.

Vocabulary

14.1

剑桥	**Jiànqiáo**	Cambridge
牛津	**Niújīn**	Oxford
伦敦	**Lúndūn**	London
青岛	**Qīngdǎo**	Qingdao; Tsingdao (a coastal city in China)
海滨	**hǎibīn**	seaside
办公楼	**bàngōnglóu**	office block
教学楼	**jiàoxuélóu**	block teaching
小卖部	**xiǎomàibù**	shop (in school, college, factory, etc.)
实验室	**shíyànshì**	laboratory

14.2

位置	**wèizhi**	location; position
拐角	**guǎijiǎo**	corner
迷路	**mí lù**	to get lost; to lose one's way
聊天	**liáotiān**	to chat
矗立	**chùlì**	to stand tall and upright
大厦	**dàshà**	large building; sky scraper; tower
宏伟	**hóngwěi**	magnificent; grand
壮丽	**zhuànglì**	magnificent; majestic
坐落	**zuòluò**	to be located; to be situated
繁华	**fánhuá**	busy; bustling
超级市场	**chāojí shìchǎng**	supermarket
耸立	**sǒnglì**	to tower up
侧	**cè**	side
山水画	**shānshuǐhuà**	landscape painting
崭新	**zhǎnxīn**	brand-new
奔驰	**Bēnchí**	Mercedes-Benz

14.3

建筑物	**jiànzhùwù**	building
别墅	**biéshù**	villa
幢	**zhuàng**	(a measure word for buildings)
红砖	**hóng zhuān**	red brick
典雅美观	**diǎnyǎ měiguān**	elegant and attractive
造型别致	**zàoxíng biézhì**	uniquely designed; unusual design
简陋	**jiǎnlòu**	simple and crude; shabby
装饰一新	**zhuāngshì yìxīn**	re-decorated; renovated
富丽堂皇	**fùlì tánghuáng**	sumptuous; gorgeous; splendid
巍然屹立	**wēirán yìlì**	to tower imposingly
瓦房	**wǎfáng**	tile-roofed house
公寓	**gōngyù**	apartment
壮观	**zhuàngguān**	magnificent

豪华	háohuá	luxurious, sumptuous
古色古香	gǔsègǔxiāng	with a style of antiquity
别具一格	bié jù yì gé	in a unique style
结构精巧	jiégòu jīngqiǎo	exquisitely constructed
历史悠久	lìshǐ yōujiǔ	with a long history
庙宇	miàoyǔ	temple
占地面积	zhàn dì miànjī	ground area
鲜明	xiānmíng	striking; distinct
对比	duìbǐ	contrast

14.4

灿烂	cànlàn	bright
乌云翻滚	wūyún fāngǔn	dark clouds are rolling in
瓢泼大雨	piáopō dàyǔ	to bucket down with rain
晴朗	qínglǎng	sunny
飘	piāo	to float
漫步	mànbù	to stroll; to ramble; to roam
欣赏	xīnshǎng	to enjoy
阴沉沉	yīnchénchén	cloudy
红彤彤	hóngtōngtōng	red
迷人	mírén	enchanting
星斗	xīngdǒu	stars
闪闪发光	shǎnshǎn fā guāng	sparkling; glittering
晴空万里	qíng kōng wànlǐ	it is a clear and boundless sky
云开雾散	yún kāi wù sàn	the clouds roll away and the mists disperse
灰蒙蒙	huīméngméng	grey
火红	huǒhóng	flaming; fiery red
鲜红	xiānhóng	bright red
火辣辣	huǒlàlà	scorching
明媚	míngmèi	bright and beautiful
微弱	wēiruò	faint; weak
朦胧	ménglóng	dim; hazy
明亮	míngliàng	bright
柔和	róuhé	soft
阴冷	yīnlěng	gloomy and cold
闪光	shǎnguāng	sparkling; glittering
亮晶晶	liàngjīngjīng	glittering; sparkling
盼望	pànwàng	to hope for; to long for
中秋节	Zhōngqiūjié	the mid-autumn festival
月饼	yuèbing	moon cake
赏月	shǎng yuè	to enjoy looking at the moon
倒映	dàoyìng	to reflect; in retrospect

14.5

| 台风 | táifēng | typhoon |
| 倾盆大雨 | qīngpén dàyǔ | heavy downpour |

鹅毛大雪	**émáo dàxuě**	heavy snow in big flakes
银装世界	**yínzhuāng shìjiè**	silver-coated world
洁白	**jiébái**	pure white; spotlessly white
白茫茫	**báimángmáng**	a vast expanse of whiteness
冒着	**màozhe**	braving
狂风暴雨	**kuángfēng bàoyǔ**	a violent storm
寒风	**hán fēng**	cold wind
飓风	**jùfēng**	hurricane
阵雨	**zhènyǔ**	shower
毛毛雨	**máomáoyǔ**	drizzle
暴雨	**bàoyǔ**	torrential rain
满天飞扬	**mǎntiān fēiyáng**	to fill the sky
满天飞舞	**mǎntiān fēiwǔ**	to dance in the sky
暴风骤雨	**bàofēng zhòuyǔ**	a violent storm
顶着	**dǐngzhe**	heading into
不顾	**búgù**	ignoring
糟糕	**zāogāo**	bad; awful
湿透	**shītòu**	wet through; to be soaked (with water)
寻找	**xúnzhǎo**	to look for; to search for

第十五单元: 贸易信函
Unit Fifteen: Business correspondence

It goes without saying that not everyone has to write business letters. However, more and more people would like to learn how to write business letters in Chinese. This is probably due to the increasing contacts between Western business communities and their counterparts in China. There are various types of business letters and they often require the use of business jargon. In this unit, we focus on business letters to promote the sale of goods, letters inquiring about their prices, letters quoting prices, letters ordering goods, and letters confirming shipment.

15.1 商品推销函 Letters promoting the sale of goods

范文 *1, Text 1*

敬启者:

首先请原谅本人冒昧去函向贵公司介绍本公司的各类出口商品。

本公司专门经营各种家电设备的出口,已有近四十年的历史。客户遍及北美、欧洲、澳大利亚、东南亚等国家和地区,其商品因质量可靠,造型优美,价格合理等优点在国际市场享有盛誉。

若能为贵公司提供彩电、冰箱、空调等家电商品,本公司将深感荣幸,并将竭诚为贵公司提供最佳服务。

为使贵公司了解本公司的出口商品,随函寄去本公司出口商品目录和价格表各一份,请查收。若贵公司能在收到此函后一个月内订货,本公司愿在价格上给予贵公司15%的特别折扣。

希望不久能收到贵公司的回信。

　　　　　　敬请

业安!

　　　　　　中国太平洋电器集团公司国际部主任　王耀光

　　　　　　2001年4月30日

Notes to Text 1

a. The phrase 敬启者 is used in formal letters, and it has a meaning similar to the English phrase '*To whom it may concern*'.

b. In formal business letters, it is common practice to use 本人 instead of 我, to use 本公司 instead of 我(们)公司, to use 贵公司 instead of 你(们)公司, to use 函 instead of 信, and to use 若 instead of 如果.

c. The phrase '首先请原谅本人冒昧去函 . . .' (*Please first of all forgive me for taking the liberty of writing to you . . .*) is often used at the beginning of a formal letter approaching someone you are not familiar with. This phrase can be replaced by other phrases, such as '今冒昧去函 . . .' (*Today I am taking the liberty of writing to you . . .*), '今去函 . . .' (*Today I am writing to you . . .*).

d. To promote your company and your products, the following phrases can be useful:
'本公司专门经营 . . .' (*our company specialises in the business of . . .*);
'已有 . . . 年的历史' (*have a history of . . . years*);
'本公司客户 (or 产品) 遍及......等国家和地区' (*we have clients from countries and regions such as . . . ; or we have sold our products to countries and regions such as . . .*);
'本公司商品(or 产品)质量可靠，造型优美，价格合理' (*our company's goods/products are of reliable quality, beautifully designed and reasonably priced*);
'本公司的商品 (or 产品) 在 . . . 享有盛誉' (*our company's goods / our company's products enjoy(s) a high reputation in . . .*).

e. To win over a customer, one often uses the following phrases:
'若能为贵公司提供 . . .，本公司将深感荣幸' (*we would feel greatly honoured if our company could supply your company with . . .*);
'本公司将竭诚为贵公司提供最佳服务' (*our company will endeavour to provide the best possible service to your company*);
'本公司愿给予贵公司 . . .% 的特别折扣' (*our company is happy to offer a special discount of . . .% to your company*);
'若能在 . . . 前订货，本公司将给予 . . .% 的优惠' (*if you can place an order by . . . , our company will be happy to give you a . . .% discount*).

f. With a business letter, you may have to enclose something besides the letter. In this case, you can use phrases like '随函寄去 . . .' or '随函附上 . . .' (*I am enclosing . . .*). The phrase 请查收 (*lit.: please check*) is often used immediately afterwards.

g. In business letter writing, the quantity and the measure word are usually put after, rather than before, the noun, as in 出口商品目录一份 (*a copy of the list of goods for export*) and 价格表两张 (*two copies of the price list*).

h. The phrase 敬请 业安！ is a closing remark, which literally means '*Respectfully wishing you a peaceful business*'. It is a common practice that the first two characters and the last two in this kind of closing remark are put on two different lines.

Exercises for 15.1

1 Complete the following letter with the words and phrases provided.

贵，价格，遍及，敬启，质量，订单，冒昧，优惠，若，盛誉，
业安，最佳，本，已有，了解，随函，一份，荣幸，优美

＿＿＿者:

今＿＿＿去信向贵公司介绍本厂生产经营的各种运动鞋。

＿＿＿厂生产经营各种运动鞋＿＿＿＿八十余年的历史，其客户
＿＿＿＿世界各地。由于本公司的产品＿＿＿可靠，造型＿＿＿，
＿＿＿合理，在国际市场上一直享有＿＿＿。

为帮助贵公司＿＿＿本厂生产的各类运动鞋，＿＿＿附上本厂的
产品介绍＿＿＿，其中包括各种产品的价格。＿＿＿能接到贵公司的
＿＿＿，本厂将深感＿＿＿，并将竭诚为贵公司提供＿＿＿服务。
对六万美元以上的订货，本厂将给予10%的＿＿＿。

衷心希望＿＿＿公司能对本厂的产品给予积极的考虑，并希望不久
能接到贵公司的订单。

敬请

＿＿＿！

中国力士运动鞋厂
销售部经理　于光远
2001年2月18日

2 Imagine you are working in the sales department of a mountain bicycle (山地自行车) factory in China, which has a history of over 50 years and has a good market in North and South America, Europe and Australia, but not in Southeast Asia. The head of the department has asked you to write to the largest bicycle shop in Singapore to promote the factory's products. He has given you authority to offer 10–15% discount to potential customers.

15.2 商品询价函 Letters inquiring about prices

范文 *2, Text 2*

敬启者:

　　从贵公司的网页上得知，贵公司经营高档纯毛西服。现去函索取贵公司的西服样品手册和价格表各一份。

　　回信烦请注明各类西服的详细规格，包装形式，可供数量，以及运抵青岛的到岸价。

　　本公司系中国蓝岛市最大的西服经销商，并在中国各大城市设有分公司。如贵公司的西服款式新颖，质量优良，价格合理，我公司将定期大量订货。

　　　　　　敬请
业安！

　　　　　　　　　　　　　　　　　蓝岛西服实业有限公司
　　　　　　　　　　　　　　　　　供销部经理　朱宏达
　　　　　　　　　　　　　　　　　2001年5月8日

Notes to Text 2

a. When inquiring about prices, you can start the letter by stating 从 . . . 得知 or 从 . . . 获悉 (*I have learned from . . . that*), as in '从贵公司的网页上得知' (*We have learned from the webpage of your company that . . .*).

b. Here the verb 索取, rather than 要, should be used for the meaning of '*requesting for* (something)'.

c. '回信烦请 . . .' means '*when you reply please . . .*'. The verb following 请 can be 注明 (*to specify*), 提供 (*to supply*), 告知 (*to let me know*), etc.

d. The verb 运抵 means '*to be shipped to*'. In a less formal situation, it can be replaced by the verb 运到.

e. The term '青岛的到岸价' means '*CIF Qingdao*'. CIF is an abbreviation of Cost, Insurance and Freight. Another often quoted price is 离岸价, which means '*FOB*', an abbreviation of Free On Board, as in 伦敦离岸价 (*FOB London*).

f. In '本公司系...', the verb 系 can be replaced by 是, but the former is more formal than the latter.

g. To obtain a better deal, one can state '如/若..., 我公司将定期大量订货' (*if..., our company will place regular and substantial orders regularly and in a large quantity*). Here the phrase 定期 can be replaced by 长期 (*over a long period of time*), and 大量 by 大批 (*in large quantities*).

Exercises for 15.2

1 Complete the following letter with the words and phrases provided.

新颖，大批，烦请，经营，质量，离岸，获悉，索取，合理

敬启者：

　　从贵公司在《世界贸易》杂志上刊登的广告中＿＿＿＿＿＿，贵公司＿＿＿＿＿各种中国工艺品的出口。现去函＿＿＿＿贵公司的样品目录和价格表。

　　回信＿＿＿＿告知贵公司的商品包装形式，以及上海＿＿＿＿价。本公司在英国各地都有工艺品连锁店，若贵公司的商品式样＿＿＿＿，＿＿＿＿优良，价格＿＿＿＿，本公司将会长期、＿＿＿＿订购。

　　希望早日得到贵公司的回信。

英国伦敦工艺品公司
副总经理: 江大伟
2000. 12. 12

2 Imagine you work for a company which is the largest trader in silk products in the USA. You have learned from the internet (互联网) that 中国龙海市丝绸公司 produces and exports silk products of high quality. Write to that company asking for a catalogue of their products and a price list. Also ask for product specifications information on packaging, and the price CIF Boston (波士顿). You should promise to place regular and substantial orders if the products are good and the prices are reasonable.

15.3 商品报价函 Letters quoting prices

范文 3, Text 3

蓝岛西服实业有限公司供销部

尊敬的朱宏达经理：

很高兴收到您五月八日发来的询价函。首先我愿借此机会对贵公司有意购买本公司的高档西服表示感谢。

按贵公司的要求，现寄去本公司的西服样品手册和价格表各一份。本公司极为重视贵公司的询价，并愿为贵公司做如下优惠报价。

商品：高档全毛西服
尺寸：小号，中号，大号，特大号
价格：对于数量不少于两千套的订货，青岛到岸价为每十套一千二百美元

如贵公司接受上述报价，本公司保证在收到信用证后两周内发货。本公司期待早日收到贵公司的订货单。

敬请
业安！

利物浦华通服装公司销售部经理　戴马克
2001年5月18日

Notes to Text 3

a. 询价函 means '*a letter inquiring about prices*'. A letter quoting a price is called 报价函.

b. To acknowledge receipt of the letter of inquiry, one can use the phrases '很高兴收到您 ... 发来的询价函，首先我愿借此机会对 ... 表示感谢'.
Here 收到 can be replaced by 接到 and 发来 by 寄来.

c. The phrase '极为重视贵公司的询价' means '*to attach great importance to your company's price inquiry*'.

d. The phrase '做(...)优惠报价' means '*to offer preferential prices*'.

e. In '如贵公司接受上述报价' (*if your company accepts the prices quoted above*), 上述 can be replaced with 以上.

f. In '青岛到岸价为每十套一千二百美元' (*CIF Qingdao is US$1,200 per ten sets*), the character 为 can be replaced with 是.

g. One often uses a sentence like '本公司保证在 … 内/前发货' (*our company guarantees that the goods will be delivered in/by …*) to give potential customers some assurance about the delivery time.

h. 信用证 means '*L/C*', an abbreviation of letter of credit.

Exercises for 15.4

1 Complete the following letter with the words and phrases provided.

优惠　　尺寸　　到岸价　　有意　　目录　　订货　　报价
寄来　　尊敬　　向　　　　附上　　保证

_____的欧阳山先生：

很高兴收到您二月十八日_____的询价函，并非常感谢贵公司_____购买本公司的高档男式皮鞋。

按来函要求，现_____贵公司做如下优惠_____：
商品：高档黑色男式皮鞋
____：39号–45号
价格：伦敦_____为每一千双四万八千英镑

随函_____本公司的皮鞋样品_____和价格表各一份。若贵公司对以上_____报价感到满意，本公司将_____按时供货。

衷心希望早日收到贵公司的_____。

华东皮革公司
销售部主任　康士杰
2002年3月6日

2 Imagine you work in the sales department of a glassware company. You have received a letter dated January 10th, 2002, inquiring about the prices of crystal vases (水晶玻璃花瓶). The letter is from 中国北京东方大酒店采购部主任鲁浩年, who asks for a catalogue of the vases, the size specification of the vases, and CIF Tianjin. You have three different sizes of vase in stock: 20cm high, 40cm high and 60cm high, and after investigations and calculations, you have worked out that CIF Tianjin is £4,600 for 120 crystal vases, including 40 vases of each size. Now write a letter of reply quoting the price.

15.4 商品订购函 Letters ordering goods

范文 *4, Text 4*

利物浦华通服装公司
销售部经理

尊敬的戴马克先生：

　　您五月十八日的来信收悉。本公司对贵公司提供的高档纯毛西服价格感到满意，现向贵公司订购下列货物：

　　货物名称：华通纯毛西服
　　数量：小号600套，中号1200套，大号1000套，特大号800套

　　本公司要求上述货物在7月底之前运抵青岛港。若逾期未至，本公司保留要求赔偿和拒收货物的权利。

　　如贵公司认为这批订货可以接受，请速来电确认。

　　　　　　此致
敬礼！

　　　　　　　　　　　　　　　　　　　蓝岛西服实业有限公司
　　　　　　　　　　　　　　　　　　　供销部经理　朱宏达
　　　　　　　　　　　　　　　　　　　2002年5月22日

Notes to Text 4

a. The phrase '收悉' literally means '. . . *has received and understood*'. It is much more formal than 收到了.

b. The phrase '对 . . . 感到满意' means '*to be satisfied with. . .*'.

c. To place an order, one can use the phrase '向 . . . (company) 订购 . . . (goods)'.

d. The word 下列 can be replaced with 以下 and 下述; and the word 上述 can be replaced with 以上 and 上列.

e. The phrase 运抵 (*to be shipped/transported to*) can be replaced with 运到 (*to be shipped/transported to*), but the former is more formal than the latter.

f. '若逾期未至' is a conditional clause, meaning '*if . . . fail to arrive by the specified date*'. Here 逾期 means '*to be overdue* or *to exceed the time limit*'; 未 means '*not*', and 至 means '*to arrive*'.

g. '保留……的权利' means '*to reserve the right to . . .*', as in '保留要求赔偿和拒收货物的权利' (*to reserve the right to ask for compensation and refuse to accept the goods*).

h. Here 批 (*batch; lot*) is a measure word for 货物 or 订货.

i. '请速来电确认' literally means '*Please immediately send us telegram/fax/email to confirm*'.

Exercises for 15.4

1 Complete the following letter with the words and phrases provided.

货物　要求　确认　满意　以下　逾期　收悉　上述　来函　保留

尊敬的陈文启先生：

贵厂六月二十日的_____及随函寄来的产品目录和价格表均已____
____。本公司对贵厂黑色女式手提包的报价感到_____，现向贵厂订购
_____货物：

_____名称: 黑色女式手提包
数量: 小号200个，中号400个，大号600个

本公司急需该批货物，因此_____贵厂务必在九月十五日之前将
_____货物运抵波士顿港。若_____未至，本公司_____要求赔偿和追
究法律责任的权利。

望能速来电_____贵厂是否接受此批订货。

　　　　　　此致
敬礼！

美国波士顿皮革贸易有限公司: 李约翰
2002年7月2日

2 Imagine you work in a trading company dealing in woollen jumpers. You have just received a reply, dated June 24, from Mr. 丁石岩 of 中国毛衣制品进出口公司 quoting prices for men's woollen jumpers which your company is interested in buying. Also enclosed is a catalogue of their products. Your company is pleased with the prices and has decided to place an order for 2,000 men's woollen jumpers, which includes 200 Size S, 600 Size M, 800

165

Size L and 400 Size XL. Your company requires that the goods arrive in New York (纽约) by the end of October. Now write a letter ordering the goods. You should state in the letter that your company reserves the right to ask for compensation if the goods do not arrive by the date specified.

15.5 商品装运确认函 Letters confirming shipment

范文 5, *Text 5*

蓝岛西服有限公司供销部

尊敬的朱宏达先生：

    现确认本公司已收到贵公司通过中国银行开出的第1644号信用证，金额为432,000美元。

    贵公司订购的3,600套西服已于昨日装大不列颠号货轮，预计将于七月底之前运抵青岛港。

    本公司希望这批货物能安全抵达并使贵公司满意。再次感谢贵公司订购本公司的货物，并希望经常得到贵公司的惠顾。

             敬请
业安！

                利物浦华通服装公司销售部经理：戴马克
                2002年5月18日

Notes to Text 5

a. '现确认 . . .' means '*This is to confirm . . .*'.
b. '金额为 . . .' means '*the sum of money is . . .*'.
c. Note that in '已于昨日 . . .', the words 于 and 日 are used instead of 在 and 天. This is because it is a formal letter.
d. 预计 here means '*it is anticipated that . . .*' or '*it is expected that . . .*'.
e. In this letter, the verbs 运抵 and 抵达 have similar meanings. However, the former, but not the latter, requires an object, as in '运抵青岛港'.
f. The phrase 惠顾 (*your patronage*) is often used by business people to show respect to customers, as in '希望经常得到贵公司的惠顾' (*we hope we can frequently enjoy your company's patronage*).

Exercises for 15.5

1   Complete the following letter with the words and phrases provided.

预计，于，惠顾，确认，抵达，满意，日，批，表示

尊敬的白玛丽女士：

今去函_____贵公司订购的3,600个黑色羊皮公文箱已_____今晨装上长江号货轮，明_____将起程开往美国，_____该轮将于五月三十日_____纽约港。

本公司衷心希望此_____货物能安全，准时到达，并希望贵公司对本公司的服务感到_____。

本人愿借此机会对贵公司订购本公司的货物再次_____感谢，并希望本公司能得到贵公司的长期_____。

敬请

业安！

中国办公用品进出口公司：纪高峰
2001年4月20日

2   Imagine you are working for a computer company. Now write a letter to Ms. 赵容范 of 中国计算机进出口公司. In the letter, you need to tell her that the cheque for £95,000 she sent you has arrived. Also confirm that the 100 computers that she has ordered have been loaded onto the cargo ship *Edinburgh* (爱丁堡号), which will leave London this weekend and is expected to arrive in Shanghai within one month. In your letter, you should thank her again for purchasing the computers from your company, and express your hope that her company will order more goods from yours.

Vocabulary

15.1

推销	**tuīxiāo**	to promote sales
函	**hán**	letter
冒昧	**màomèi**	to take the liberty; to be bold enough
经营	**jīngyíng**	to manage; to run; to trade in

家电	**jiādiàn**	domestic electric/electronic products
设备	**shèbèi**	equipment
客户	**kèhù**	client
造型优美	**zàoxíng yōuměi**	beautifully designed
享有盛誉	**xiǎngyǒu shèngyù**	to enjoy a high reputation
若	**ruò**	if
空调	**kōngtiáo**	air-conditioner
深感荣幸	**shēn gǎn róngxìng**	to feel deeply honoured
竭诚	**jiéchéng**	to endeavour to
最佳	**zuìjiā**	the best
目录	**mùlù**	catalogue
订货	**dìng huò**	to place an order
折扣	**zhékòu**	discount
订单	**dìngdān**	order (for goods)
销售部	**xiāoshòu bù**	sales department

15.2

询价	**xún jià**	to inquire about prices
网页	**wǎngyè**	web page
高档	**gāodàng**	high-quality
纯毛	**chún máo**	pure wool
索取	**suǒqǔ**	to request
注明	**zhùmíng**	to give a clear indication of
规格	**guīgé**	specifications
包装形式	**bāozhuāng xíngshì**	packaging format
运抵	**yùndǐ**	to be shipped to; to be transported to
到岸价	**dào'ànjià**	CIF; Cost, Insurance and Freight
经销商	**jīngxiāoshāng**	distributor
款式新颖	**kuǎnshì xīnyǐng**	new and original design
实业有限公司	**shíyè yǒuxiàn gōngsī**	industrial (or commercial) limited company
供销部	**gōngxiāo bù**	supply and sales department
刊登	**kāndēng**	to publish; to carry (in a newspaper or magazine)
获悉	**huòxī**	to learn
离岸价	**lí'ànjià**	FOB; Free On Board
伦敦	**Lúndūn**	London
工艺品	**gōngyìpǐn**	handicraft
样品	**yàngpǐn**	sample
连锁店	**liánsuǒdiàn**	chain store
丝绸	**sīchóu**	silk
波士顿	**Bōshìdùn**	Boston

15.3

报价	**bào jià**	to quote a price
有意	**yǒu yì**	to have the intention

手册	shǒucè	handbook
优惠	yōuhuì	preferential; favourable
尺寸	chǐcùn	size
信用证	xìnyòngzhèng	L/C; letter of credit
期待	qīdài	to look forward to
利物浦	Lìwùpǔ	Liverpool
发货	fā huò	to dispatch goods
供货	gōng huò	to supply goods
衷心	zhōngxīn	wholeheartedly
水晶	shuǐjīng	crystal
采购部	cǎigòu bù	purchasing department

15.4

订购	dìnggòu	to place an order (for something)
收悉	shōuxī	to have received
逾期未至	yúqī wèi zhì	to fail to arrive by the specified date
保留...的权利	bǎoliú . . . de quánlì	to reserve the right to . . .
赔偿	péicháng	compensation
拒收	jù shōu	to refuse to accept
均	jūn	all; both
港	gǎng	port
追究法律责任	zhuījiū fǎlǜ zérèn	to investigate and assign the legal responsibility
皮革	pígé	leather
纽约	Niǔyuē	New York

15.5

装运	zhuāngyùn	to load and transport; to ship
金额	jīn'é	the sum of money
预计	yùjì	to anticipate; to expect
装	zhuāng	to load
大不列颠号货轮	Dàbùlièdiānhào huòlún	the cargo ship *Great Britain*
抵达	dǐdá	to arrive
惠顾	huìgù	your patronage
公文箱	gōngwénxiāng	business briefcase

The following are answers to all the closed questions. They are not necessarily the only correct answers.

Unit One

1.1 1. (a) 过 guò (b) 大寿/寿辰/生日 dàshòu/shòuchén/shēngri 祝寿 zhùshòu
(c) 尊敬的 大寿 寿比 东海 敬上
1.2 1. 愉快/快乐 心想
1.3 喜 伉俪 甜蜜/美满/幸福 早生 恩爱 白头
1.4 (a) 哀悼/悼念 āidào/dàoniàn (b) 去世/离开了这个世界 qùshì/líkāile zhège shìjiè
(c) 惊悉 逝世/去世 悲痛 深感/深表 同情 哀悼 垂 朽

Unit Two

2.1 1. (a) 本 果 给我 以 (b) 为 天 上 个 我
(before 可能)
2.3 1. (a) 帮 做 (b) 做/办 (c) 会 的
2.6 1. 先 再/然后 然后/接着/接下来 最后

Unit Three

3.1 1. (a) 您 (b) 身体 (c) 亲爱的 (d) 您的孙女
(1) 亲爱的奶奶: (2) 您好 (3) 祝您身体健康! (4) 您的孙女
2. (a) 我昨天收到了你的来信。得知你在那儿一切都好，我真为你高兴。
(b) 好久没收到你们的来信，不知近况如何，是否适应了新环境?
(c) 很抱歉，没有尽早给你回信。最近我正忙着写我的学位论文。
(d) 请代我向你们全家问好！Or向你全家问好。

练习答案

Key to Some Exercises

3.2

> 710061
>
> 西安市西城大街38号16楼2室
>
> 王和平　收
>
> 北京大学留学生宿舍6楼3号
> 100081

3.3 1. (1) (d) 务请原谅　(2) (a) 敬请光临　(3) (c) 你要是能来，那就太好了。
(4) (e) 是我的荣幸。　(5) (b) 真遗憾 . . . 无法前来参加。

3.4 1. (1) (g) 来信　(2) (c) 上个月寄去的照片是否收到　(3) (e) 相处得很好
(4) (a) 你如果那时候在上海的话　(5) (f) 对了
(6) (d) 希望尽快收到你的回信
(7) (b) 又: 秀芳生了个女孩，起名叫荷芝

Unit Four

4.3.1 1. 拾到　认领

4.3.3 1. (a) 为了　(b) 今收到　整　据　(c) 因　特　为盼
(d) (i) 本人　拾到　一个　若干　者　认领　(ii) 不慎　拾到者　联系

Unit Six

6.1 (a) 方华说他根本没有告诉小平那件事。
(b) 李一建失望地说他这次考试考得很一般。
(c) 明雨对她妈妈说她准备第二天带她的男朋友回家见她的父母。
(d) 林林高兴地对他妈妈说万万没想到她会来。
(e) 小王的哥哥问小王是否用了他的手机，小王说没用。

6.2 1. (a) 强调　(b) 介绍　(c) 警告说　(d) 坚信　(e) 声称
2. (b) 认为　指出　承认　相信　建议　重申　警告说　表示　透露

Unit Seven

7.1–7.3 1. (a) 换 . . . 句话说　(b) 总之　(c) 例如　(d) 比方说　(e) 一句话
(f) 具体 . . . 地说

Unit Eight

8.1 1. (a) 与　不同的　(b) 跟　相似　(c) 却完全不一样　(d) 跟　完全一样
8.2 1. (a) <u>真像</u>　(b) <u>就好比　就如同　恰似</u>　(c) <u>是</u>　(d) <u>变成</u>

Unit Nine

9.1 1. c b f a e d
9.2 1. (a) 最初　后来　(b) 开始的时候　接着　后来　不久　接下来
　　　(c) 起初　后来　不久　最后　(d) 最初　后来　接着　以后　很快
9.3 1. 首先　其次　最令人头疼的是　不仅如此…还　除此之外
　　　更认人失望的是

Unit Ten

10.1 1. (a) 白发苍苍(满头银发)　(b) 头发蓬乱(披头散发)
　　　(c) 头发稀疏(秃顶，谢顶)　(d) 谢顶(秃顶)
　　　(e) 头发乌润(头发油亮，头发光洁)
　　2. (a) 齐耳的短发　(b) 花白的头发(灰白的头发)
　　　(c) 金黄的头发(卷曲的头发，波浪式的头发，乌黑的头发，披肩的长发)
　　　(d) 细长的小辫　(e) 灰白的头发(花白的头发)
10.2–10.3 1. Positive 明亮的，有神的，敏锐的，热情的，亲切的，含笑的，亮
　　　晶晶的，信任的，乌黑的
　　　Negative 冷酷的，凶狠的，迟钝的，痴呆的
　　　Neutral 严肃的，试探的
10.4–10.6 2. (a) 满脸羞愧(脸上红一阵白一阵)
　　　(b) 愁眉苦脸(愁容满面，满脸愁容)　(c) 神采奕奕
　　　(d) 脸刷地一白了(面无血色，面如土色，面色苍白)
　　　(e) 面如土色(面黄肌瘦，面色苍白，脸色蜡黄，面无血色)
　　　(f) 嬉皮笑脸　(g) 满脸笑容(眉开眼笑，喜笑颜开，满脸春风)
　　　(h) 板着脸(绷着脸，拉长了脸，脸色铁青)

Unit Eleven

11.1 1. 热爱　2. 朝思暮想　3. 情深似海　4. 情意绵绵　5. 爱好　6. 爱戴
11.2 1. (a) 兴高采烈地　(b) 乐开了花　(c) 得眼泪都流出来了　(d) 不好意思地
　　　(e) 得喊了起来
11.4 1. (a) 愁眉苦脸　闷闷不乐　(b) 忧心忡忡的　很苦恼　(c) 很忧虑
　　　(d) 闷闷不乐的
11.5 1. (a) 心惊肉跳　(b) 大惊失色的　(c) 很恐惧　(d) 吓得出了一身冷汗

11.6 1. (a) 勃然大怒　(b) 火冒三丈　两眼冒金星　(c) 恼火
11.7 1. (a) 后悔　(b) 懊悔　(c) 惭愧　内疚
11.8 1. (a) 他画的这幅画表明他对自己家乡的怀念。
　　　(b) 那个老农民对他儿子的期待是娶一个漂亮的媳妇，早点给他生个孙
　　　　子。
　　　(c) 她从来没有表露她对女儿的挂念。
　　2. (a) 我期望他在这次比赛中拿冠军。
　　　(b) 大家都意识到他思念他的母亲。
　　　(c) 这封家信说明了父母惦念女儿。

Unit Twelve

12.2 1. 无忧无虑—多愁善感　缺乏信心—充满信心　冷淡—热情　慷慨—吝啬
　　　自馁—自信　悲观—乐观　大方—小气　狭窄—开朗
　　2. (a) 自信　(b) 吝啬　(c) 悲观　(d) 开朗　(e) 冷淡　(f) 小气
　　　(g) 多愁善感
12.3 1. 彬彬有礼　谦虚谨慎　平易近人　谨小慎微　胆小怕事
　　2. 内向—外向　腼腆—放肆　虚心—自满　拘谨—大方　谦虚—骄傲
　　3. (a) 拘谨　(b) 内向　(c) 谦虚　(d) 腼腆　(e) 虚心
12.4 1. 表里如一　言行一致　机智勇敢　老老实实　光明正大　精明强干
　　2. 狡猾—老实　聪明—愚蠢　迟钝—敏锐　凶恶—善良　机灵—愚笨
　　　虚伪—诚实
　　3. (a) 老实　(b) 善良　(c) 聪明　(d) 诚实　(e) 敏锐　(f) 机灵

Unit Thirteen

13.1 1. (a) 迈着沉重的步伐　(b) 迈着矫健的步伐　(c) 迈着犹豫的步伐
　　　(d) 迈着坚定的步伐
　　2. (a) 走起路来东倒西歪的　(b) 走起路来摇摇晃晃的
　　　(c) 走起路来一瘸一拐的
　　3. (a) 的脚步显得很沉重　(b) 的脚步显得非常从容
13.2 1. 拔腿就跑　上气不接下气　气喘吁吁　像插上了翅膀　扭头就跑
　　2. (a) 拔腿就跑　(b) 像插上了翅膀　(c) 得上气不接下气
　　　(d) 像一只只乌龟
13.3 1. (a) 观看　观望　观察　(b) 注视　凝视　(c) 看望　探望　观望
　　　(d) 观察　视察
　　2. (a) 视察　(b) 打量　(c) 看望　(d) 观看　(e) 注视　(f) 瞧
13.4 1. (a) 听候　(b) 偷听　(c) 倾听　(d) 听从　(e) 旁听　(f) 聆听
13.5 1. (a) 谈论　议论　讨论　辩论　争论　(b) 讲话　讲解　讲授　讲演
　　　(c) 谈话　说话　讲话
　　2. (a) 议论　讨论　(b) 讲授　(c) 争吵　(d) 讲演　(e) 谈话　(f) 辩论

Unit Fourteen

14.1 1. (a) 位于　距离　(b) 在　东南部　(c) 西北边　(d) 在　南边
       (e) 在　南边　在　东北边

14.2 1. (a) 小河边坐着一群孩子，又说又笑。
       (b) 火车站的西侧耸立着两座高楼，一座是邮电大楼，一座是和平宾馆。
       (c) 走进他的房间，你会看到四周的墙上挂着很多中国画。
    2. (a) 有一座电视塔矗立在八关山的山腰，电视台就在八关山的山脚下。
       (b) 有很多书放在她的桌子上，有中文的，也有英文的。
       (c) 我记得当时有两辆崭新的德国奔驰汽车停在他家门口。
    3. 对面　左边　左边　对面　中间

14.3 1. (a) 古色古香　历史　(b) 古色　造型　精巧　(c) 壮观
       (d) 破旧　豪华　(e) 座　式

14.4 1. 阳光灿烂　云开雾散　天气晴朗　晴空万里　乌云翻滚
    2. (a) 亮晶晶　(b) 火辣辣　(c) 阳光灿烂　朵　飘　(d) 明媚　(e) 闪闪发光
       (f) 阴沉沉

14.5 3. (a) 瓢泼大雨　(b) 下　飘　刮　(c) 倾盆大雨　(d) 飞舞　白茫茫

Unit Fifteen

15.1 1. 敬启　冒昧　本　已有　遍及　质量　优美　价格　盛誉　了解
       随函　一份　若　订单　荣幸　最佳　优惠　贵　业安

15.2 1. 获悉　经营　索取　烦请　离岸　新颖　质量　合理　大批

15.3 1. 尊敬　寄来　有意　向　报价　尺寸　到岸价　附上　目录
       优惠　保证　订货

15.4 1. 来函　收悉　满意　以下　货物　要求　上述　逾期　保留　确认

15.5 1. 确认　于　日　预计　抵达　批　满意　表示　惠顾

Chinese–English Glossary

哀悼	āidào	condolences	1.4
唉声叹气	āishēngtànqì	to sigh in despair	11.4
矮人	ǎirén	short people	6.2
矮小	ǎixiǎo	small and short	6.2
爱不释手	ài bú shìshǒu	cannot put down	11.1
爱戴	àidài	to love and esteem	11.1
爱护	àihù	to take good care of	8.2
爱慕	àimù	admiration; affection	9.2, 11.1
爱情	àiqíng	love	6.2
爱上	àishang	to fall in love	6.2
安	ān	to fix; to install; to lay	8.2
安慰	ānwèi	to comfort	11.7
暗示	ànshì	to hint; to imply	6.2
暗喻	ànyù	metaphor	8.2
熬夜	áoyè	to stay up all night	6.1
懊悔	àohuǐ	to feel remorse and regret	11.7
捌	bā	eight	4.3.2
八字胡	bāzìhú	moustache	10.2
白茫茫	báimángmáng	a vast expanse of whiteness	14.5
白纱	bái shā	white gauze	8.2
白头到老	bái tóu dào lǎo	to grow old together	1.3
佰	bǎi	hundred	4.3.2
百忙之中	bǎimángzhīzhōng	amid one's busy life	5.4
百年夫妻	bǎi nián fūqī	to be husband and wife for a hundred years	1.3
百年佳偶	bǎi nián jiā ǒu	to be happily married for a hundred years	1.3
百年偕老	bǎi nián xié lǎo	to be together for a hundred years	1.3
搬	bān	to move	3.3
板着脸	bǎnzhe liǎn	to have a stern expression	10.6
办公楼	bàngōnglóu	office block	2.3, 14.1
办事处	bànshìchù	office; branch	5.1
伴随	bànsuí	to accompany	10.6
包装形式	bāozhuāng xíngshì	packaging format	15.2
保护	bǎohù	to protect	9.3
保留 . . . 的权利	bǎoliú . . . de quánlì	to reserve the right to . . .	15.4
保重	bǎozhòng	take care of yourself	1.4
宝马汽车	bǎo mǎ qìchē	BMW (car)	11.6
饱受战争磨难	bǎoshòu zhànzhēng mónàn	to suffer a great deal from the hardship of the war	8.1
报答	bàodá	to repay	11.1

报到	bàodào	to register	5.4
报价	bào jià	to quote a price	15.3
报名费	bàomíng fèi	registration fee	5.4
报社	bàoshè	newspaper (as an organisation)	2.2
暴风骤雨	bàofēng zhòuyǔ	a violent storm	14.5
暴雨	bàoyǔ	torrential rain	14.5
抱歉	bàoqiàn	to apologise; apologies	2.5, 3.3, 10.8
抱歉地	bàoqiànde	apologetically	6.1
抱头痛哭	bàotóu tòngkū	to cry on each other's shoulders	11.3
悲观	bēiguān	pessimistic	12.2
悲伤	bēishāng	sadness; sad; sorrowful	10.3, 10.8, 11.3
悲痛	bēitòng	grief; painfully sad	1.4, 11.3
北岛公园	Běidǎo Gōngyuán	Beidao Park	9.4
奔驰	Bēnchí	Mercedes-Benz	14.2
奔跑	bēnpǎo	to run	8.1
绷着脸	běngzhe liǎn	to look displeased; to pull a long face	10.6
笔	bǐ	(a measure word for a business deal)	11.6
笔试	bǐshì	written exam	5.1
笔挺	bǐtǐng	straight	10.4
笔译	bǐyì	translation	5.1
必有重谢	bì yǒu zhòng xiè	there will be a generous reward	4.3.1
编	biān	to compile	3.4
编辑部	biānjì bù	editorial department	3.2
编目	biānmù	to catalogue	5.1
边远	biānyuǎn	remote	11.1
扁平的鼻子	biǎnpíngde bízi	flat nose	10.4
辩论	biànlùn	to debate; to argue	13.5
表达	biǎodá	to express	9.2
表姐	biǎo jiě	cousin (female and older)	1.3
表里如一	biǎo lǐ rúyī	to be consistent in thought and deed	12.4
表露	biǎolù	to show; to reveal	11.8
表示	biǎoshì	to state	6.2
别具一格	bié jù yì gé	in a unique style	14.3
别墅	biéshù	villa	14.3
彬彬有礼	bīnbīn yǒulǐ	refined and courteous	12.3
波浪式的	bōlàngshìde	wavy	10.1
波士顿	Bōshìdùn	Boston	15.2
勃然大怒	bórán dànù	to fly into a rage	11.6
不道德	bú dàodé	immoral	13.4
不负…期望	bú fù … qīwàng	will not let … down	5.1
不顾	búgù	ignoring	14.5
不慎	búshèn	carelessly	4.3.1
不胜悲痛	búshèng bēitòng	great sorrow	1.4
不幸	búxìng	unfortunately; sadly	1.4

不正确	bú zhèngquè	incorrect	6.2
不管怎么说	bùguǎn zěnmeshuō	no matter what you say	6.2
不仅如此	bù jǐn rú cǐ	in addition	5.2
不及格率	bù jígé lǜ	failure rate	9.4
不予考虑	bù yǔ kǎolǜ	will not be considered	5.1
不知不觉	bù zhī bù jué	without realising	3.4
补充说	bǔchōngshuō	to add	6.2
步伐	bùfá	step; pace	9.2, 13.1
步履蹒跚	bùlǚ pánshān	stumbling along; walking haltingly	13.1
布满了皱纹	bùmǎnle zhòuwén	full of wrinkles	10.6
布置	bùzhì	to assign (homework)	9.3
材料	cáiliào	material	2.2
财政	cáizhèng	fiscal; financial	7.3
彩电	cǎi diàn	colour TV	4.2
采购部	cǎigòu bù	purchasing department	15.3
采用	cǎiyòng	to adopt	9.2
参观	cānguān	to visit	4.1, 9.4
参加	cānjiā	to take part	4.1
参议院	Cānyìyuàn	Senate	8.1
残废	cánfèi	crippled; disabled	11.4
惭愧	cánkuì	(to be) ashamed	11.7
灿烂	cànlàn	bright	14.4
苍白	cāngbái	pale; pallid; wan	10.5
侧	cè	side	14.2
查出	cháchū	to find out	6.2
尝尝	chángchang	to have a taste; to try	9.1
长期驻外	chángqī zhù wài	to work elsewhere on a long-term basis	5.1
长寿	chángshòu	long life	1.1
超过	chāoguò	to surpass; to exceed	8.1
超级市场	chāojí shìchǎng	supermarket	14.2
朝鲜	Cháoxiǎn	(North) Korea	8.1
炒	chǎo	to stir-fry	2.6, 9.1
车祸	chē huò	traffic accident	10.6
车棚	chēpéng	bike-shed	2.3
乘	chéng	to take (e.g. bus, train)	2.6
呈	chéng	to show; to display	9.4
承包责任制	chéngbāo zérèn zhì	contract and responsibility system	9.2
承担	chéngdān	to bear (responsibility)	6.2
承认	chéngrèn	to admit	6.2
城东	chéng dōng	east of the city	3.3
城南	chéng nán	south of the city	3.3
惩罚	chéngfá	punishment	6.2
成年人	chéngniánrén	adult	13.4
成千上万	chéng qiān shàng wàn	thousands and thousands	7.3
成员	chéngyuán	member	8.1
诚聘	chéngpìn	to sincerely recruit	5.1
诚实	chéngshí	honest	12.4

痴呆	chīdāi	dull-witted	10.3
迟钝	chídùn	slow	10.3
持平	chípíng	to be level; to be flat	9.4
尺寸	chǐcùn	size	15.3
宠爱	chǒng'ài	to dote on	
厨房	chúfáng	kitchen	2.6
出口创汇额	chūkǒu chuànghuì 'é	export earnings	
处理	chǔlǐ	to see to; to deal with	2.1
矗立	chùlì	to stand tall and upright	14.2
创汇大户	chuànghuì dàhù	companies and factories which earn large amounts of foreign currency	6.2
纯毛	chún máo	pure wool	15.2
唇无血色	chún wú xuěsè	pallid lips	10.5
磁带	cídài	tape	2.4
磁盘	cípán	disk	4.3.1
辞谢	cíxiè	to decline with regret	3.3
辞职	cízhí	to resign; to quit	9.2
此据	cǐ jù	hereby confirm	4.3.2
此外	cǐwài	furthermore; in addition	5.2
此致 敬礼	cǐ zhì jìnglì	with best wishes	5.1
葱	cōng	spring onion	2.6
葱丝	cōngsī	sliced spring onion	9.1
从容	cóngróng	calm	13.1
从事	cóngshì	to do; to engage in . . .	5.1
粗壮	cūzhuàng	sturdy; strong	10.7
醋	cù	vinegar	9.1
错过	cuòguò	to miss	3.3
打呵欠	dǎ hāqian	to yawn	13.4
打量	dǎliang	to look at . . . up and down; to size up	13.3
打碎	dǎsuì	to break into pieces	6.1
打碎的	dǎsuìde	beat-up; beaten	2.6
打招呼	dǎ zhāohu	to greet	9.2
打字	dǎzì	typing	5.2
大不列颠号货轮	Dàbùlièdiānhào huòlún	the cargo ship *Great Britain*	15.5
大发雷霆	dàfā léitíng	to be furious; explode with fury	11.6
大方	dàfang	generous	12.2
大家	dàjiā	everyone	4.1
大街	dàjiē	avenue	3.2
大惊失色	dàjīng shīsè	to turn pale with fright	11.5
大力扶持	dàlì fúchí	to provide ample support	6.2
大礼堂	dàlǐtáng	assembly hall	4.1
大厦	dàshà	large building; sky scraper; tower	14.2
大使馆	dàshǐguǎn	embassy	3.3
大寿	dà shòu	birthday (for older people)	1.1
大喜	dàxǐ	happy event	1.3
大院	dàyuàn	compound	2.6

178

大跃进	dàyuèjìn	Great Leap Forward	7.3
代办	dàibàn	to do (something for somebody)	9.4
代我	dài wǒ	on my behalf; for me	3.3
带上	dàishang	to bring with	3.3
单位	dānwèi	work unit	2.1
单眼皮	dān yǎnpí	single eyelid	10.3
耽误	dānwu	to delay; to take up (time)	2.5
担心	dānxīn	to be worried; be concerned	2.2
胆小怕事	dǎnxiǎopàshì	timid	12.3
党纪国法	dǎng jì guó fǎ	Party discipline and national law	6.2
档次	dàngcì	grade	2.3
倒	dào	to pour	9.1
倒映	dàoyìng	to reflect, in retrospect	14.4
道	dào	(a measure word for wrinkles)	10.6
道德	dàodé	morality; moral	7.2
到岸价	dào'ànjià	CIF; Cost, Insurance and Freight	15.2
到时(候)	dào shí(hou)	when the time comes	2.1
稻子	dàozi	rice; paddy	8.2
得知	dézhī	to know	5.1
登记	dēngjì	to list; to register	5.1
的确	díquè	indeed	6.2
抵达	dǐdá	to arrive	15.5
第四册	dìsì cè	the 4th volume	2.1
地下电缆	dìxià diànlǎn	underground electric cable	8.2
地形	dìxíng	topography; terrain	13.3
典雅美观	diǎnyǎ měiguān	elegant and attractive	14.3
电脑	diànnǎo	computer	6.1
电器	diànqì	electrical appliances	4.2
电源	diànyuán	power	2.6
电子邮件	diànzǐ yóujiàn	e-mail	5.3
惦念	diànniàn	to keep thinking of; to worry about	11.8
调动	diàodòng	to boost; to arouse	9.2
盯	dīng	to gaze at	13.3
顶着	dǐngzhe	heading into	14.5
订单	dìngdān	order (for goods)	15.1
订购	dìnggòu	to place an order (for something)	15.4
订货	dìng huò	to place an order	15.1
定单	dìngdān	order	6.2
定勤勉	dìng qíngmiǎn	will definitely work hard	5.1
丢失	diūshī	to lose	4.3.1
丢失者	diūshī zhě	the person who has lost it	4.3.1
东倒西歪	dōng dǎo xī wāi	staggering along	13.1
栋	dòng	block	3.2
动用	dòngyòng	to use	7.1
兜	dōu	pocket	4.3.1

逗人喜爱	dòu rén xǐ'ài	amusing; lovable	10.4
独特	dútè	unique	3.4
端详	duānxiáng	to look (someone) up and down; to scrutinze	13.3
短期	duǎn qī	short term	5.1
短训班	duǎnxùn bān	short training course	5.3
断言	duànyán	to state with certainty	6.2
对比	duìbǐ	contrast	14.3
对外汉语教学	duìwài hànyǔ jiàoxué	teaching Chinese as a foreign language	5.3
多愁善感	duō chóu shàn gǎn	gloomy and over-emotional	12.2
多寿多福	duō shòu duō fú	long life and good fortune	1.1
哆嗦	duōsuo	to tremble	11.5
鹅毛大雪	émáo dàxuě	heavy snow in big flakes	14.5
贰	èr	two	4.3.2
发财	fā cái	to get rich; to make a fortune	8.2
发动	fādòng	to launch	8.1
发黄	fā huáng	to become yellow	10.5
发货	fā huò	to dispatch goods	15.3
发言人	fāyánrén	spokesperson	6.2
发紫	fā zǐ	to turn blue	10.5
乏味	fá wèi	dull; uninteresting	12.1
法官	fǎguān	judge	6.2
法律	fǎlǜ	law	6.2
法庭	fǎtíng	court	6.2, 13.4
法西斯	fǎxīsī	fascist	8.1
法治	fǎ zhì	to rule by law	7.3
翻弄	fānnòng	to stir	9.1
翻译	fānyì	translator; to translate	5.1
繁华	fánhuá	busy; bustling	14.2
繁荣景象	fánróng jǐngxiàng	scene of prosperity; prosperity	7.3
烦闷	fánmèn	unhappy; worried	11.4
烦恼	fánnǎo	vexed; worried	11.4
反驳说	fǎnbóshuō	to reject	6.2
反攻	fǎngōng	counter-attack	8.1
犯	fàn	to make (mistake)	7.3
犯罪率	fànzuì lǜ	crime rate	7.1
仿佛	fǎngfú	to seem; as if	8.2
仿效	fǎngxiào	to emulate; to imitate	9.2
放鞭炮	fàng biānpào	to set off firecrackers	9.1
放声大哭	fàngshēng dàkū	to cry loudly	11.3
放肆	fàngsì	unrestrained; reckless	12.3
放映	fàngyìng	to show (a film)	4.3.3
非	fēi	non	4.1
非法	fēifǎ	illegal	6.2
肺	fèi	chest; lung	11.6
飞奔	fēibēn	to dash	8.2
翡翠	fěicuì	jadeite	8.2
吩咐	fēnfu	to tell; to instruct	13.4

分类	fēnlèi	to classify; to sort out	5.1
愤怒	fènnù	indignant	11.6
丰富	fēngfù	to enrich	4.1
丰富多彩	fēngfù duōcǎi	splendid	1.1
丰满	fēngmǎn	robust; bulky	10.7
丰收	fēngshōu	rich harvest	11.2
风景	fēngjǐng	scenery	3.3
风趣	fēngqù	witty	12.1
风雨无阻	fēng yǔ wú zǔ	rain or shine	3.3, 11.1
奉陪	fèngpéi	to accompany	3.3
否认	fǒurèn	to deny	6.2
夫妻恩爱	fūqī ēn'ài	loving couple	1.3
福如东海	fú rú dōng hǎi	happiness as great as the eastern sea	1.1
浮现	fúxiàn	to appear before one's eyes; to materialize	13.3
腐败	fǔbài	corruption	7.1
附	fù	attached; enclosed	4.3.3
附上	fùshang	attached are/as . . .	5.4
富贵年年	fù guì nián nián	to be prosperous year after year	1.2
富丽堂皇	fùlì tánghuáng	sumptuous; gorgeous; splendid	14.3
负责人	fùzérén	the person in charge	5.3
副作用	fù zuòyòng	side effects	6.2, 7.1
改革	gǎigé	reform	9.2
改革开放	gǎigé kāifàng	reform and opening up	7.1
改善	gǎishàn	to improve	7.2
盖	gài	to build	9.2
尴尬	gāngà	embarrassed; awkward	12.3
赶	gǎn	to try to finish	6.1
赶不回来	gǎn bu huílai	can't come back in time	2.2
刚毅	gāngyì	fortitude; steadfast; resolute	10.6
港	gǎng	port	15.4
高档	gāodàng	high-quality; superior quality	8.2, 15.2
高寿	gāoshòu	long life	1.1
高效率	gāoxiàolǜ	high efficiency	7.2
告诫说	gàojièshuō	to warn	6.2
歌迷	gēmí	fan of a singer/singers	11.8
隔三天	gé sān tiān	every three days	2.3
个体经营	gètǐ jīngyíng	individual business; private business	9.2
个性	gèxìng	character	10.1
给 . . . 带来 . . .	gěi . . . dàilái . . .	to bring . . .	1.1
给以	gěiyǐ	to give	5.4
跟 . . . 似的	gēn . . . shìde	to be just like . . .	8.2
根子	gēnzi	root	7.1
公关	gōngguān	public relations	5.1
公款	gōng kuǎn	public funds	7.1, 13.5
公文箱	gōngwénxiāng	business briefcase	15.5
公寓	gōngyù	apartment	14.3

恭贺新禧	**gōnghè xīn xǐ**	New Year congratulations	1.2
恭喜发财	**gōngxǐ fācái**	Congratulations and wishing you prosperity	1.2
工会	**gōnghuì**	trade union	4.1
工艺品	**gōngyìpǐn**	handicraft	15.2
工作报告	**gōngzuò bàogào**	working report	7.3
供货	**gōng huò**	to supply goods	15.3
供销部	**gōngxiāo bù**	supply and sales department	15.2
功绩	**gōngjì**	achievement; contribution	7.3
共同努力	**gòngtóng nǔlì**	joint efforts	6.2
贡献	**gòngxiàn**	contribution	5.2
狗	**gǒu**	dog	1.2
购买力	**gòumǎilì**	purchasing power	9.3
购物中心	**gòuwù zhōngxīn**	shopping centre	9.2
孤独	**gūdú**	loneliness; lonely	10.3
孤峰岭	**Gūfēng Lǐng**	Gufeng Mountain	3.3
估计	**gūjì**	to estimate	2.1
孤僻	**gūpì**	unsociable and eccentric	12.1
股票市场	**gǔpiào shìchǎng**	stock market	9.2
古色古香	**gǔsègǔxiāng**	with a style of antiquity	14.3
故意	**gùyì**	intentionally; deliberately	6.2
雇佣	**gùyōng**	to employ	6.2
雇主	**gùzhǔ**	employer	6.2
瓜子脸	**guāzǐ liǎn**	oval face	10.6
挂号信	**guàhào xìn**	registered letter	5.4
挂念	**guàniàn**	to miss; to worry about	11.8
拐角	**guǎijiǎo**	corner	14.2
观察	**guānchá**	to observe; to watch	13.3
观望	**guānwàng**	to look on from the sidelines; to wait and see	13.3
官僚作风	**guānliáo zuòfēng**	bureaucratic way of working	13.4
关系网	**guānxì wǎng**	network	9.3
馆长	**guǎnzhǎng**	head of the library	5.1
管理	**guǎnlǐ**	management	6.2
冠军	**guànjūn**	champion	13.2
光洁	**guāngjié**	shiny and neat	10.1
光明正大	**guāngmíng zhèngdà**	open and above board; just and honourable	12.4
广大	**guǎngdà**	all members of . . .	4.1
规范作用	**guīfàn zuòyòng**	regulating function	8.2
规格	**guīgé**	specifications	15.2
归为己有	**guī wéi jǐ yǒu**	to take as one's own	8.1
贵	**guì**	your (polite form)	5.1
锅	**guō**	pan; wok	9.1
国会	**Guóhuì**	Congress	8.1
国家六合彩抽奖	**guójiā liùhécǎi chōu jiǎng**	national lottery draw	11.2
国家元首	**guójiā yuánshǒu**	head of state	8.1
国内外	**guónèiwài**	at home and abroad	6.2
国庆	**guóqìng**	National Day	3.3

过期	guò qī	to be past the deadline	5.1
海报	hǎibào	announcement (for a film, concert, etc.)	4.1
海滨	hǎibīn	seaside	14.1
海外华人	hǎiwài huárén	overseas Chinese	9.3
函	hán	letter	15.1
寒风	hán fēng	cold wind	14.5
含酒精	hán jiǔjīng	to contain alcohol	9.4
含笑	hánxiào	smiling	10.3
毫无疑问	háowú yíwèn	without doubt	9.3
毫无根据	háo wú gēnjù	without grounds; groundless	6.2
毫无区别	háo wú qūbié	no difference at all	8.1
豪华	háohuá	luxurious, sumptuous	14.3
好比	hǎobǐ	to be just like; can be compared to	8.2
好客	hàokè	hospitable	12.2
好评	hǎopíng	high opinion; favourable comments	5.2
好似	hǎosì	to be like; to seem	8.2
好友	hǎo yǒu	good friend	1.1
号	hào	number	3.2
号召	hàozhào	to call on; summon	7.3, 9.2
喝醉	hēzuì	drunk	6.2
合唱团	héchàngtuán	choir	2.5
合家欢乐	hé jiā huānlè	happy family reunion	1.2
合同	hétong	contract	5.4
合同期	hétong qī	length of contract	5.4
合资企业	hézī qǐyè	joint venture	5.2
合作	hézuò	cooperation	5.1
黑暗	hēi'àn	dark	8.2
很有把握地	hěn yǒu bǎwòde	confidently	6.1
红润	hóngrùn	ruddy; rosy	10.6
红彤彤	hóngtōngtōng	red	14.4
红卫兵	hóngwèibīng	Red Guard	7.3
红一阵白一阵	hóng yízhèn bái yízhèn	to turn red then pale	10.6
红砖	hóng zhuān	red brick	14.3
宏伟	hóngwěi	magnificent; grand	14.2
猴	hóu	monkey	1.2
后悔	hòuhuǐ	to regret	11.7
后悔莫及	hòuhuǐ mò jí	too late to repent	11.7
后者	hòuzhě	the latter	8.1
忽视	hūshì	to neglect; to overlook	7.3
呼啸	hūxiào	to whistle; to whizz	8.2
呼吁	hūyù	to call for; to appeal	6.2
胡同	hútong	lane	2.6
虎	hǔ	tiger	1.2
互联网	húlianwǎng	Internet	
护照	hùzhào	passport	11.2
花白	huābái	grey	10.1
画廊	huàláng	art gallery	4.1

怀念	**huáiniàn**	cherish the memory of	11.8
欢乐	**huānlè**	happiness	1.1
欢声笑语	**huān shēng xiào yǔ**	laughter	1.1
欢迎各位	**huānyíng gè wèi**	all are welcome	4.1
换乘	**huàn chéng**	to change (e.g. bus)	2.6
黄澄澄	**huángdēngdēng**	glistening yellow; golden	8.2
灰白	**huībái**	grey	10.1
灰蒙蒙	**huīméngméng**	grey	14.4
诙谐	**huīxié**	humorous; jocular	12.1
回复	**huífù**	to reply; reply	5.1
回音	**huíyīn**	to reply; response	3.2
惠顾	**huìgù**	your patronage	15.5
悔恨	**huǐhèn**	(to be) bitterly remorseful	11.7
绘画	**huìhuà**	painting; drawing	11.1
贿赂	**huìlù**	bribe	6.2
昏倒	**hūndǎo**	to faint	10.6
婚礼	**hūnlǐ**	wedding	3.3
活力	**huólì**	vitality; vigour; energy	10.7
活泼	**huópo**	lively; vivacious	8.1, 12.1
活跃	**huóyuè**	to enliven; to liven up	6.2
活字典	**huó zìdiǎn**	walking dictionary	8.2
火车头	**huǒchētóu**	locomotive	8.2
火锅	**huǒguō**	hot pot	2.2
火红	**huǒhóng**	flaming; fiery red	14.4
火辣辣	**huǒlàlà**	scorching	14.4
火冒三丈	**huǒ mào sānzhàng**	to flare up	11.6
获取	**huòqǔ**	to obtain	6.2
获悉	**huòxī**	to have heard	5.1, 15.2
鸡	**jī**	rooster	1.2
鸡蛋	**jīdàn**	egg	2.6
基本待遇	**jīběn dàiyù**	basic terms of employment	5.1
激动不已	**jīdòng bùyǐ**	to be tremendously excited	3.3
几乎	**jīhū**	almost	7.3
机会	**jīhuì**	opportunity	3.3
机灵	**jīling**	clever; intelligent	10.8, 12.4
机智勇敢	**jīzhì yǒnggǎn**	clever and resourceful	12.4
积极性	**jījíxìng**	enthusiasm	9.2
极大的	**jídàde**	enormous; great	7.3
极愿	**jí yuàn**	would very much like	5.1
集合	**jíhé**	to gather; to get together	3.3
即将	**jíjiāng**	soon; to be about to	1.2
急剧	**jíjù**	dramatically	9.4
急购	**jí gòu**	to buy urgently	4.2
急事	**jí shì**	urgent matter	2.1
急租	**jí zū**	accommodation needed urgently	4.2
济南	**Jǐ'nán**	[a city in China]	3.4
给予	**jǐyǔ**	to give	6.2
计划经济	**jìhuà jīngjì**	planned economy	9.2
计划生育	**jìhuà shēngyù**	family planning	7.3
计算机房	**jìsuànjī fáng**	computer room	4.3.1

纪律	jìlǜ	discipline	8.2
记者	jìzhě	reporter	2.2
记者招待会	jìzhě zhāodàihuì	press conference	6.2
夹	jiā	to put in between; insert	9.2
家电	jiādiàn	domestic electric/electronic products	15.1
家教	jiājiào	private tuition	4.2
加速	jiāsù	to speed up	9.2
假冒	jiǎmào	imitations	6.2
价钱	jiàqian	price	2.3
尖鼻子	jiān bízi	pointed nose	10.4
坚持	jiānchí	to adhere to; without fail	7.3, 11.1
坚信	jiānxìn	to believe strongly	7.3
简单易用	jiǎndān yì yòng	simple and easy to use	2.6
简陋	jiǎnlòu	simple and crude; shabby	14.3
简历	jiǎnlì	curriculum vitae	5.1
简直	jiǎnzhí	simply	8.2, 11.1
减慢	jiǎnmàn	to slow down	9.2
减税	jiǎnshuì	tax reduction	9.3
建立	jiànlì	to establish	7.2, 9.2
建设	jiànshè	construction	7.2
建议	jiànyì	to suggest	6.2
建筑物	jiànzhùwù	building	14.3
健美	jiànměi	vigorous and graceful; strong and handsome	10.7
剑桥	Jiànqiáo	Cambridge	14.1
讲解	jiǎngjiě	to explain	13.5
讲授	jiǎngshòu	to lecture	13.5
讲演	jiǎngyǎn	to make a speech	13.5
奖学金	jiǎngxuéjīn	scholarship	5.4
酱油	jiàngyóu	soya sauce	2.6
浇	jiāo	to water	2.3
交	jiāo	to hand in	2.5
交通事故	jiāotōng shìgù	traffic accident	9.4
交往	jiāowǎng	contact	9.2
焦急	jiāojí	anxiety; worry	10.3
狡猾	jiǎohuá	cunning; sly; crafty	12.4
矫健	jiǎojiàn	vigorous	13.1
教练	jiàoliàn	coach; trainer	13.4
教学	jiàoxué	teaching	7.2
教学楼	jiàoxuélóu	block teaching	14.1
教育部	jiàoyùbù	Ministry of Education	13.4
接上	jiēshàng	to connect (power)	2.6
接受	jiēshòu	to accept	3.3
节哀	jié āi	to restrain one's grief	1.4
洁白	jiébái	clean and white	10.5, 14.5
竭诚	jiéchéng	to endeavour to	15.1
结构精巧	jiégòu jīngqiǎo	exquisitely constructed	14.3
结为	jiéwéi	to tie the knot; to become married	1.3
截然相反	jiérán xiāngfǎn	completely the opposite	8.1

解释说	jiěshìshuō	to explain	6.2
介绍	jièshào	to introduce	6.2
借条	jiètiáo	receipt	4.3.2
借物人	jiè wù rén	the borrower of sth.	4.3.2
戒指	jièzhi	ring	13.3
金额	jīn'é	the sum of money	15.5
金黄	jīnhuáng	blond; golden	10.1
金子	jīnzi	gold	8.2
津津有味	jīnjīnyǒuwèi	with great interest	13.4
紧接着	jǐnjiēzhe	straight after that	2.6
仅仅	jǐnjǐn	only	7.2
谨小慎微	jǐnxiǎoshènwēi	overcautious	12.3
进口额	jìnkǒu'é	imports; import volume	9.4
进修班	jìnxiū bān	refresher course	5.4
近况	jìn kuàng	recent situation	3.1
近视眼	jìnshìyǎn	short-sighted	10.3
近照	jìn zhào	recent photograph	5.1
尽早	jìn zǎo	as early as possible	3.2
精彩	jīngcǎi	brilliant; wonderful; splendid	13.3
精明强干	jīngmíng qiánggàn	intelligent and capable	12.4
精神文明	jīngshén wénmíng	spiritual civilization	7.2
精通	jīngtōng	be an expert on; be good at	5.1, 7.3
惊慌	jīnghuāng	panic-stricken	11.5
惊恐	jīngkǒng	terrified and panic-stricken	11.5
惊恐万状	jīngkǒng wànzhuàng	to be in a total panic	11.5
惊喜	jīngxǐ	pleasant surprise	1.1
惊喜万分	jīngxǐ wànfēn	to be pleasantly surprised	11.2
惊悉	jīng xī	to be shocked to hear	1.4
经济萧条	jīngjì xiāotiáo	economic recession	9.3
经济效益	jīngjì xiàoyì	economic efficiency	6.2
经济形势	jīngjì xíngshì	economic situation	7.3
经济学	jīngjìxué	economics	2.4
经销商	jīngxiāoshāng	distributor	15.2
经营	jīngyíng	to manage; to run; to trade in	15.1
警告说	jǐnggàoshuō	to warn	6.2
景色	jǐngsè	scenery	3.4
敬酒	jìngjiǔ	to offer a toast	9.1
敬上	jìngshàng	sincerely	1.1
玖	jiǔ	nine	4.3.2
拘谨	jūjǐn	cautious; reserved	12.3
沮丧地	jǔsàngde	depressed; dejectedly	6.1, 11.4
举办	jǔbàn	to hold (an event)	4.1, 9.4
举行	jǔxíng	to hold	3.3
飓风	jùfēng	hurricane	14.5
聚会	jùhuì	get-together; party	3.3
俱佳	jù jiā	to be good at both	5.1
拒收	jù shōu	to refuse to accept	15.4
具体地	jùtǐ de	specifically	7.2
捐款	juānkuǎn	donation (of money)	4.3.2
绝对	juéduì	absolutely	9.2

均	jūn	both; all	6.2, 15.4
俊俏	jùnqiào	pretty; charming	10.4
俊秀	jùnxiù	pretty; of delicate beauty	10.6
开除	kāichú	to expel; to fire; to dismiss	11.6, 13.4
开发	kāifā	development	5.1
开朗	kāilǎng	open and clear; cheerful	8.1, 12.2
开设	kāishè	to open	9.4
开心地	kāixīnde	happily	11.2
刊登	kāndēng	to print; to carry (in a newspaper or a magazine)	5.1, 15.2
康乐	kāng lè	heathy and happy	3.3
慷慨	kāngkǎi	generous	12.2
伉俪	kànglì	married couple; husband and wife	1.3
靠	kào	to rely on; to depend on	8.2
科学技术	kēxué jìshù	science and technology	7.3
科研基地	kēyán jīdì	scientific research centre	13.3
科长	kēzhǎng	section head	5.1
可靠	kěkào	reliable	12.4
可喜现象	kěxǐ xiànxiàng	gratifying achievements	6.2
渴望	kěwàng	to be eager to; to long for	5.2, 11.8
课程	kèchéng	(academic) course	5.1
客观	kèguān	objective	7.3
客户	kèhù	client	15.1
客人	kèrén	guest	3.3
刻着	kèzhe	be carved; to be engraved (used metaphorically here)	10.6
恳切	kěnqiè	sincerely	5.3
空调	kōngtiáo	air-conditioner	15.1
恐慌	kǒnghuāng	terror-stricken	11.5
恐惧	kǒngjù	frightened	11.5
控制	kòngzhì	control; to control	6.2
控制在 . . . 以内	kòngzhì zài . . . yǐnèi	to control . . . within . . .	6.2
口才	kǒucái	eloquence	5.1
哭泣	kūqì	to cry; to weep	11.3
苦闷	kǔmèn	depressed	11.4
苦恼	kǔnǎo	vexed; worried	11.4
酷爱	kù'ài	to love ardently; to be very fond of	11.1
快递	kuài dì	express delivery; express letter or parcel	2.4
款式新颖	kuǎnshì xīnyǐng	new and original design	15.2
狂风暴雨	kuángfēng bàoyǔ	a violent storm	14.5
魁梧	kuíwǔ	big and strong; powerfully-built	10.7
昆明	Kūnmíng	[a city name]	2.3
拉长了脸	lāchángle liǎn	to pull a long face	10.6
拉出	lāchū	to pull out	2.6
拉链	lāliàn	zipper; zip fastener	8.2
蜡黄	làhuáng	sallow; waxy yellow	10.6

来临	láilín	to arrive	1.2
朗诵	lǎngsòng	to recite (poetry); to give a reading	11.8
浪费	làngfèi	waste	12.2
浪漫色彩	làngmàn sècǎi	romantic colour	1.1
老虎	lǎohǔ	tiger	8.2
老老实实	lǎolǎo shíshí	honestly; conscientiously; in earnest	12.4
老舍	Lǎo Shě	[name of a well-known Chinese writer]	11.1
乐观	lèguān	optimistic	12.2
乐开了花	lèkāile huā	to be filled with joy	11.2
乐享余年	lè xiǎng yú nián	to enjoy the rest of your life	1.1
泪如泉涌	lèi rú quán yǒng	tears well up like water from a well	11.3
泪水夺眶而出	lèishuǐ duókuàng ér chū	tears well from one's eyes	11.3
类似	lèisì	similar	8.1
冷冰冰的	lěngbīngbīng de	cold and unfriendly; frigid	10.6
冷淡	lěngdàn	cold; indifferent	12.2
冷酷	lěngkù	unfeeling; callous	10.3
离岸价	lí'ànjià	FOB; Free On Board	15.2
理想	lǐxiǎng	ideal	8.2
利大于弊	lì dà yú bì	advantages outnumber disadvantages	9.3
利物浦	Lìwùpǔ	Liverpool	15.3
利用	lìyòng	to take advantage of	4.2
历史悠久	lìshǐ yōujiǔ	with a long history	14.3
连鬓胡	liánbìnhú	whiskers; side-burns	10.2
连锁店	liánsuǒdiàn	chain store	15.2
联欢会	liánhuānhuì	party	4.1
联系	liánxì	to get in touch; to contact	2.3, 5.4
廉洁奉公	liánjié fènggōng	fulfil duties honestly	6.2
脸红脖子粗	liǎn hóng bózi cū	one's face becomes red	11.6
脸色铁青	liǎnsè tiěqīng	the face turns livid/angry	10.6
良药	liángyào	good medicine; effective remedy	6.2
两眼冒金星	liǎng yǎn mào jīnxīng	to see red	11.6
两者	liǎngzhě	both	8.1
亮晶晶	liàngjīngjīng	glistening; shiny	10.3, 14.4
聊天	liáotiān	to chat	14.2
吝啬	lìnsè	stingy; mean; miserly	12.2
聆听	língtīng	to listen attentively to	13.4
另	lìng	p.s.	3.1
领导干部	lǐngdǎo gànbù	leading cadre	
溜达	liūda	to stroll	13.1
流传	liúchuán	(the rumour) says; to spread	6.2
流行歌手	liúxíng gēshǒu	pop singer	11.8
留着	liúzhe	to be growing; to have (a beard)	10.2
陆	liù	six	4.3.2

龙	lóng	dragon	1.2
龙凤齐飞	lóng fèng qí fēi	dragon and phoenix fly together	1.3
龙年	lóng nián	Year of the Dragon	1.2
楼	lóu	building	3.2
炉子	lúzi	cooker	2.1, 9.1
鲁迅	Lǔ Xùn	[name of a Chinese writer]	5.4
路	lù	road	3.2
露出	lùchū	to reveal	10.5
录取通知书	lùqǔ tōngzhīshū	admission letter	11.2
录下来	lùxialai	to record it	2.4
录音机	lùyīnjī	recorder	2.4
旅途	lǚtú	journey	10.8
略微	lüèwēi	slightly; a little	10.5
伦敦	Lúndūn	London	14.1, 15.2
论文	lùnwén	thesis; dissertation	6.1
落	luò	to fall; to drop	8.2
络腮胡	luòsāihú	full beard	10.2
麻烦	máfan	to bother; to cause trouble	2.4
马	mǎ	horse	1.2
埋怨	mányuàn	to complain	6.1
满不在乎地	mǎn bú zàihude	nonchalantly	6.1
满脸不高兴地	mǎn liǎn bù gāoxìngde	unhappily	6.1
满脸愁云	mǎn liǎn chóuyún	to look extremely worried	10.6
满脸羞愧	mǎn liǎn xiūkuì	to look ashamed	10.6
满面春风	mǎn miàn chūnfēng	beaming with satisfaction; radiant with happiness	10.6
满脸疑惑	mǎnliǎn yíhuò	to look unconvinced; to look to have doubts	10.6
满天飞舞	mǎntiān fēiwǔ	to dance in the sky	14.5
满天飞扬	mǎntiān fēiyáng	to fill the sky	14.5
满足和暇逸	mǎnzú hé xiáyì	comfort and contentment	1.1
漫步	mànbù	to stroll; to ramble; to roam	14.4
毛毛雨	máomáoyǔ	drizzle	14.5
冒昧	màomèi	to take the liberty; to be bold enough	5.2, 15.1
冒着	màozhe	braving	14.5
眉飞色舞	méifēi sèwǔ	enraptured with dancing eyebrows and radiant face; to be pleased with oneself	10.6
眉开眼笑	méikāi yǎnxiào	to beam with joy; to be all smiles	10.6
眉目	méimù	sign of a positive outcome (*lit.* eyebrow and eye)	3.4
眉清目秀	méiqīng mùxiù	to have delicate features	10.6
没精神	méi jīngshen	to have no energy	9.3
美术馆	Měishù Guǎn	Art Gallery	2.6
魅力	mèilì	charm	10.1
闷闷不乐	mènmèn bú lè	depressed	11.4
朦胧	ménglóng	dim; hazy	14.4

蒙受	méngshòu	to suffer; to sustain	8.1
猛	měng	fierce; vigorous	8.2
猛烈	měngliè	vigorous; fierce	8.1
梦	mèng	dream	8.2
迷路	mí lù	to get lost; to lose one's way	14.2
迷人	mírén	enchanting; charming; fascinating	10.5, 14.4
秘密	mìmì	secret	13.4
秘书	mìshū	secretary	5.2
苗条	miáotiao	slender; slim	10.7
免费	miǎnfèi	free of charge	4.1, 5.1
免税	miǎnshuì	tax exemption; tax-free	9.3
腼腆	miǎntiǎn	shy; bashful	12.3
面不改色	miàn bù gǎi sè	to remain calm; not to change colour	10.6
面红耳赤	miàn hóng ěr chì	to be red in the face; to flush with embarrassment	10.6
面黄肌瘦	miàn huáng jī shòu	sallow and emaciated; thin and haggard	10.6
面孔	miànkǒng	face	11.5
面临	miànlín	to be faced with	7.3, 8.2 9.3
面临着	miànlínzhe	to be faced with	6.2
面试	miànshì	interview	5.1, 13.3
妙趣横生	miàoqù héngshēng	full of wit and humour	12.1
妙语连珠	miàoyǔ liánzhū	one witty remark after another	12.1
庙宇	miàoyǔ	temple	14.3
民主	mínzhǔ	democratic	8.1
民族	mínzú	nation	8.2
敏锐	mǐnruì	sharp	10.3
名列前茅	míng liè qiánmáo	to be among the best	5.2
名画展	mínghuà zhǎn	famous painting exhibition	4.1
明亮	míngliàng	bright	14.4
明媚	míngmèi	bright and beautiful	14.4
明清史	Míng Qīng shǐ	history of Ming and Qing Dynasties	2.5
明显	míngxiǎn	obvious; clear	9.4
明喻	míngyù	simile	8.2
抹掉	mǒdiào	to erase	7.3
默默地	mòmòde	quietly; silently	11.3
默许	mòxǔ	consent	9.2
陌生	mòshēng	strange; unfamiliar	10.6
母语	mǔyǔ	mother tongue	5.1
目录	mùlù	catalogue	15.1
拿 ... 工资	ná ... gōngzī	to be paid	5.2
南岭植物园	Nánlǐng Zhíwùyuán	Nanling Botanic Garden	9.4
难舍难分	nán shě nán fēn	to be loath to part from each other	11.1
恼火	nǎohuǒ	annoyed	11.6

闹洞房	nào dòngfáng	to hold house-warming activities in the bridal chamber	9.1
内疚	nèijiù	to feel guilty	11.7
内向	nèixiàng	introverted	8.1, 12.3
能力	nénglì	to feel ability	5.1
能文能武	néng wén néng wǔ	to be both cultured and brave; to be able to wield both the pen and the gun	
拟	nǐ	to intend; to plan	5.1
年年有余	niánnián yǒu yú	to have an abundance every year	1.2
年薪	niánxīn	annual salary	5.1
凝视	níngshì	to stare at	
牛	niú	ox	1.2
牛津	Niújīn	Oxford	14.1
纽约	Niǔyuē	New York	15.4
浓密	nóngmì	thick; dense	10.6
浓眉大眼	nóngméi dàyǎn	heavy eyebrows and big eyes; heavy features	10.3
农田	nóngtián	farmland	9.2
奴隶	núlì	slave	8.1
女车	nǚ chē	woman's bike	4.2
女王	nǚwáng	queen	8.1
欧洲	Ōuzhōu	Europe	8.1
牌	pái	brand (of product)	6.2
徘徊	páihuái	to pace up and down	13.1
排练	páiliàn	rehearsal	2.5
盼望	pànwàng	to look forward to	11.8, 14.4
旁观	pángguān	to view as an onlooker	13.3
旁听	pángtīng	to listen as a visitor (at a meeting or in a school class)	13.4
赔偿	péicháng	compensation	15.4
蓬勃朝气	péngbó zhāoqì	youthful and rigorous	10.7
蓬乱	péngluàn	dishevelled	10.1
披肩长发	pījiān cháng fà	shoulder-length hair	10.1
披头散发	pītóu sǎnfà	with dishevelled hair; with hair in disarray	10.1
皮肤	pífū	skin	10.6
皮革	pígé	leather	15.4
飘	piāo	to float	14.4
瓢泼大雨	piáopō dàyǔ	to bucket down with rain	14.4
贫富不均	pín fù bù jūn	gap between the rich and the poor	7.1
聘为	pìnwéi	to be employed as	5.4
聘用	pìnyòng	to employ	5.4
平易近人	píngyìjìnrén	amiable and approachable	12.3
迫害	pòhài	to purge; a purge	7.3
破坏	pòhuài	damage; destruction	7.3
迫切	pòqiè	eager; urgent	5.3
铺	pū	to pave; to surface	8.2

柒	qī	seven	4.3.2
期待	qīdài	to look forward to; to expect	5.1, 8.2, 11.8, 15.3
期间	qījiān	period	7.3, 9.4
欺骗	qīpiàn	to deceive; to cheat	12.4
期望	qīwàng	to hope; to expect	11.8
旗	qí	flag; banner	8.2
齐耳	qí'ěr	trimmed to the ears	10.1
泣不成声	qì bù chéngshēng	to choke with sobs	11.3
气喘吁吁	qìchuǎn xūxū	to pant hard	13.2
气氛	qìfēn	atmosphere	6.2
气愤	qìfèn	furious	11.6
谦虚谨慎	qiānxū jǐnshèn	modest and prudent	12.3
前来观看	qiánlái guānkàn	to come and watch	4.1
前苏联	qián Sūlián	the former Soviet Union	8.1
前途	qiántú	future; prospect	11.4
前者	qiánzhě	the former	8.1
潜在	qiánzài	potential	9.3
谴责说	qiǎnzéshuō	to denounce	6.2
墙	qiáng	wall	2.3
强调指出	qiángdiào zhǐchū	to emphasise	6.2
强奸	qiángjiān	to rape	8.1
悄悄地	qiāoqiāode	quietly	13.5
憔悴	qiáocuì	wan and sallow; thin and pallid	10.6
切碎的	qiēsuìde	chopped-up	2.6
窃听	qiètīng	to eavesdrop; to bug	13.4
侵略者	qīnlüèzhě	invader	8.1
侵占	qīnzhàn	to invade and occupy	8.1
清晨	qīngchén	early morning	11.1
清瘦	qīngshòu	thin; lean	10.6
清秀	qīngxiù	delicate and pretty	10.6
青岛	Qīngdǎo	Qingdao; Tsingdao (a coastal city in China)	14.1
倾盆大雨	qīngpén dàyǔ	heavy downpour	14.5
倾听	qīngtīng	to listen attentively to	13.4
晴空万里	qíng kōng wànlǐ	it is a clear and boundless sky	14.4
晴朗	qínglǎng	sunny	14.4
情深似海	qíng shēn sì hǎi	to love . . . as deeply as the ocean	11.1
情意绵绵	qíngyì miánmián	endless affection	11.1
请查收	qǐng cháshōu	please find . . .	5.1
请假条	qǐngjià tiáo	written request for leave	4.3.3
请批准	qǐng pīzhǔn	please grant me leave	4.3.3
庆祝	qìngzhù	to celebrate	3.3
球讯	qiúxùn	announcement (for football, and other ball games)	4.1
求租	qiúzū	seeking accommodation	4.2
趋势	qūshì	trend; tendency	9.4
娶	qǔ	to marry (a woman); to take a wife	3.3, 11.8

鬈曲	quánqū	curly	10.1
劝	quàn	to urge; to try to persuade	9.2
缺	quē	to be missing; to lack	2.1
缺乏	quēfá	to lack; to be short of	12.2
缺少	quēshǎo	to lack; to be short of	12.1
确定	quèdìng	to determine; to decide on	7.3
确认	quèrèn	to confirm	2.3
然而	rán'ér	however; but	8.1
燃烧	ránshāo	to burn	8.2
热爱	rè'ài	to love	5.1
热血沸腾	rèxuè fèiténg	extremely excited (*lit.* hot blood boiling)	9.2
人情	rén qíng	human relationship	9.3
人权	rén quán	human rights	7.3
人治	rén zhì	to rule by people	7.3
人事科	rénshìkē	personnel department	5.1
仍然	réngrán	still	2.1
忍不住	rěnbúzhù	cannot help (doing something)	10.6
忍痛割爱	rěn tòng gē ài	to part with what one treasures	11.1
认领	rènlǐng	to claim	4.3.1
认为	rènwéi	to think	6.2
认准	rènzhǔn	to double-check	6.2
任务	rènwù	task	7.3
日出	rìchū	sunrise	3.4
日趋	rìqū	day by day	9.2
容光焕发	róngguāng huànfà	face glows with health	10.6
荣幸	róngxìng	pleasure; honour	3.3
柔和	róuhé	soft	14.4
如蒙录用	rú méng lùyòng	if (I am) employed	5.1
如同	rútóng	like; as	8.2
入学申请表	rù xué shēnqǐng biǎo	application form for entering educational establishment	5.3
若	ruò	if	15.1
若干	ruògān	a certain amount; a certain number	4.3.1
撒腿就跑	sātuǐ jiù pǎo	to run off at once; to flee	13.2
叁	sān	three	4.3.2
三七开	sān qī kāi	to divide into 30% and 70%	7.3
杀害	shāhài	to kill	8.1
杀死	shāsǐ	to kill	6.2
山水画	shānshuǐhuà	landscape painting	14.2
山羊胡	shānyánghú	goatee	10.2
闪光	shǎnguāng	sparkling; glittering	14.4
闪闪发光	shǎnshǎn fā guāng	sparkling; glittering	14.4
善良	shànliáng	kind-hearted; kind	9.2
商定	shāngdìng	to negotiate	4.2
商业区	shāngyè qū	commercial district	9.2
赏月	shǎng yuè	to enjoy looking at the moon	14.4
上不成	shàng bu chéng	cannot attend	2.4
上级	shàngjí	higher authorities	13.4
上面列有	shàngman liè yǒu	listed in . . . are	5.2

上气不接下气	shàngqì bù jiē xiàqì	to become out of breath	13.2
上升	shàngshēng	to increase	9.4
上司	shàngsi	boss; superior	12.2
上旬	shàngxún	the first half (of a month)	5.1
上议院	Shàngyìyuàn	House of Lords	8.1
上涨	shàngzhǎng	to rise; a rise	9.2
烧杀掠夺	shāo shā lüèduó	to burn, to kill and to rob	8.1
烧热	shāorè	to heat up	2.6, 9.1
少了	shǎo le	to be short of; to be missing	3.3
少数民族	shǎoshù mínzú	ethnic minority; minority nationality	7.3
少许	shǎoxǔ	a little	2.6
蛇(小龙)	shé (xiǎo lóng)	snake (small dragon)	1.2
设备	shèbèi	equipment	15.1
摄氏度	shèshìdù	degree centigrade; Celsius	8.1
社长	shèzhǎng	head of a publishing firm	5.1
社会活动	shèhuì huódòng	social activities	5.2
深表同情	shēn biǎo tóngqíng	to express deepest sympathy	1.4
深感荣幸	shēn gǎn róngxìng	to feel deeply honoured	15.1
深感惋惜	shēn gǎn wǎnxī	to feel the loss keenly	1.4
深切哀悼	shēnqiè āidào	heartfelt condolences	1.4
深圳	Shēnzhèn	[name of a city in China]	9.2
申请	shēnqǐng	to apply	5.1
申请费	shēnqǐng fèi	application fee	5.4
身材	shēncái	stature; physique	6.2
身体健康	shēntǐ jiànkāng	good health	1.1
神采奕奕	shéncǎi yìyì	glowing with health	10.6
声称	shēngchēng	to claim	6.2
生活甜蜜	shēnghuó tiánmì	sweet life	1.3
生意	shēngyi	business; deal	11.6
胜任	shèngrèn	be competent	to 5.1
失物	shī wù	lost item	4.3.1
失恋	shīliàn	to be disappointed in love; be broken-hearted	11.4
失眠	shīmián	to be unable to sleep	9.3
失去	shīqù	to lose	6.2
失声痛哭	shīshēng tòngkū	to burst out crying loudly	11.3
失望	shīwàng	disappointment	10.3
失望地	shīwàngde	disappointedly	6.1
师生员工	shīshēng yuángōng	students and staff	4.1
湿透	shītòu	wet through; to get soaked	8.2, 14.5
诗意	shīyì	poetic flavour	1.1
拾	shí	ten	4.3.2
拾到	shídào	to have found; to have picked up	4.3.1
识别	shíbié	to distinguish; to detect; to recognise	12.4
实行	shíxíng	to implement	9.2
实验室	shíyànshì	laboratory	14.1
实业有限公司	shíyè yǒuxiàn gōngsī	industrial (or commercial) company/limited	15.2

实在	shízài	indeed	2.5
时装	shízhuāng	fashionable clothes; fashions	8.2
市	shì	city	3.2
市民监督	shìmín jiāndū	supervision by citizens	6.2
室	shì	flat	3.2
视察	shìchá	to inspect	9.2, 13.3
视为	shìwéi	to treat as; to regard as	8.1
市场	shìchǎng	marketing; market	5.1
市场经济	shìchǎng jīngjì	market economy	9.2
是否	shìfǒu	if; whether	6.1
世界	shìjiè	world	4.1
逝世	shìshì	to pass away	1.4, 11.3
试探的	shìtànde	probing	10.3
事项	shìxiàng	particulars; relevant items	5.4
事业	shìyè	career	6.2, 8.2
收获	shōuhuò	gain; benefit	
收款人	shōukuǎnrén	recipient of cash	4.3.2
受贿	shòuhuì	to accept bribes	6.2
刷地一下白了	shuāde yíxià báile	to suddenly turn pale	10.6
耍贫嘴	shuǎ pínzuǐ	to be garrulous	12.1
帅	shuài	handsome	13.3
双眼皮	shuāng yǎnpí	double eyelids	10.3
水晶	shuǐjīng	crystal	15.3
睡过了头	shuìguòletóu	overslept	6.1
税务	shuìwù	taxation	7.3
说服	shuōfú	to convince	13.5
丝绸	sīchóu	silk	15.2
丝毫	sīháo	the slightest amount/degree	10.7
思念	sīniàn	to miss and long for	11.8
死板	sǐbǎn	inflexible; rigid	12.1
肆	sì	four	4.3.2
四方脸	sìfāng liǎn	square face	10.6
速度	sùdù	speed; pace	8.1
随信寄去	suí xìn jìqu	enclosed are . . .	3.1
随便	suíbiàn	to do as one pleases	2.6
随时	suíshí	at any time; at all times	13.4
随时举报	suíshí jǔbào	to inform at any time	6.2
岁岁平安	suì suì píng'ān	to have peace year after year	1.2
松柏	sōngbǎi	pine and cypress	1.1
耸立	sǒnglì	to tower up	14.2
锁	suǒ	to lock	2.3
所登的	suǒ dēng de	carried; printed (e.g. in newspaper)	5.1
所在公司	suǒ zài gōngsī	the company where one works	5.2
所作所为	suǒ zuò suǒ wéi	behaviour	8.1, 11.7
索取	suǒqǔ	to obtain	5.3
索取	suǒqǔ	to request	15.2
台风	táifēng	typhoon	14.5
泰山	Tài Shān	Mount Taishan; Taishan Mountain	3.4
瘫痪	tānhuàn	to paralyse	7.3

探听	tàntīng	to fish for information; to try to find out	13.4
探望	tànwàng	to visit	13.3
陶醉不已	táozuì bù yǐ	to be completely intoxicated	3.4
腾地一下红了	tēngde yíxià hóngle	to suddenly turn red	10.6
疼爱	téng'ài	to love dearly	11.1
特安排	tè ānpái	to specially arrange	4.1
特此请假	tècǐ qǐngjià	hence ask for leave	4.3.3
特邀请	tè yāoqǐng	to specially invite	4.1
提包	tíbāo	handbag	8.2
提倡	tíchàng	to advocate	7.3
提供	tígōng	to provide	5.4
提高	tígāo	to increase; to improve	6.2, 7.2
提议	tíyì	to propose	6.2
替	tì	on one's behalf; for	2.2
T恤衫	tìxùshān	T-shirt	10.1
添	tiān	to add	2.4
天使	tiānshǐ	angel	8.2
天真活泼	tiānzhēn huópo	vivacious	12.1
天真烂漫	tiānzhēn lànmàn	unaffected	12.1
天真无邪	tiānzhēn wúxié	simple and unaffected	12.1
填好	tiánhǎo	to fill in (forms)	5.4, 8.2
贴	tiē	stick	8.2
铁塔	tiě tǎ	iron tower	10.7
铁轨	tiěguǐ	rail track	8.2
听从	tīngcóng	to listen and obey; to listen and comply with	13.4
听候	tīnghòu	to wait for	13.4
亭亭玉立	tíngtíngyùlì	slim and graceful	10.7
挺直的鼻子	tǐngzhíde bízi	straight nose	10.4
同伴	tóngbàn	companion	3.3
同情	tóngqíng	sympathy	10.3
同期	tóngqī	the same period	9.4
同事	tóngshì	colleague	9.2
通过	tōngguò	to pass	7.3
通货膨胀	tōnghuò péngzhàng	inflation	6.2, 7.1
通讯地址	tōngxùn dìzhǐ	postal address	5.3
痛苦	tòngkǔ	pain	6.2, 10.3
偷听	tōutīng	to listen secretly to	13.4
投	tóu	to cast; to throw	10.3
投降	tóuxiáng	surrender	8.1
投资	tóuzī	to invest	9.3
投资环境	tóuzī huánjìng	investment environment	6.2
透露	tòulù	to reveal	6.2
秃顶	tūdǐng	bald	10.1
图书管理员	túshū guǎnlǐyuán	librarian	5.1
兔	tù	rabbit	1.2
兔子	tùzi	rabbit	13.2
推荐人	tuījiàn rén	referee	5.4
推荐信	tuījiàn xìn	reference letter	5.4

推销	tuīxiāo	marketing	5.2, 15.1
推销员	tuīxiāo yuán	sales person	5.2
挖	wā	to dig	8.2
瓦房	wǎfáng	tile-roofed house	14.3
外貌	wàimào	physical appearance	10
外商	wàishāng	foreign businessmen	6.2
外向	wàixiàng	extroverted	12.3
弯弯的	wānwānde	bent	10.8
玩具	wánjù	toy	13.5
碗	wǎn	bowl	6.1
晚婚	wǎn hūn	to marry late	7.3
晚宴	wǎnyàn	evening banquet	3.3
晚育	wǎn yù	to have children late	7.3
万事如意	wàn shì rú yì	everything goes as you wish	1.2
万万没想到	wàn wàn méi xiǎngdào	completely unexpectedly	6.1
万分同情	wànfēn tóngqíng	deepest sympathy	1.4
往东走	wǎng dōng zǒu	walk towards the east	2.6
网页	wǎngyè	web page	15.2
望准为盼	wàng zhǔn wéi pàn	hoping that the leave will be granted	4.3.3
微波炉	wēibōlú	microwave oven	2.1, 4.2
微弱	wēiruò	faint; weak	14.4
巍然屹立	wēirán yìlì	to tower imposingly	14.3
为	wéi	to be	5.4
为了	wèile	in order to	4.1
唯一	wéiyī	only; unique	6.2
位置	wèizhi	location	2.3, 14.2
文才	wéncái	talent in writing	5.1
文化大革命	wénhuà dàgémìng	Cultural Revolution	7.3
文静	wénjìng	gentle and quiet	10.4
文明	wénmíng	civilisation	7.1
文学	wénxué	literature	5.4
文字处理	wénzì chǔlǐ	word processing; to word-process	5.1
稳步	wěnbù	steadily	9.4
我(们学)院	wǒ(men xué)yuàn	our college	4.1
乌龟	wūguī	tortoise	13.2
乌黑发亮	wūhēi fāliàng	dark and shiny	10.1
乌润	wūrùn	glossy	10.1
乌云翻滚	wūyún fāngǔn	dark clouds are rolling in	14.4
无比思念	wúbǐ sīniàn	to miss . . . very much	11.8
无辜	wúgū	innocent; innocent person	8.1
无穷的	wúqióngde	endless	1.1
无瑕	wú xiá	flawless	8.2
无限	wúxiàn	boundless	1.4
无意中	wúyì zhōng	unintentionally	6.1
无忧无虑	wú yōu wú lǜ	carefree	12.2
伍	wǔ	five	4.3.2
五官端正	wǔguān duānzhèng	to have regular features	10.6
物价	wùjià	price	9.2

物价上涨	wùjià shàngzhǎng	prices rising	6.2
物质	wùzhì	material	7.2
物质文明	wùzhì wénmíng	material civilization	7.2
务请原谅	wùqǐng yuánliàng	please excuse me; apologies	3.3
吸毒	xīdú	to take drugs	11.6
嬉皮笑脸	xīpí xiàoliǎn	grinning cheekily; smiling	10.6
稀疏	xīshū	thinning	10.1
西山动物园	Xīshān Dòngwùyuán	Xishan Zoo	9.4
西藏	Xīzàng	Tibet	13.4
吸血鬼	xīxuèguǐ	bloodsucker; vampire	8.2
吸引力	xīyǐn lì	attractive; attraction	9.3
媳妇	xífù	daughter-in-law; wife	11.8
喜出望外	xǐ chū wàng wài	to be overjoyed	11.2
喜结良缘	xǐ jié liáng yuán	happily married	1.3
喜酒	xǐjiǔ	wedding banquet	3.3
喜闻	xǐ wén	to be pleased to hear	1.3
喜笑颜开	xǐxiào yánkāi	to light up with pleasure; to be wreathed in smiles	10.6
洗衣粉	xǐyī fěn	washing powder	2.6
细长	xìcháng	thin and long	10.1
细眉细眼	xì méi xì yǎn	fine eyebrows and narrow eyes	10.3
夏时制	xiàshí zhì	summer time	9.2
下海	xiàhǎi	to go into business	9.2
下降	xiàjiàng	to decrease	9.4
下水道	xiàshuǐdào	sewer	8.2
下议院	Xiàyìyuàn	House of Commons	8.1
鲜红	xiānhóng	bright red	14.4
鲜明	xiānmíng	striking; distinct	14.3
闲逛	xiánguàng	to stroll	13.1
显而易见	xiǎn ér yì jiàn	obvious	7.1
显示	xiǎnshì	to show; to display; to demonstrate	8.2
县	xiàn	county	3.2
线条	xiàntiáo	line (of the mouth)	10.5
现象	xiànxiàng	phenomenon	7.1
宪法	xiànfǎ	constitution	7.3, 8.1
相似	xiāngsì	similar; alike	8.1
香油	xiāngyóu	sesame oil	9.1
详(细)情(况)	xiáng(xì) qíng(kuàng)	details	2.3, 5.3
想必	xiǎngbì	to reckon	3.4
想念	xiǎngniàn	to miss	11.8
享有盛誉	xiǎngyǒu shèngyù	to enjoy a high reputation	15.1
相片	xiàngpiān	photo	5.4
消费者	xiāofèizhě	consumers	6.2
销量	xiāoliàng	amount of sales; sales volume	9.4
销售部	xiāoshòu bù	sales department	5.1, 15.1
削瘦	xiāoshòu	emaciated; thin	10.6
小辫	xiǎobiàn	short braid; pigtail	10.1
小卖部	xiǎomàibù	shop (in school, college, factory, etc.)	14.1

小气	xiǎoqi	stingy; mean; miserly	12.2
小巧玲珑	xiǎoqiǎo línglóng	small and exquisite	11.1
笑容可掬	xiàoróng kějū	to be radiant with smiles	10.6
笑嘻嘻	xiàoxīxī	grinning; smiling broadly	10.6
协助	xiézhù	assistance	8.1
谢顶	xièdǐng	bald	10.1
新春愉快	xīn chūn yúkuài	Happy New Year	1.2
新婚快乐	xīn hūn kuàilè	happy marriage	1.3
心地善良	xīndì shànliáng	kindhearted	12.4
心烦	xīnfán	upsetting; disturbing; troublesome	9.3
心花怒放	xīnhuā nùfàng	to burst with joy; to be wild with joy	11.2
心惊胆战	xīnjīng dǎnzhàn	to tremble with fear; to shake with fright	11.5
心惊肉跳	xīnjīng ròutiào	to twitch with anxiety	11.5
心思	xīnsi	mood; state of mind	8.2
心想事成	xīn xiǎng shì chéng	achieve your heart's desires	1.2
心胸狭窄	xīnxiōng xiázhǎi	narrow-minded	12.2
欣赏	xīnshǎng	to enjoy	14.4
欣喜若狂	xīnxǐ ruòkuáng	to be wild with joy	11.2
信任的	xìnrènde	trusting	10.3
信用证	xìnyòngzhèng	L/C; letter of credit	15.3
星斗	xīngdǒu	stars	14.4
行贿	xínghuì	to bribe	6.2
幸福和成功	xìngfú hé chénggōng	happiness and success	1.1
兴高采烈	xìnggāo cǎiliè	in great delight; in high spirits	11.2
兴高采烈地	xìnggāo cǎiliède	happily; in high spirits	6.1
性格	xìnggé	nature; disposition; temperament	8.1, 12.2
凶狠	xiōnghěn	vicious	10.3
修长	xiūcháng	tall and slim; slender	10.7
休假	xiūjià	to be on holiday	3.4
羞愧	xiūkuì	(to be) ashamed	11.7
秀丽	xiùlì	beautiful; pretty	10.4
宣布	xuānbù	to declare	6.2, 8.1
旋钮	xuánniǔ	knob	2.6
选举	xuǎnjǔ	election	8.1
学术报告会	xuéshù bàogàohuì	academic talk	4.1
学术会议	xuéshù huìyì	academic conference	3.3
学生会	xuéshēng huì	student union	5.2
学完	xuéwán	to finish studies	4.2
学问	xuéwèn	knowledge; learning; scholarship	12.3
学者	xuézhě	scholar	10.3
血海	xuèhǎi	sea of blood	8.2
寻	xún	to look for	4.3.1
寻找	xúnzhǎo	to look for; to search for	14.5
询价	xún jià	to inquire about prices	15.2
迅速发展	xùnsù fāzhǎn	to develop rapidly	7.3

鸭蛋脸	yādàn liǎn	oval face	10.6
亚太地区	Yà-Tài dìqū	Asian Pacific Region	9.3
亚洲	Yàzhōu	Asia	8.1
盐	yán	salt	2.6, 9.1
严格	yángé	strictly	7.3
严厉惩罚	yánlì chéngfá	severe punishment	6.2
沿海城市	yánhǎi chéngshì	coastal city	6.2
研究	yánjiū	research	5.4
言行一致	yánxíng yízhì	to be as good as one's word	12.4
演出	yǎnchū	to give a performance	4.1
羊	yáng	sheep	1.2
阳台	yángtái	balcony	2.3
样品	yàngpǐn	sample	15.2
腰包	yāobāo	purse; pocket	8.2
要求	yāoqiú	demands; requirements	5.2
邀约	yāoyuē	invitation	3.3
摇篮	yáolán	cradle	8.2
摇摇晃晃	yáoyáohuànghuàng	with faltering steps	13.1
钥匙	yàoshi	key	2.3
业余	yèyú	spare time	4.1
壹	yī	one	4.3.2
医疗事故	yīliáo shìgù	medical negligence	11.6
医学院	yīxuéyuàn	medical college	4.1
一定	yídìng	certain (specific)	5.1
一定的	yídìngde	a certain degree of . . .	5.2
一个接一个	yíge jiē yíge	one by one	9.2
一系列	yíxìliè	a series	7.1, 9.3
一帆风顺	yì fān fēng shùn	smooth progress	1.2
一分为二	yì fēn wéi èr	looking at both sides of the coin	7.3
一番	yìfān	(a verbal measure word)	13.3
一瘸一拐	yìqué yìguǎi	limping along	13.1
一游	yì yóu	for a visit	3.3
移动电话	yídòng diànhuà	mobile phone	11.1
移民	yímín	immigrant	6.2
姨妈	yímā	aunt (on mother's side)	2.4
遗憾	yíhàn	shame that . . . ; pity that . . .	3.3
遗像	yíxiàng	a portrait of a deceased person	13.3
以	yǐ	in order to	6.2
以笔代口	yǐ bǐ dài kǒu	write a letter instead of talking	9.3
议会	yìhuì	parliament	8.1
意识到	yìshìdào	to realise	7.1, 11.3
阴沉沉	yīnchénchén	cloudy	14.4
阴冷	yīnlěng	gloomy and cold	14.4
阴森森的	yīnsēnsēn de	cold and unfriendly; forbidding	10.6
音响	yīnxiǎng	hi-fi	4.2
银发	yínfà	grey hair	10.1
银装世界	yínzhuāng shìjiè	silver-coated world	14.5
鹰钩鼻子	yīnggōu bízi	Roman nose; aquiline nose	10.4
英俊	yīngjùn	handsome	10.6

樱桃	yīngtáo	cherry	10.5
营业收入	yíngyè shōurù	business income; trading income	9.4
应聘	yìng pìn	to apply (for a job)	5.1
应试方法	yìng shì fāngfǎ	method for applying	5.1
应聘条件	yìngpìn tiáojiàn	requirements for application	5.1
应聘者	yìngpìnzhě	applicant	5.1
永偕伉俪	yǒng xié kànglì	be married forever	1.3
永垂不朽	yǒngchuíbùxiǔ	to be immortal	1.4
用具	yòngjù	appliance	2.6
忧愁	yōuchóu	sad and depressed	11.4
忧虑	yōulù	worried; concerned	11.4
忧伤	yōushāng	distressed	11.4
忧心忡忡	yōuxīn chōngchōng	to be down-hearted	11.4
优厚	yōuhòu	generous	5.1
优惠	yōuhuì	favourable; preferential	6.2, 9.3, 15.3
优美	yōuměi	beautiful	3.3, 8.2
优异成绩	yōuyì chéngjì	excellent results	5.1
幽默	yōumò	humorous	12.1
游	yóu	to visit; to tour	3.3
游览	yóulǎn	to visit	9.4
游艇	yóutǐng	boating; boat	9.4
油	yóu	cooking oil	9.1
油亮	yóuliàng	glossy; sleek	10.1
邮编	yóubiān	postcode	3.2
由于	yóuyú	due to	3.3, 4.1
犹豫	yóuyù	hesitant	13.1
有发现者	yǒu fāxiàn zhě	whoever has found it	4.3.1
有关	yǒuguān	relevant	5.2
有权有势	yǒu quán yǒu shì	the powerful and influential	7.1
有神	yǒushén	piercing	10.3
有拾到者	yǒu shídào zhě	whoever has found it	4.3.1
有信心地	yǒu xìnxīnde	confidently	6.1
有兴趣者	yǒu xìngqù zhě	anyone interested	4.2
有兴致	yǒu xìngzhì	to be interested	3.4
有意	yǒu yì	to have the intention	15.3
有约	yǒu yuē	to have had things arranged	3.3
又及	yòují	p.s.	3.1
愚笨	yúbèn	foolish; stupid; clumsy	12.4
逾期未至	yúqī wèi zhì	to fail to arrive by the specified date	15.4
与......联系	yǔ . . . liánxì	to contact	4.3.1
预订	yùdìng	to reserve	2.1
预定的	yùdìngde	predetermined; scheduled	7.3
预计	yùjì	to predict; anticipate; expect	9.4, 15.5
预料	yùliào	to predict	6.2
郁金香	yùjīnxiāng	tulip	3.3
渊博	yuānbó	broad and profound	11.1
圆满	yuánmǎn	successfully	7.3

远视眼	yuǎnshìyǎn	long-sighted	10.3
愿	yuàn	wishing; to wish	1.1
愿意	yuànyì	willing	6.2
约	yuē	to arrange; to invite	3.3
月饼	yuèbing	moon cake	14.4
云开雾散	yún kāi wù sàn	the clouds roll away and the mists disperse	14.4
匀称	yúnchèn	well-proportioned	10.7
允许	yǔnxǔ	to permit; to allow	9.2, 13.4
运抵	yùndǐ	to be shipped to; to be transported to	15.2
杂技	zájì	acrobatics	13.3
杂技团	zájì tuán	acrobatic troupe	4.1
灾难	zāinàn	disaster; catastrophe	8.1
在此	zài cǐ	here; in this	1.2
在 . . . 之际	zài . . . zhī jì	at the time when . . .	1.2
葬礼	zànglǐ	funeral	13.1
遭到	zāodào	to suffer from	7.3
糟糕	zāogāo	bad; awful	14.5
早生贵子	zao sheng guizi	to have a boy soon	1.3
早日	zǎorì	early; soon	5.1
造成	zàochéng	to cause	9.4
造反	zàofǎn	to rebel	7.3
造型别致	zàoxíng biézhì	uniquely designed; unusual design	14.3
造型优美	zàoxíng yōuměi	beautifully designed	15.1
责任	zérèn	responsibility	6.2
责任心强	zérèn xīn qiáng	strong sense of responsibility	5.1
增高	zēnggāo	to increase the height; to make taller	6.2
增强	zēngqiáng	to strengthen	9.3
增长	zēngzhǎng	to increase	6.2
扎着	zhāzhe	to be wearing	10.1
炸	zhà	to explode	11.6
宅	zhái	house	3.2
崭新	zhǎnxīn	brand-new	14.2
占	zhàn	to occupy	2.5
占	zhàn	to constitute; to make up	7.3
占地面积	zhàn dì miànjī	ground area	14.3
掌声	zhǎngshēng	clapping; applause	11.8
障碍	zhàng'ài	barrier; obstacle	9.3
招待会	zhāodàihuì	reception	3.3
招呼	zhāohu	to look after	2.2
招架不了	zhāojià bùliǎo	to be unable to cope	9.3
招领	zhāolǐng	to look for the owner	4.3.1
招聘	zhāopìn	to recruit; to invite application	5.1
朝思暮想	zhāo sī mù xiǎng	to yearn for . . . day and night	11.1
朝气	zhāoqì	vigour; vitality	10.1
着了迷	zháolemí	to become spellbound	13.4
折扣	zhékòu	discount	15.1

哲学家	zhéxuéjiā	philosopher	13.4
真不巧	zhēn bùqiǎo	unfortunately	3.3
真可惜	zhēn kěxī	what a shame	3.3
阵雨	zhènyǔ	shower	14.5
争吵	zhēngchǎo	to quarrel; to squabble	13.5
争论	zhēnglùn	to argue; to dispute	13.5
整	zhěng	only	4.3.2
政策	zhèngcè	policy	6.2, 7.3, 9.3
政府	zhèngfǔ	government	6.2, 7.3
政府官员	zhèngfǔ guānyuán	government official	7.1
政治	zhèngzhì	political	8.1
证明	zhèngmíng	certificate	4.3.3
知识分子	zhīshi fènzǐ	intellectual	7.3
直不起腰来	zhí bù qǐ yāo lai	couldn't hold one's back straight	11.2
直飞航班	zhífēi hángbān	direct flight	9.4
职位	zhíwèi	position	6.2
植物	zhíwù	plant	2.3
执行	zhíxíng	to implement	7.3
指出	zhǐchū	to point out	6.2
指挥	zhǐhuī	order; direction	13.4
指责	zhǐzé	to accuse; to criticise	7.3
至	zhì	to	7.3
至于	zhìyú	as for	5.2
制度	zhìdù	system	8.1
制定	zhìdìng	to formulate; to draw up	7.3, 9.3
治理	zhìlǐ	to run; to govern	7.3
治疗	zhìliáo	to cure; treatment	6.2
质量	zhìliàng	quality	7.2
致死	zhì sǐ	to cause death	7.3
秩序	zhìxù	order	7.2
猪	zhū	pig	1.2
珠子	zhūzi	pearl	11.3
逐年	zhúnián	year by year	9.3
逐年改善	zhúnián gǎishàn	to improve year by year	7.3
主持人	zhǔchírén	presenter	12.1
主任	zhǔrèn	director	5.1
主厅	zhǔtīng	main hall	3.3
主席	zhǔxí	chairman	5.2
主页	zhǔyè	home page	5.3
注册商标	zhùcè shāngbiāo	trade mark	6.2
注明	zhùmíng	to give a clear indication of	15.2
注视	zhùshì	to look attentively at	13.3
祝寿	zhù shòu	to celebrate (an older person's) birthday	1.1
祝贺	zhùhè	to congratulate; congratulations	1.1
住宿	zhùsù	accommodation	5.1
住宅楼	zhùzhái lóu	residential buildings	9.2

抓	zhuā	to pay attention to	7.2
抓紧	zhuājǐn	to pay special attention to	7.2
专车	zhuānchē	special car	9.1
转	zhuàn	to turn	2.6
转移	zhuǎnyí	to shift; to move	9.3
赚钱	zhuàn qián	to make money	9.2, 12.4
装	zhuāng	to load	15.5
装饰一新	zhuāngshì yìxīn	re-decorated; renovated	14.3
装运	zhuāngyùn	to load and transport; to ship	15.5
壮观	zhuàngguān	magnificent	14.3
壮丽	zhuànglì	magnificent; majestic	14.2
追求	zhuīqiú	to pursue; to seek	7.3
忠厚老实	zhōnghòu lǎoshi	kind and honest	12.4
中等	zhōngděng	medium	10.7
终生难忘	zhōngshēng nánwàng	will never forget as long as one lives	11.8
准假...为盼	zhǔn jià ... wéi pàn	to hope permission will be given for . . . (duration)	4.3.3
准时	zhǔnshí	to be on time; timely	3.3
有资格	yǒu zīgé	to be qualified	7.1
自豪地	zìháode	proudly	6.1
自满	zìmǎn	complacent; self-satisfied	12.3
自馁	zìněi	to lose confidence; to be discouraged	12.2
棕红色	zōnghóngsè	brown	10.6
总起来	zǒng qǐlái	in general	6.2
总经理	zǒngjīnglǐ	general manager	6.2
总统	zǒngtǒng	president	8.1
租房	zū fáng	seeking accommodation	4.2
租期	zū qī	rental period	4.2
组织	zǔzhī	to organise	5.2
嘴唇	zuǐchún	lip	10.5
最佳	zuìjiā	the best	15.1
尊敬的	zūnjìngde	respected	1.1
尊重	zūnzhòng	to respect	12.3
做鬼脸	zuò guǐliǎn	to pull a face	12.1
做生意	zuò shēngyi	to do business	9.2
坐落	zuòluò	to be located; to be situated	14.2